Contents

access to history

Race Relations in the USA 1863–1980 THIRD EDITION

Vivienne Sanders

Hodder Murray

A MEMBER OF THE HODDER HEADLINE GROUP

The publishers would like to thank the following individuals, institutions and companies for permission to reproduce copyright illustrations in this book:
Courtesy of the African American Museum and Library at Oakland (AAMLO), page 65; © Bettmann/CORBIS, pages 8, 9, 34, 55, 68, 70, 75, 76, 78, 92, 109, 111, 121, 154, 156, 183, 186, 197; © CORBIS, pages 19, 47; Getty Images, page 42; BILL HUDSON/AP/EMPICS, page 133; © Hulton-Deutsch Collection/CORBIS, page 153; Southern Media Archives, Special Collections, University of Mississippi Libraries, page 101; © Ted Streshinsky/CORBIS, page 162; Time Life Pictures/Getty Images, page 91; Wisconsin Historical Society (Image ID: 2381), page 127.

The publishers would also like to thank the following for permission to reproduce material in this book:
Oxford, Cambridge and RSA (OCR) examinations for extracts used on pages 36, 59, 207.

Orders: please contact Bookpoint Ltd, 130 Milton Park, Abingdon, Oxon OX14 4SB. Telephone: (44) 01235 827720. Fax: (44) 01235 400454. Lines are open 9.00–5.00, Monday to Saturday, with a 24-hour message answering service. Visit our website at www.hoddereducation.co.uk

First published in 2006 by
Hodder Murray, an imprint of Hodder Education,
a member of the Hodder Headline Group
338 Euston Road
London NW1 3BH

Impression number 10 9 8 7 6 5 4 3 2
Year 2010 2009 2008 2007 2006

The front cover illustration shows Martin Luther King reproduced courtesy of Associated Press.
Typeset in Baskerville 10/12pt and produced by Gray Publishing, Tunbridge Wells.
Printed in Malta

A catalogue record for this title is available from the British Library

ISBN-10: 0 340 90705 3
ISBN-13: 978 0 340 90705 4

Dedication

Keith Randell (1943–2002)

The *Access to History* series was conceived and developed by Keith, who created a series to 'cater for students as they are, not as we might wish them to be'. He leaves a living legacy of a series that for over 20 years has provided a trusted, stimulating and well-loved accompaniment to post-16 study. Our aim with these new editions is to continue to offer students the best possible support for their studies.

1 Introduction

POINTS TO CONSIDER

Relations between the different races in the United States have frequently been tense. Originally inhabited by Native Americans, the North American continent experienced an influx of immigrants from the seventeenth century onwards. Most were voluntary immigrants, initially from Europe and subsequently from Asia. The black slaves who were imported from Africa were involuntary immigrants. This chapter gives an overview of the different racial groups and examines the relationships between them, asking:

- When and why relationships between the different racial groups in the United States were tense
- What suggestions were made to improve the relationships between the different groups in the United States

It does this through the following sections:

- America's racial groups – an overview
- Underlying reasons for racial tensions
- Escalating tensions 1600–1860
- Suggested solutions to problems of racial tensions

Key dates

Pre-1600	North American continent inhabited by Native Americans
1600s	White immigrants began to take land from Native Americans and imported black slaves from Africa
1776	The Declaration of Independence
1787	Constitution of the new United States of America
1800s	Whites moved Westward and took more Native American land
1860s	Asian American immigration to West Coast began
1861–5	Civil War between Southern slave states and Northern states
1882	Chinese Exclusion Act
1887	Dawes Act

1 | America's Racial Groups – An Overview

Key question
Who are 'Americans'?

All residents of the area now known as the United States of America are referred to as Americans throughout this book. Americans have used colour and/or place of origin to try to distinguish between different **racial** groups in the USA. This book deals with the history of the interrelationship between five racial groups:

- White Americans
- African Americans
- Native Americans
- Hispanic Americans
- Asian Americans.

Key terms

Racial
Pertaining to a group of people connected by common descent from distinct ethnic stock.

Hispanic
Relating to Spain, for example, having Spanish ancestry and/or speaking Spanish.

Most white Americans have European/Mediterranean ancestry. For example, there are Americans of British, German, Italian, Irish and Jewish descent. Black Americans are descended from slaves imported from Africa, or from African or Caribbean emigrants. Previously known as 'Indians', Native Americans are the descendants of the earliest inhabitants of North America.

Hispanic Americans are Spanish speaking, but few are of relatively pure Spanish (white European) ancestry. Most Hispanic Americans have predominantly Native American ancestry. The Asian American group includes Americans with Chinese, Japanese, Indian and Southeast Asian ancestry.

How these groups became 'Americans'

Key question
How and when did the different racial groups become 'Americans'?

From the fifteenth century onwards, white Europeans extended their influence over continents inhabited by peoples with different skin colours and different cultures. These non-European peoples were generally at earlier stages of economic, technological and political development than Europeans. The Europeanisation of the North American continent had a dramatic impact upon the native inhabitants (whose land was increasingly taken by the Europeans) and upon the inhabitants of the African continent (whom the whites imported into North America as slaves). Whites of British ancestry dominated the new nation that was established in 1783 as the United States of America.

Key date
Chinese Exclusion Act: 1882

During the nineteenth century, whites from eastern and southern Europe arrived in America. These were slowly accepted as part of the dominant white group. Whites controlled the legal, social and economic status of blacks and Native Americans, and were wary of allowing non-white racial groups to enter America. Asians were the first racial group to be legally excluded from America, by the 1882 Chinese Exclusion Act.

Slowly the black minority grew more assertive, culminating in a mid-twentieth century campaign for political, legal, social and economic equality (the **civil rights** movement). In the later twentieth century the United States saw an influx of immigrants from Asia and from nearby Spanish-speaking areas. The latter

Key term

Civil rights
- Having the vote in free elections.
- Equal treatment under the law.
- Equal opportunities, e.g. in education and work.
- Freedom of speech, religion and movement.

spoke Spanish because of Spanish conquest and colonisation of Central and South America.

During the second half of the twentieth century, the racial minority populations of the United States rose dramatically due to the relaxation of immigration restrictions and natural population increase. Between 1970 and 1980, non-whites grew from 12 to 18 per cent of America's population.

2 | Underlying Reasons for Racial Tensions

Key question
Have the races mixed successfully within the USA?

Early twentieth-century Americans spoke of an American 'melting pot', in which nationalities and racial groups fused into one. However, there were frequent ethnic antagonisms, even amongst the white majority. For example, mid-nineteenth-century New England houses and places of employment often displayed 'NO IRISH WANTED' signs. There was also racial hostility between whites and non-whites, and between different non-white groups. For example, in the 1960s Martin Luther King tried to decrease hostility between blacks and whites, but found that some of his associates did not want to co-operate with Hispanic victims of inequality.

There are several reasons why the different racial groups failed to get along:

- One reason is clearly human nature. Before the arrival of white men, Native American tribes warred amongst themselves.
- Throughout history, people have been hostile towards those from another culture/country/race. People often dislike those who are different from them.
- Some peoples consider themselves superior to others. The European Christians who conquered the North American continent and imported and enslaved black Africans, generally assumed that they were superior. Why?
  - Some Christians believed that non-Christians had 'got it wrong'. Native Americans and Africans taken as slaves were not Christians and were therefore 'inferior'.
  - When Europeans found the Native Americans and Africans to be technologically less advanced, particularly in armaments, that seemed to confirm their cultural and racial inferiority.
- When Europeans wanted to acquire Native American land and African slaves, their sense of superiority was a necessary part of the moral justification for conquest.
- The majority of the individuals who peopled the North American continent from the fifteenth to the twentieth centuries were motivated primarily by the desire for personal improvement. While some sought political freedom, the vast majority sought 'to get rich'. Anyone who got in their way was a threat. Thus a main and continuing source of racial hostility was economic.

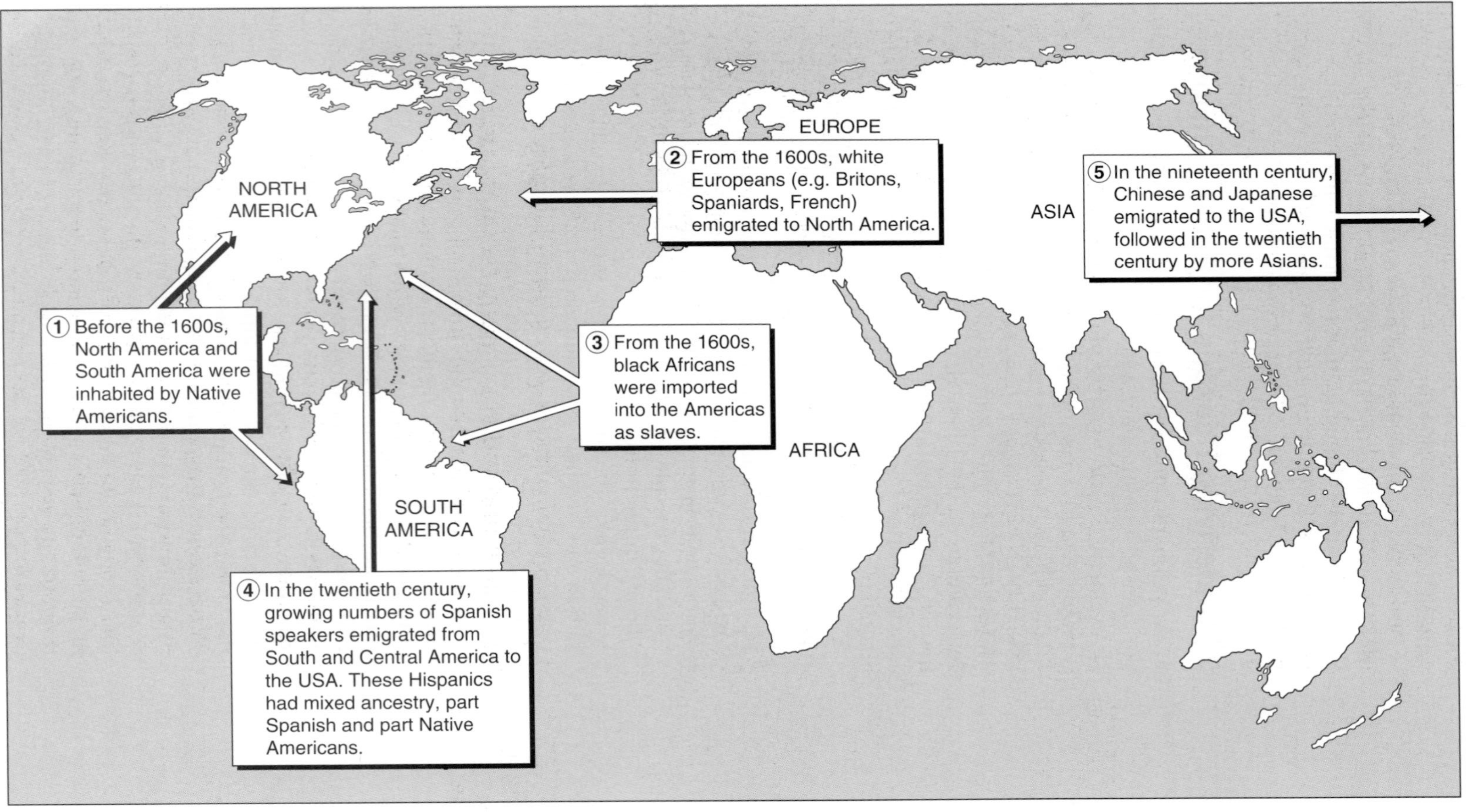

Map 1.1: Racial groups in the USA and their origins.

Most white Americans have always felt superior to, yet threatened by, other racial groups. When the non-white minorities became increasingly assertive, whites grew anxious. This book concentrates on the history of the relations between the white and the non-white races in the twentieth century, a history of uneasy coexistence and occasional violence. Some ethnic groups quietly accepted discrimination, and retreated into their own community, as with Chinese Americans. The most discriminated against ethnic group, African Americans, have protested most, which is why this book concentrates upon them. Less assertive minorities are also studied, and compared to African Americans.

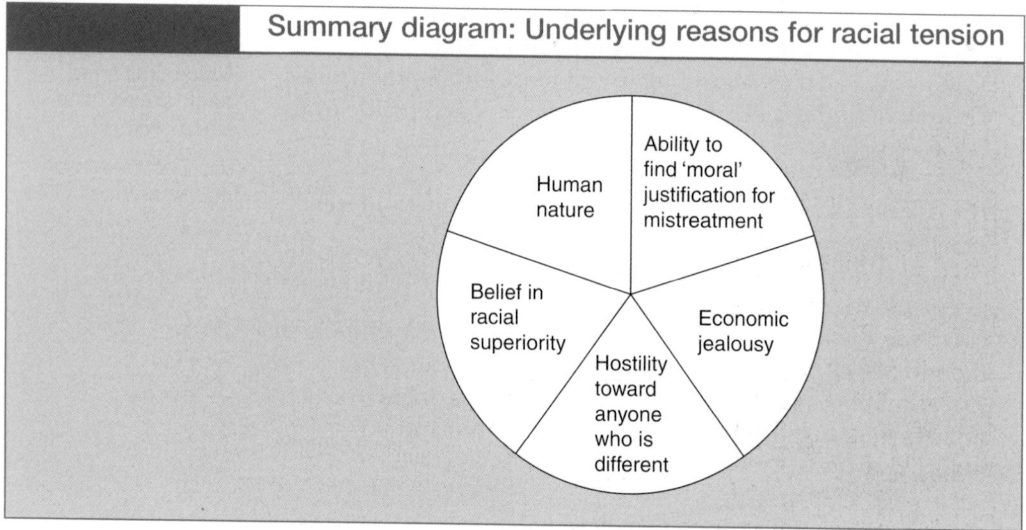

Key question
When and why did the first racial tensions arise?

3 | Escalating Tensions c1600–c1860

(a) Whites and Indians – early racial tensions

Before the arrival of white European explorers in the fifteenth century, several million people already inhabited North America. Europeans described them as red-skinned and called them 'Indians'. Hence Native Americans were known for a long time as 'Red Indians'.

Relations between white Europeans and 'Indians' soon deteriorated, because of two main reasons:

- The Europeans' attitude to the Indians was condescending. Europeans thought cultures that were different to their own were inferior: seventeenth century English settlers on the East coast of North America thought non-Christian Indians were Satan's agents and responsible for evil, such as the tempting of white women settlers into excessive 'cutting, curling and immodest laying out of their hair'!
- Whites felt entitled to take Indian lands, which caused tension, then outright hostility. In 1622 the Indians attacked the English in Virginia and killed one-third of the white population, which

gave the English a good excuse to wipe out any tribes who got in their way. Some Indians were enslaved: there were 1400 Indian slaves in the South Carolina colony by 1708.

White immigration had led to cultural and economic clashes with the native population: racial tension had been introduced to North America.

(b) The introduction of black people and slavery

Key question
Why was it considered acceptable to enslave blacks?

In the early seventeenth century, the Southern colony of Virginia had a persistent labour problem. Therefore, European merchants began to sell black Africans to the English in Virginia. By 1660, slavery was both common and legal. Vast numbers of ill-armed blacks were easily acquired from western Africa, where some African tribal leaders were willing to sell blacks from other tribes to white slave traders. The English considered it acceptable to use blacks as slaves because:

Key dates
Whites imported black slaves from Africa: 1600s
The Declaration of Independence: 1776

- The Africans had a different, non-Christian culture and were therefore perceived as uncivilised heathens.
- They looked very different to Europeans, so it seemed acceptable to treat them differently.
- There was work that needed to be done and too few white men to do it. Slaves provided cheap and plentiful labour. The expansion of the profitable and labour-intensive tobacco industry in the Southern colonies increased demand for imported African slave labour.

All these factors made slavery seem acceptable.

By 1776 British North America contained 2,500,000 people, one-fifth of whom were black slaves. There were occasional armed rebellions: New York City slaves attacked their white oppressors in 1712. Such unsuccessful revolts demonstrated black resentment and powerlessness. White belief in their supremacy and the overriding importance of white economic needs had led to the development of more racial tension.

Key term
Constitution
The rules and system by which a country's government works. The USA has a written constitution.

In 1776 the white American colonists demanded freedom from British rule in their Declaration of Independence. However, few slave owners recognised the contradiction between their ideas of freedom and the existence of slavery. The Declaration's beautiful words on equality were not meant to apply to blacks nor to what the Declaration called 'merciless Indian Savages'.

(c) The Constitution and race relations

Key question
How did the Constitution deal with slavery?

In 1783 the British government recognised American independence. The Americans needed to establish their own form of government for the 13 ex-colonies, now to be called states. Delegates from the states (the Founding Fathers) discussed a new **constitution**.

The Founding Fathers debated a crucial question on black slaves: did a black slave deserve political representation like other (white) human beings or was he merely a piece of property? The

Key date

The Constitution of the new United States of America: 1787

Key terms

Congress
The American equivalent to Britain's parliament, consisting of the Senate and the House of Representatives. Voters in each American state elect two senators to sit in the Senate and several congressmen (the number depends on the size of the state's population) to sit in the House of Representatives.

Federal government
The USA, as a federation of many separate states (such as South Carolina and New York), has a federal government. The federal government consists of the President, Congress and the Supreme Court.

Southern states wanted their black slaves to count as human beings for purposes of representation, so that although the slaves could not vote, the South would nevertheless have the maximum number of representatives in **Congress**. However, Southerners did not want their slaves to count as human beings if that meant having to pay more taxes. The resulting Three-Fifths Compromise settled the issue: five slaves were to equal three free persons for purposes of taxation and representation in Congress. The new American Constitution thus enshrined the inferiority of black slaves. The Constitution also guaranteed the continuation of the slave trade until 1808.

The Constitution contained great potential for a clash between the powers of state governments (such as Virginia and Georgia) and the powers of the national or **federal government** (in Washington DC). The Constitution gave each state government control over the make-up of the electorate and ensured that only privileged white males could vote. The Constitution of the new nation set out to protect rights, liberties and freedom – but only of white men.

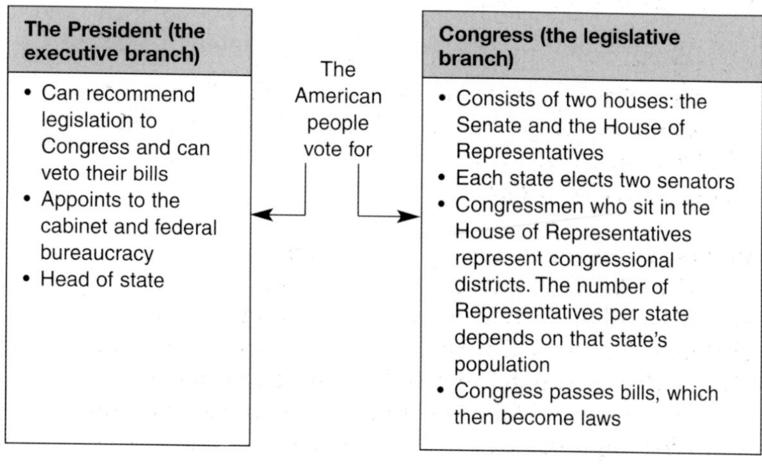

Figure 1.1: Federal government in the USA.

Key questions
How did contemporaries view race and slavery?

How did President Jefferson feel about non-whites?

(d) Early reactions to racism and slavery

(i) Thomas Jefferson, racism and slavery

The unequal treatment of non-whites was frequently overlooked by the Founding Fathers of the new nation. Thomas Jefferson had been influential in the production of the ringing declaration of 1776 that 'all men are created equal'. However, he said that

Americans would be 'obliged' to drive the 'backward' Indians into the mountains like 'beasts of the forests'. As Indians did not farm or value private property like whites, it was unreasonable that they retain so much land. On the other hand, Jefferson was hopeful that Indians might eventually blend into and adopt white American 'civilisation'.

Profile: Thomas Jefferson 1743–1826

1743	–	Born in the Southern colony of Virginia, into a relatively prosperous and slave-owning family
1767	–	Became a lawyer
1775	–	Represented Virginia at Continental Congress, which discussed American independence
1776	–	Principal author of Declaration of Independence
1779	–	Elected Governor of Virginia
1782	–	Published 'Notes on Virginia' in which he said he opposed slavery, but that blacks and whites could never live together in harmony
1784–9	–	United States ambassador to France, where he began his long-term relationship with his slave, Sally Hemmings, by whom he had many children
1787	–	Approved of the new United States Constitution, including its acceptance of slavery
1789	–	Served in new United States government
1801–9	–	Twice elected as president of the United States
1826	–	Died

Jefferson is important in illustrating and understanding the racial position of influential whites in the early years of the new American nation. Highly intelligent (he designed his beautiful home Monticello) and idealistic (he wrote eloquently on 'freedom'), he nevertheless considered blacks intellectually inferior and did little in practice to make a reality of his avowed opposition to slavery.

Jefferson was ambivalent about blacks and slavery. He never publicly admitted his affection for his long-standing slave-mistress, nor did he publicly acknowledge their children, only freeing them in his will. He said that he despised slavery and once spoke of freeing all his slaves, but never did. He said it was difficult to decide whether blacks were inferior to whites or simply made so by the 'peculiar institution' of slavery. Rather conveniently for a slave owner, he said that freeing those brought up in slavery would be like abandoning children.

(ii) Southerners and slavery

Key question
Why were Southerners keen to keep slavery?

Unlike Jefferson, most people were decisively pro- or anti-slavery. Slavery had been abolished in most Northern states by the early nineteenth century and some Northerners advocated the

How were slaves treated?

Escape, simulated illness, self-inflicted injury, broken tools, deliberate accidents and ignorance, and the occasional rebellion demonstrated slave discontent. Most slaves lacked freedom of choice over movement, work, family life and culture. Some whites did not overwork the slaves, and allowed them to eat well, to have a stable family life to attend religious meetings, and to learn to read and write. Some were exceptionally cruel. A drunken Kentuckian dismembered his slave and threw him bit by bit into the fire. Whippings were quite common. Occasionally, slaves retaliated. One beaten Kentucky slave strangled her mistress.

White women and black men rarely had a sexual relationship. However, as a result of relationships between white men and black female slaves, there were 411,000 mulatto slaves, out of a total slave population of 3.9 million, by 1860. The figure might have been higher, as many mulattos passed as whites.

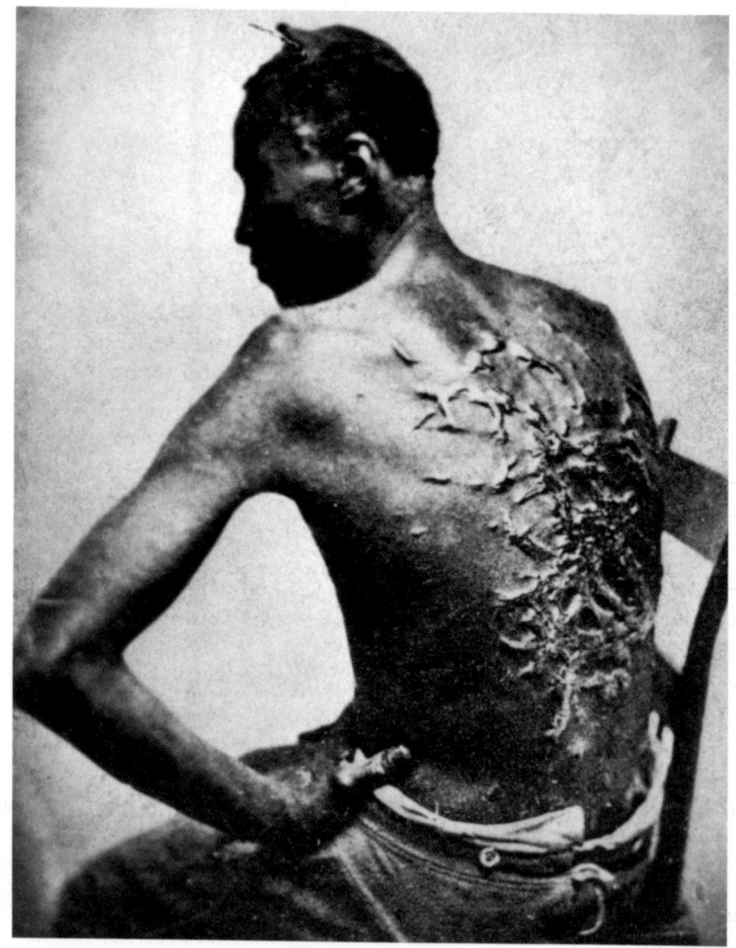

The scarred back of a Louisiana slave who had been beaten by his owner.

abolition of slavery throughout the USA. However, most Southerners were pro-slavery, because:

- Wealthy Southerners thought that the profitability of their plantations depended upon slave labour.
- Non-slave-owning white Southerners feared that freed slaves would be competition for wage-paying jobs.
- Rich and poor white Southerners were frightened by the potential hostility of freed black slaves.
- Over 90 per cent of American blacks lived in the South. Slaves outnumbered whites in states such as South Carolina and Mississippi. If slaves were freed, they would threaten white supremacy and racial purity.

(iii) Southern justification for slavery

Key question
How did Southerners justify slavery?

When **abolitionists** increasingly criticised slavery, resentful Southerners sought new justification. The 'necessary evil' argument was replaced by the 'positive good' argument. This gave Southerners more reasons to maintain slavery. The 'positive good' argument claimed that blacks were happy-go-lucky, lazy, ignorant and inferior to whites. This made slavery desirable, it was argued. How could this inferior race survive, if not worked, fed and clothed by caring white slave owners?

Key term
Abolitionists Those who wanted to end slavery.

The introduction and maintenance of slavery in America had led to what seemed like an insoluble problem.

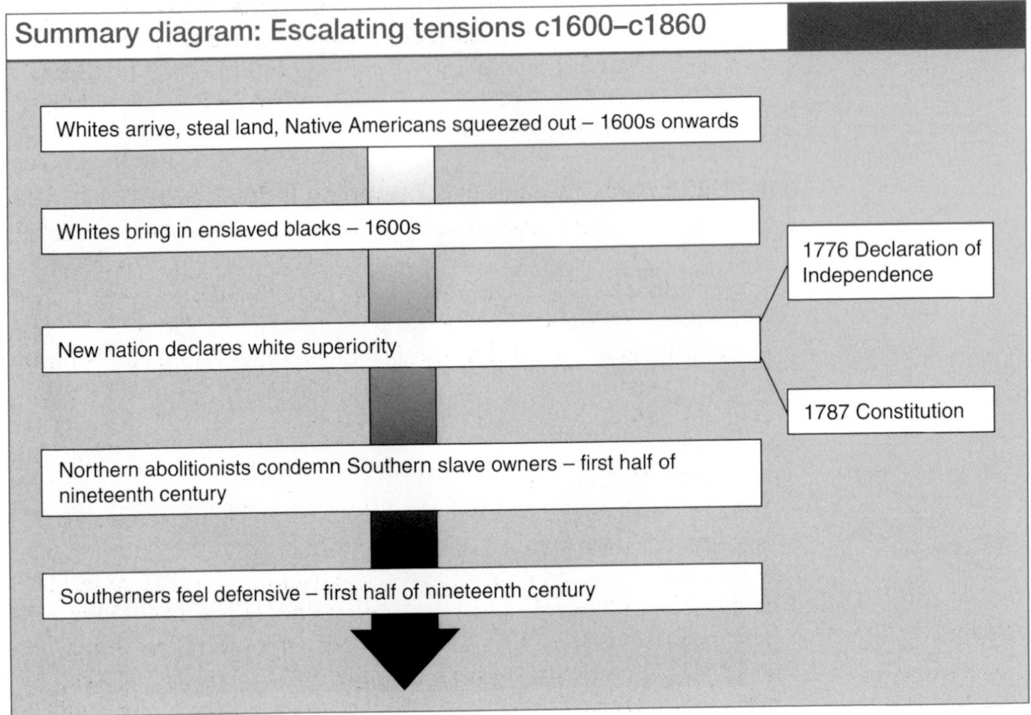

Key questions

What solutions to the race problems were suggested by nineteenth century Americans?

How did whites handle the 'Indian problem'?

4 | Suggested Solutions to the Problem of Racial Tensions

Several answers to America's race problems were suggested in the nineteenth century.

(a) Indians – military, legal, educational and segregationist solutions

As whites moved westward and took ever more Indian land, they used six methods for dealing with the 'Indian problem':

(i) Force

The whites, with better weapons and more men, gained land in battle with the Indians.

(ii) Biological warfare

In 1763, a white general thought infecting the Indians with smallpox might be easier than conventional warfare. Blankets and handkerchiefs from a smallpox hospital were distributed amongst the Delaware Indians. Whether that early attempt at biological warfare was responsible for the smallpox epidemic that soon raged amongst the Delawares is difficult to determine.

(iii) Ethnic cleansing and genocide

Key term

Genocide
The murder of an entire race.

Many whites favoured 'ethnic cleansing', while some Indian leaders felt death in battle preferable to a living death under white rule. Thus Indians contemplated suicide and whites contemplated (and almost committed) **genocide** as solutions to the clash between the red and white races. In practice, white treatment of the Indians approached genocide. Before the whites arrived in America, there were several million Indians; by 1900, there were a quarter of a million.

(iv) Diplomacy, treaties and obtaining Indian land

The Indians signed many treaties with white Americans. Treaties were often synonymous with trickery: in 1809, several Indian chiefs 'mellowed' by an American official with alcohol, signed away three million acres of land in Indiana. The treaties supposedly guaranteed that the Indians retained some lands but whites broke the treaties when it suited them. Between 1829 and 1866 the Winnebago tribe was moved six times.

(v) 'Americanisation'

Key date

Indian children 'Americanised' in boarding schools: 1880s

After whites had obtained most of the Indians' land, the racial problem still remained. Sympathetic whites thought the Indians' best chance of survival lay in 'Americanisation' – the rejection of traditional Indian culture and the assimilation of white culture. This integrationist solution climaxed in the 1880s when Indian children were taken away from parental influence and 'civilised' in federal-funded boarding schools. The policy failed. Whites and Indians both rejected 'educated' Indians. The Indian children often suffered greatly. For example, the federal government ordered that all male Indians in the schools should cut their hair, because long hair represented resistance to civilisation. On some reservations, Indian boys had to be shackled for their hair cutting, because they believed that long hair had supernatural significance for rain ceremonies and that they were doomed if their hair fell into enemy hands.

(vi) Separation on reservations

Key date: Dawes Act: 1887

Whites kept the defeated and 'undesirable' Indians geographically separate. By the late nineteenth century, most Indians had been settled on reservations on land that whites did not want. Sometimes whites changed their minds. When gold was found in the Black Hills of Dakota, the Indians were forced to move to a reservation elsewhere.

The Dawes Act allotted land to Indians. Whites frequently obtained allotted lands cheaply from uncomprehending Indians. Between 1887 and 1934, Indians lost 86 million out of a total of 138 million acres. Most of that which remained was undesirable semi-desert.

So, after three centuries of struggle, white domination over the Indians was total. By 1900, whites considered the Indian problem solved.

(b) Hispanics – the 'no more imperialism' solution

Key question
How did whites handle the 'Hispanic problem'?

When white Americans expanded over large parts of the North American continent they acquired Western territories (such as California, New Mexico and Texas) that had belonged to Mexico. By the mid-nineteenth century whites of North European ancestry outnumbered Hispanics in the American West. Light-skinned Hispanics were frequently accepted as equals by white Americans, but darker skinned Hispanics were kept socially, politically and economically inferior.

Some Americans favoured the acquisition of Mexico itself. However, many whites did not want the United States to acquire any more Hispanics. Thus, rarely, the United States desisted from imperialist expansion to avoid further racial tension.

(c) Chinese – the 'stop immigration' solution

Key question
How did whites handle the 'Chinese problem'?

Immigrants flocked to the increasingly prosperous United States. Up to the mid-nineteenth century most were of white, Protestant, north European stock, but soon immigrants flooded in from other areas. Chinese immigrants were particularly unpopular. Chinese men were first attracted by the discovery of gold in California in the 1840s. They were encouraged to come to the West as cheap labour for the transcontinental railroad building in the 1860s. By 1870, 100,000 Chinese constituted about 10 per cent of California's population. White mob violence frequently drove Chinese workers out. Whites considered it a joke to cut off the pigtail of Chinese men, which would make them unacceptable if they returned to China. White Californians felt threatened by

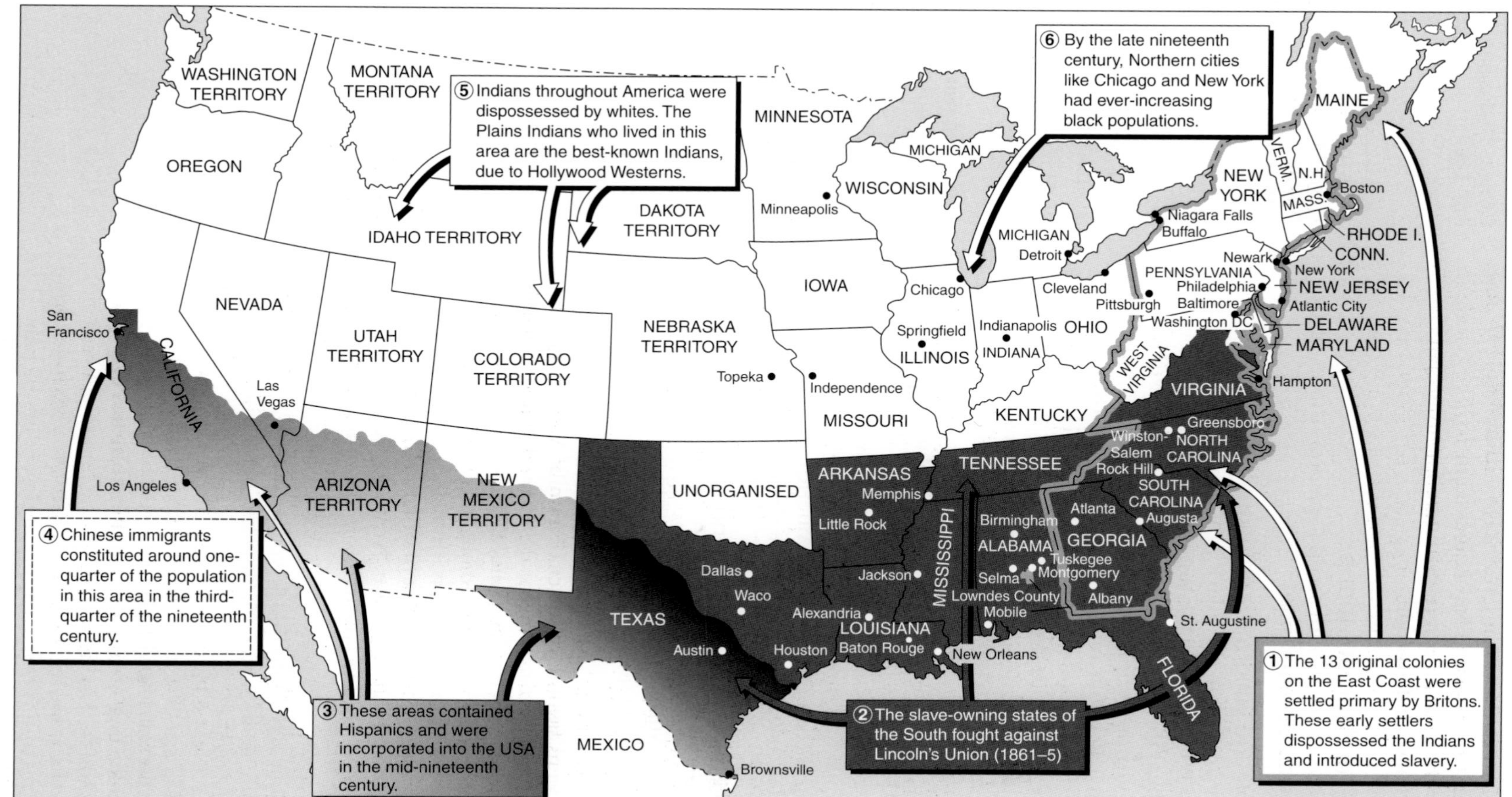

Map 1.2: Race relations in the United States in the mid-nineteenth century

Chinese willingness to work for lower wages, culminating in anti-Chinese riots in Chinatown in San Francisco in 1877. Consequently, Congress passed the Chinese Exclusion Act (1882) prohibiting Chinese immigration.

Key date
Chinese Exclusion Act: 1882

(d) Blacks – multiple solutions

Whites and blacks came up with several solutions to the 'black problem' in the nineteenth century.

Key question
How did whites handle the 'black problem'?

(i) Repatriation and emigration solutions

One suggested solution to the 'black problem' was the **repatriation** of freed slaves. The American Colonisation Society aimed to compensate slave owners and send their slaves back to Africa. Under this programme, about 12,000 blacks returned to Africa to the new Republic of Liberia (founded in 1822). However, Liberia was not a popular solution. Black people considered North America their home. They did not want to leave, but wanted to get better treatment. Repatriation became unfashionable after 1830 but it revived in the 1850s when some white politicians and blacks argued that black freedom necessitated departure from America. Some **black separatists** emigrated to Haiti to escape American racism. Others, subsidised by the federal government, went to live in Panama and the Caribbean islands, but these black migrations were never very popular among the majority of black Americans. Clearly, attempts to get rid of blacks were an unworkable solution.

Key terms

Repatriation
In the context of American race relations this meant people of African descent (black Americans) being returned to Africa.

Black separatists
Blacks who desired to live apart/away from whites.

Free blacks
In the North in particular, many blacks had been freed from slavery by their owners.

Democratic Party
Dominated American politics in the first half of the nineteenth century. It was pro-slavery and against a powerful central/federal government.

Republican Party
Emerged in the 1850s. It was against slavery.

(ii) Northern blacks – segregation and victimisation solutions

Before the 1860s, Northern blacks suffered from political, economic and social inequality.

Political inequality

In 1860 there were around a quarter of a million **free blacks** in the North. They were not treated as equals. Although the **Democratic Party** talked much of increasing political democracy, they did not want to give the vote to women, Indians nor blacks. One opponent of black suffrage described blacks as 'peculiar' people, 'incapable' of exercising the vote 'with any sort of discretion, prudence or independence'. Before the Civil War, New York State had disqualified 30,000 free black residents from voting.

Economic inequality

During economic recessions, black workers were the first to lose their jobs. White mobs frequently attacked black workers for accepting lower wages.

Social inequality

Many Northerners disliked blacks. 'It is certainly the wish of every patriot,' said a leading member of the **Republican Party**, that 'our union should be homogeneous in race and of our own blood.' In Northern towns, black Americans were excluded from white institutions and public facilities, and were unofficially segregated in schools, churches and housing. When a white

Key terms

Integration
The social mixing of people of different colours and cultures.

Segregation
The separation of people because of race (for example, separate housing, schools and transport).

Quaker teacher admitted a black girl to her Connecticut school, white patrons boycotted it and got the teacher arrested on trumped-up charges. The Quakers of Pennsylvania welcomed blacks to their religious services but still maintained segregated burial places. Thus Northern solutions to the 'black problem' included segregation and discrimination.

Some Northern whites favoured **integration** and the abolition of slavery. However, many Northern abolitionists looked down on blacks and did not envisage equality or integration: the French visitor De Tocqueville thought that racism was stronger in the North than the South in the 1830s.

Segregation was often the most appealing solution to blacks. They could maintain their cultural identity in their own churches, and avoid white authority while living in segregated areas. Proximity seemed to exacerbate racial tension: a high proportion of race riots occurred in areas containing a large black minority.

(iii) Southern blacks – the slavery solution

Even the 75 per cent of white Southerners who did not own slaves believed slavery was an effective method of controlling the black population. Freed slaves would be rivals for jobs. Disagreements over this Southern solution to the race problem were to contribute to the Civil War between the Northern and Southern states (see Chapter 2).

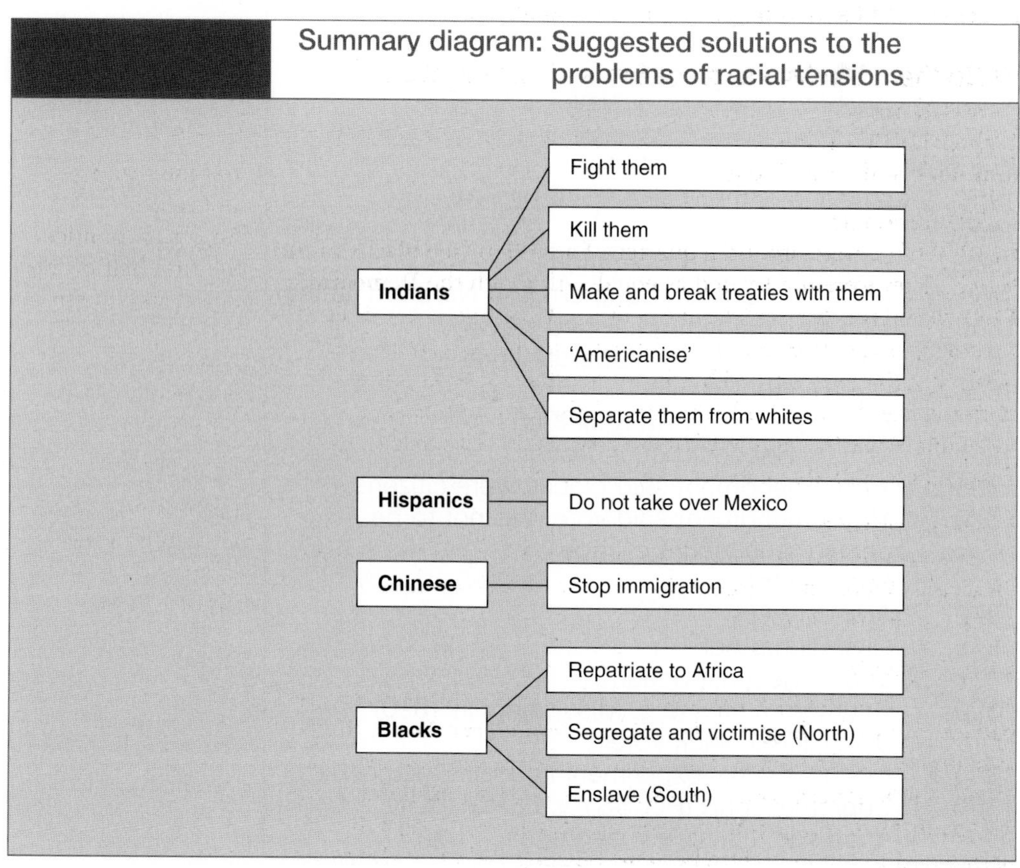

2 The Civil War, Reconstruction and Jim Crow 1861–1900

POINTS TO CONSIDER

From 1861 to 1865, the Northern states fought to keep the Southern states within the Union of the United States in a Civil War that many believed was fought over slavery. The Northern victory ensured the end of slavery and a period of 'Reconstruction' of the defeated South. Initially, freed slaves gained benefit from Reconstruction, but, after 1877, the North left the South to its own devices and white racists became dominant. They introduced the Jim Crow laws, which kept blacks inferior. This chapter looks at:

- Slavery and the Civil War
- The post-war South and the start of Reconstruction
- The situation of blacks from Reconstruction to segregation
- How Southern blacks responded to their deteriorating situation after 1877
- A summary of American race relations in 1900

Key dates

1820	Missouri compromise
1857	Dred Scott case
1862	Emancipation proclamation
1861–5	Civil War between Southern and Northern states
1865	13th Amendment abolished slavery 'Reconstruction Confederate style'
1866	Civil Rights Act Establishment of Ku Klux Klan
1867	Military Reconstruction Act
1868	14th Amendment said blacks were citizens
1870	15th Amendment said vote was not to be denied on account of race Force Acts
1872	Amnesty Act
1875	Civil Rights Act
1877	End of Reconstruction
1890s	Southern states (e.g. Mississippi in 1890) disqualified black voters
1894–8	North Carolina 'experiment in biracial democracy'
1896	Supreme Court (PLESSY v. FERGUSON) approved 'Jim Crow' segregation laws

Key question
How important were slavery and racism in causing the Civil War?

1 | Slavery and the Civil War

(a) Events leading up to the Civil War

From the early nineteenth century, as white Americans moved Westwards, new land was acquired and new states created. The question of whether to allow slavery in the new states was hotly debated. Many Northerners were opposed to the extension of slavery:

- Some had been turned against slavery by abolitionists.
- Some objected to the presence of non-whites in new territories to which Northerners might want to migrate.
- Some felt that cheap slave labour would make it harder for whites to gain employment.
- Some feared that more slave states would increase the political power of the South within the union.

In 1819 Missouri applied for admission as a state of the union. Northerners said no new state should be allowed in with slavery. Southerners were furious. Northerners appeared to be claiming moral superiority and threatening to decrease Southern influence in Congress. The answer was the Missouri Compromise (1820): Congress allowed Missouri in as a slave state but balanced it with the creation and admission of Maine as a free state.

North/South tensions over whether new territories should become slave states continued. The fact that some states were non-slave states led to the Dred Scott case in which the Supreme Court said that blacks were not US citizens and that Congress lacked the constitutional authority to exclude slavery from new states. This ruling antagonised Northerners.

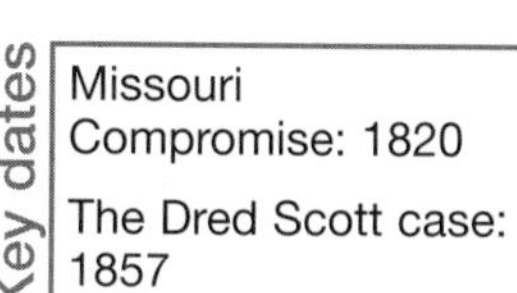

(i) The Dred Scott case 1857

Dred Scott (c1800–58) was the slave of a Missouri army surgeon. When his master worked in the free state of Illinois and the free territory of Wisconsin, Scott went with him. After they returned to Missouri, the surgeon died (1843) and Scott became the slave of the surgeon's heir. In 1846, helped by anti-slavery lawyers, Scott went to court claiming freedom, as he had resided in a free state and free territory. This case went through the US court hierarchy, right to the US Supreme Court (see diagram opposite). A Missouri state court declared Scott to be free (1850) but the Missouri Supreme Court ruled (1852) against Scott. His lawyers took the case to the federal courts. In 1857, the Supreme Court ruled that black Americans were not citizens, so Scott could not go free. Scott's embarrassed owners freed him anyway. He worked as a hotel porter for 18 months, dying in 1858.

US Court Hierarchy

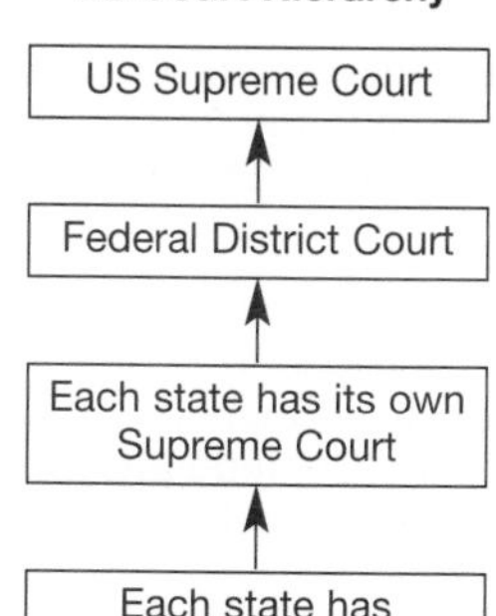

(ii) The outbreak of the Civil War

North/South tension was increased by extremism on both sides. The Republican Party opposed the extension of slavery. To Southerners, the election of the Republican President Abraham Lincoln seemed to threaten the existence of slavery. So, in

1860–1, the Southern states formed a new nation, the Confederate States of America (**the Confederacy**). When President Lincoln raised Northern armies to bring the South back into the United States, the Civil War began. After four years of bitter fighting, the North won.

(b) Was the Civil War a war to end slavery?

(i) Lincoln's views on slavery and race

Lincoln declared slavery 'the greatest wrong inflicted on any people', but had been willing to accept its continued existence in the South. He had spoken in favour of colonisation (see page 14) and the departure of all blacks. 'There must be the position of superior and inferior,' he said in a political debate in 1858. He favoured 'having the superior position assigned to the white race.' He told a black audience that, unalterably and undeniably, 'not a single man of your race is made the equal of a single man of ours.' 'It is', he said, ' better for us to be separated.'

Lincoln opposed the extension of slavery to new states, but was willing to protect it where it existed. He did not want to alienate his supporters in the slave states of Kentucky, Maryland, Missouri and Delaware, which fought on the Northern side. 'We did not go to war to put down slavery', he told Congress in December 1861. One infuriated abolitionist said Lincoln was 'a wet rag' on the slavery issue, 'halting, prevaricating [delaying], irresolute [indecisive], [and] weak'. In September 1862, however, Lincoln issued his Emancipation Proclamation.

Key terms

The Confederacy
When the Southern states left the Union, they became the Confederate States of America, known as the Confederacy for short. Supporters of the Confederacy were called Confederates.

Emancipation
In this context, freedom from slavery.

Radical Republicans
Members of the Republican Party who were most enthusiastic about ending slavery.

(ii) The Emancipation Proclamation

Key question
What motives lay behind Lincoln's Emancipation Proclamation?

Generations of black people felt grateful to the President who issued the **Emancipation** Proclamation. However, that proclamation was so cautious that Britain's Prime Minister described Lincoln's government as 'utterly powerless and contemptible'. The proclamation said slaves in Confederate States were free, but allowed slavery to continue in the slave-owning Union states and in any other state that had been occupied by Union armies or that would return to the Union before January 1863. In practice, the proclamation did not liberate a single slave, suggesting military rather than idealistic motivation. The London *Spectator* said the proclamation's philosophy was 'not that a being cannot justly own another, but that he cannot own him unless he is loyal to the United States'. So why had Lincoln issued the Emancipation Proclamation?

- Some **Radical Republicans** believed slavery was immoral and made a mockery of the Declaration of Independence. Lincoln agreed with them.
- Most Republicans blamed slave owners for the Civil War, and many believed that if slavery was not abolished, North/South divisions could not be resolved and the bloody Civil War would have been pointless.

Key dates

The North successfully fought the slave-owning South in the American Civil War: 1861–5

Lincoln's Emancipation Proclamation declared that slaves in the Confederate States were free: 1862

Profile: Abraham Lincoln 1809–65

1809 – Born in a log cabin in Kentucky
1831 – Moved to Illinois; worked as store clerk, postmaster, surveyor
1834 – Elected to Illinois state legislature
1837 – Became a lawyer
1842 – Married Mary Todd, whose Kentucky family owned slaves
1846 – Elected to the House of Representatives
1856 – Joined new Republican Party. Increasingly focused on the slavery issue
1860 – Elected President in November
– In December, the first Southern state seceded (withdrew) from the Union of the United States
1861 – The Confederate States of America established in February
– Confederate forces fired on a federal fort in April. Lincoln declared the South in rebellion; issued a Call to Arms
1862 – Lincoln issued the Emancipation Proclamation
1864 – Re-elected President
1865 – Confederacy surrendered. Lincoln assassinated by actor and Confederate sympathiser John Wilkes Booth

Lincoln is important in any history of American race relations because he began freeing the slaves with his Emancipation Proclamation of 1862. Subsequent generations of blacks revered him as the Great Emancipator, but historians argue over the relative importance of political calculation and genuine idealism in his actions, and over the extent of his racism. He was certainly vital to the defeat of the pro-slavery Confederacy, after which the South and race relations would never be the same again.

- It was thought that once Lincoln committed the North to emancipation, the Confederacy would find it impossible to receive help from foreign nations such as Britain any more.
- Army commanders had a problem with the half a million refugee slaves who came to Northern army camps situated in Southern states. By law, the slaves should have been returned to their masters, but that seemed inhumane (their masters would punish them) and unintelligent (their masters would use them to help beat the North). Evading the issue by calling slaves 'contraband of war' was tried in 1861–2, but Radical Republicans preferred outright condemnation of the institution of slavery, as that would give the North the moral high ground in the war.
- Military necessity was probably Lincoln's main motive. The North was struggling in 1862 (for example, the defeat at the Second Battle of Bull Run). This proclamation aimed to hamper the Southern war effort. In 1863, Lincoln wrote that

> black soldiers were 'a resource which, if vigorously applied now, will soon close the contest. It works doubly, weakening the enemy and strengthening us.' Nearly a quarter of a million blacks served in the Northern army, entering it just when the North's forces were becoming dangerously depleted.

In January 1863, because the Confederacy continued to fight, Lincoln said that the freedom of slaves in rebellious states was now a Union war aim, 'an act of justice', not just 'military necessity'. Finally, after Lincoln had died, in 1865, the 13th **Amendment** abolished slavery throughout the United States.

For Lincoln then, as for most Northerners, the Civil War was a war not for racial equality but for preservation of the Union. Even so, for the electorate in the 1864 presidential election, one of the Democrats' most effective anti-Lincoln criticisms was that he was a 'Negro lover' plotting **miscegenation**. However, Lincoln's views were slightly modified during the war. Initially he had not wanted Indians and blacks in the Union army. However, impressed by the performance of black soldiers, he considered giving the vote to 'the very intelligent' and most gallant.

Key terms

Amendment
Under the Constitution, Congress could add 'Amendments' (changes or new points) to the Constitution. Amendments needed ratification (approval) by 75 per cent of states.

Miscegenation
Sexual relationships between blacks and whites.

(c) The Northern view of black people during the Civil War

Key question
Were Northerners and Southerners equally racist?

Although the extension of slavery was possibly the major cause of the Civil War (1861–5), that war was not fought to end slavery. Most Northerners thought they were fighting to save the Union (of the United States) and not to free Southern slaves. Northerners feared that freed slaves would migrate to the North and flood the labour market and cause racial tension.

There was considerable hostility towards blacks in the North before and during the Civil War. Some newspapers claimed that Lincoln got America into a Civil War to help undeserving blacks. When Southern slaves first rushed to join Union forces the latter were highly suspicious. White conservatives in the North disliked the idea of arming Northern blacks whom they considered inferior and unreliable. However, by 1865, 10 per cent of Union troops were black. They came from the South as well as the North. Nearly half a million Southern slaves joined the Union army.

Key date

13th Amendment ended slavery: 1865

Black troops, although brave and enthusiastic, were given the worst and most dangerous tasks. They were usually paid less than whites. In 1863 an Irish mob had attacked black soldiers in New York, but in 1865 black soldiers were given an affectionate farewell parade there. The *New York Times* thought that signalled 'a new epoch'. The new epoch, however, did not mean that blacks attained equality. Although amendments to the Constitution from 1865 to 1870 gave rights of citizenship to the ex-slaves, real equality was far away.

Key question
What caused the US Civil War?

(d) Key debate

Historians find it hard to agree on what the Civil War was all about and have debated the following questions:

Was slavery the cause of the Civil War? and what was Lincoln's position on race?

Abraham Lincoln (1861) said that 'all knew' that slavery 'was somehow the cause of the war'.

Jefferson Davis, President of the defeated Confederacy, put the blame for the Civil War on Northern violators of states' rights and rabble-rousing abolitionists (1881).

Arthur Schlesinger Sr (1922) said that the South only used the principle of states' rights as a protection and argument for the preservation of slavery, which he saw as the main cause of the conflict.

Karl Marx saw the war as a struggle between two economic systems, between free labour and slave labour. By the 1920s, **progressive** historians such as Charles Beard (1927) followed Marx in believing that history was the record of clashes between interest groups and classes. Beard saw the war as an economic struggle, between the industrial North and agricultural South – slavery was not central to Beard's interpretation.

In the 1930s, many **revisionist** historians such as James Randall blamed abolitionist fanatics and blundering politicians for the Civil War.

In 1945, Arthur Schlesinger Jr blamed the Civil War on slavery. That has been the dominant interpretation ever since, as with Eric Foner (1980).

Given that Lincoln's ideas on slavery and race seemed to change and develop in different circumstances, it is not surprising that historians disagree over his position on race. Kenneth Stampp (1957) pointed out the irony that the president who became known as the 'Great Emancipator' emancipated reluctantly. Stampp was influenced by James Randall, who had stressed Lincoln's caution on racial issues. According to Hugh Tulloch (1999), Lincoln personally 'loathed slavery', but the majority of the Northerners whom he represented believed in white supremacy, so Lincoln had to move cautiously on the slavery issue. Stephen Oates (1977) believed that under pressure of war Lincoln became increasingly convinced of the need for racial equality.

Key terms

Progressive
A historian who is an advocate of political policies that bring about rapid progress or social reform.

Revisionist
A historian who changes a well-established interpretation.

Some key books in the debate

Charles and Mary Beard, *The Rise of American Civilisation* (1927).
Eric Foner, *Politics and Ideology in the Age of the Civil War* (1980).
Stephen Oates, *With Malice Towards None* (1977).
James Randall, *Civil War and Reconstruction* (1937).
Arthur Schlesinger Sr, *New Viewpoints in American History* (1922).
Arthur Schlesinger Jr, *The Age of Jackson* (1945).
Kenneth Stampp, *The Peculiar Institution* (1957).
Hugh Tulloch, *The Debate on the American Civil War Era* (Manchester, 1999).

Summary diagram: Slavery and the Civil War

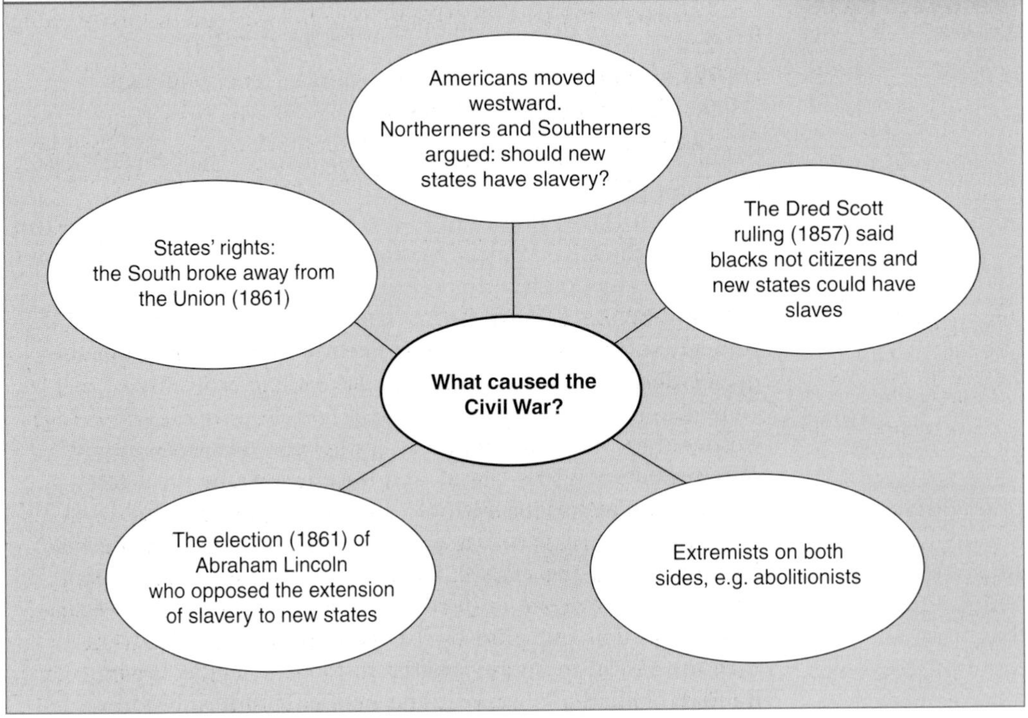

2 | The Post-war South: Starting Reconstruction

(a) 'Reconstruction Confederate style'

In April 1865 the Confederate army surrendered at Appomattox. Within days, President Lincoln was assassinated. His successor President Andrew Johnson faced the problem of what to do with the defeated Southern states. These states, with their old political system obsolete, ruined economies and changed societies (blacks were now free), had to be reincorporated into the Union. The whole process of introducing and managing change was known as **Reconstruction** (the years 1865–77 are often called the 'Age of Reconstruction').

In 1865, many Southern blacks demanded equality, and particularly the right to vote. President Johnson, however, moved to conciliate the traditional white Southern élite. Once any Southern state accepted the end of slavery and rejected the Confederacy, it was readmitted into the Union. White officials who had served the Confederacy were now elected to govern the Southern states. The ex-Confederate states introduced 'Black Codes' to ensure that blacks did not gain economic, social, political or legal equality. This was 'Reconstruction Confederate style'.

Key questions
How was the defeated South treated during Reconstruction?
What did President Johnson do with the defeated South in 1865?

Key date
Reconstruction Confederate style: 1865

Key term
Reconstruction The process of rebuilding and reforming the 11 ex-Confederate states and restoring them to the Union.

Black codes – examples of inequality

- Economic inequality – blacks were not allowed to buy or rent land.
- Social inequality – blacks were banned from schools.
- Political inequality – blacks were not allowed to vote.
- Legal inequality – of the roughly 500 white men indicted by Texas courts for murdering blacks in 1865–6, not one was convicted.

Key question
Why did Congress impose its own version of Reconstruction on the South?

(b) Congress (1865–6)

When Congress met in December 1865, Northern members were dissatisfied with 'Reconstruction Confederate style'. When newly-elected Southern Congressmen included the vice-president of the Confederacy, 58 Confederate Congressmen, and four Confederate generals, the Republican majority in Congress refused to let them sit in Congress. The Republican Congress also refused to recognise the new state governments in the South. The Republican majority clashed with President Johnson and the Democrats in Congress over issues relating to the rights of black Americans. They clashed over **bills** to improve the Freedmen Bureau (set up by Congress in 1865 to help ex-slaves, particularly through education) and to give blacks civil rights.

Key terms

Bills, Acts and **Vetos**
If a member of Congress or the President wanted a law to be made, he introduced a bill into Congress. If the bill was passed by Congress and accepted by the President, the bill became an Act or law. Under the Constitution, the President had the power to veto (reject) a bill, although if Congress persevered, it could override that veto.

Both bills became **acts** in 1866, despite Johnson's **veto**. Congress then adopted the 14th Amendment, which struck down the Black Codes, guaranteed all citizens equality before the law, and declared that the federal government could intervene if any states tried to deny rights of citizenship to any citizen. The Amendment banned most of the old Confederate élite from holding office.

However, this 14th Amendment was rejected by all the old Confederate states (except Tennessee) and therefore under the Constitution could not become law.

Northerners were now exasperated with the defeated South because:

- The Southern states did not seem to recognise that they had been defeated, as in their rejection of the 14th Amendment.
- There were race riots in Southern cities such as Memphis and New Orleans in summer 1866, in which white groups attacked blacks.
- Secret organisations such as the Ku Klux Klan (see page 28) had been set up to terrorise blacks.

Key date

Civil Rights Act: April 1866

Congress therefore decided it had to enforce its own version of Reconstruction on the South.

(c) Congressional or Radical Reconstruction

In 1867, Congress passed the Military Reconstruction Act, which said:

- No Southern state (except Tennessee) had a legal government.
- The South could not send representatives to Congress unless Congress said they could.
- The ex-Confederate states should be divided into military districts and governed by military commanders.
- In order to return to the Union, Southern states had to draw up new constitutions that would (a) allow blacks to vote, (b) ratify (accept) the 14th Amendment, and (c) disqualify Confederate office holders from political participation.

Southerners felt the Act was vicious. President Johnson thought it gave Southern blacks too much power and would 'Africanise' the South. However, there were important things that the Act did not do. It did not:

- Create any federal agencies to protect black rights.
- Give economic aid to the freed slaves.
- **Disfranchise** Southern whites.

In the 1868 presidential election General Grant (Republican) achieved a narrow victory. The Republicans wanted the black vote, so in 1869 they introduced the 15th Amendment, which said the 'right to vote should not be denied on account of race, colour or previous conditions of servitude'. Given that only eight of the Northern states allowed blacks to vote, it was revolutionary to grant all black males the right to vote. However, once again, important things were left unsaid. The Amendment did not:

- Guarantee all men the right to vote.
- Forbid states to introduce literacy, property and educational tests for would-be voters.

The 14th and 15th Amendments were ratified in 1868 and 1870, respectively, and by the next year all the Southern states had been readmitted to the Union. Southern Republicans dominated the new state governments. This was the era of Radical or **Black Reconstruction**.

Key question
How was Congressional Reconstruction introduced?

Key dates

The Military Reconstruction Act ended 'Reconstruction Confederate style' and initiated Congressional Reconstruction: 1867

The 14th Amendment said blacks were citizens with equal rights: 1868

The 15th Amendment said the vote was not to be denied on account of race: 1870

Key terms

Disfranchise
Deprive someone of their vote.

Black Reconstruction
The phrase was coined by the early twentieth-century white historian Dunning, who sympathised with Southern whites' 'suffering' when blacks gained political power during Reconstruction.

Summary diagram: Starting Reconstruction

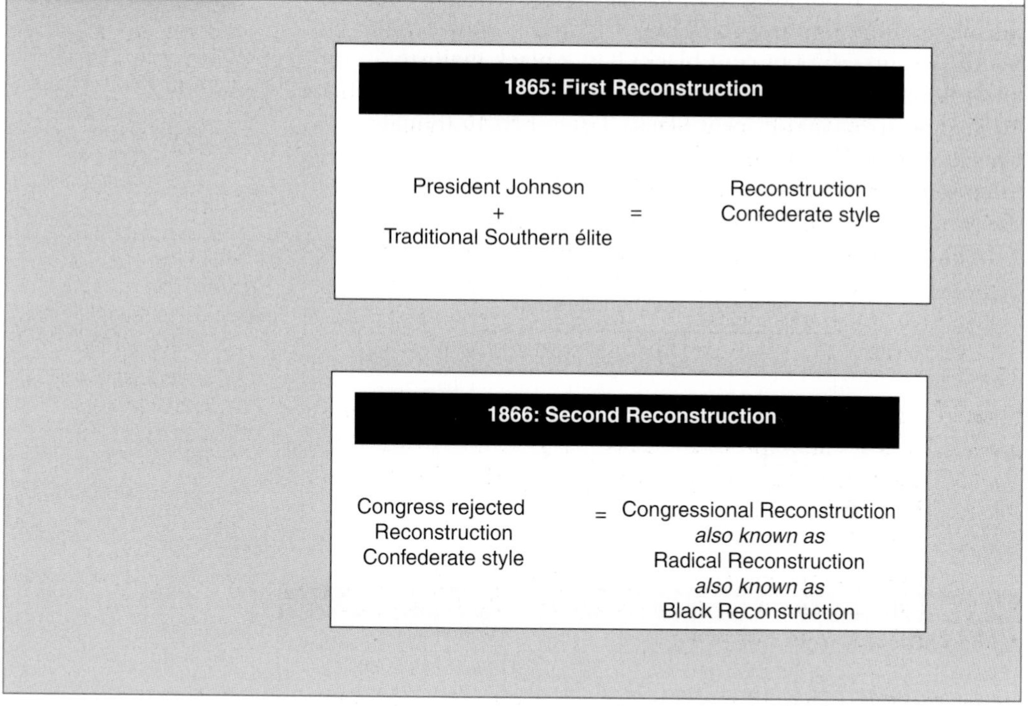

1865: First Reconstruction

President Johnson
+
Traditional Southern élite
=
Reconstruction Confederate style

1866: Second Reconstruction

Congress rejected Reconstruction Confederate style
=
Congressional Reconstruction
also known as
Radical Reconstruction
also known as
Black Reconstruction

Key questions

How did Reconstruction affect blacks?

Did the Civil War and Reconstruction bring economic equality for blacks?

Did Reconstruction bring political equality for blacks?

3 | From Reconstruction to Segregation

(a) The economic position of blacks

Reconstruction failed to bring great economic gains to blacks. Freed black slaves had acquired freedom of movement but because they lacked wealth most remained in the South and farmed. Most remained trapped in poverty, working as tenant farmers (**sharecroppers**) for the white élite in the economically backward South. Most sharecroppers produced cotton, but with the world glut in the 1870s, prices fell. Not surprisingly, Southern income was less than half that of the North. The lack of economic power kept Southern black progress slow.

Key term

Sharecropper
A white landowner provided the land, seed, tools and orders, while a black worker (the sharecropper) provided the labour. The crop produced was usually divided between the two men.

(b) The political position of blacks

(i) Black voters and black officials

After the Civil War, 700,000 blacks were registered to vote in the South, compared to 600,000 eligible whites. Radical Republicans had long advocated equal voting rights for blacks, so Lincoln's Republican Party acquired the black votes.

Southern Democrats and some historians criticised Republican rule in the South as corrupt and dominated by blacks. Black politicians were particularly blamed for the corruption, but they were neither more nor less corrupt than their white contemporaries who still dominated politics in the South and in the North.

Although outnumbered by black Republicans, white Republicans dominated the Southern states during

Reconstruction. Scores of black Republicans were elected to local and state office, but there was no black Southern governor during Reconstruction, nor any black majority in any state senate. Only South Carolina (65 per cent black) had a black majority in the lower house. There were only two black US senators, both from Mississippi (over 50 per cent black). One of them (Senator Charles Caldwell) was shot by whites in a tavern. When he begged them to let him die out in the fresh air, they took him out to the street and pumped him full of 30 extra bullets.

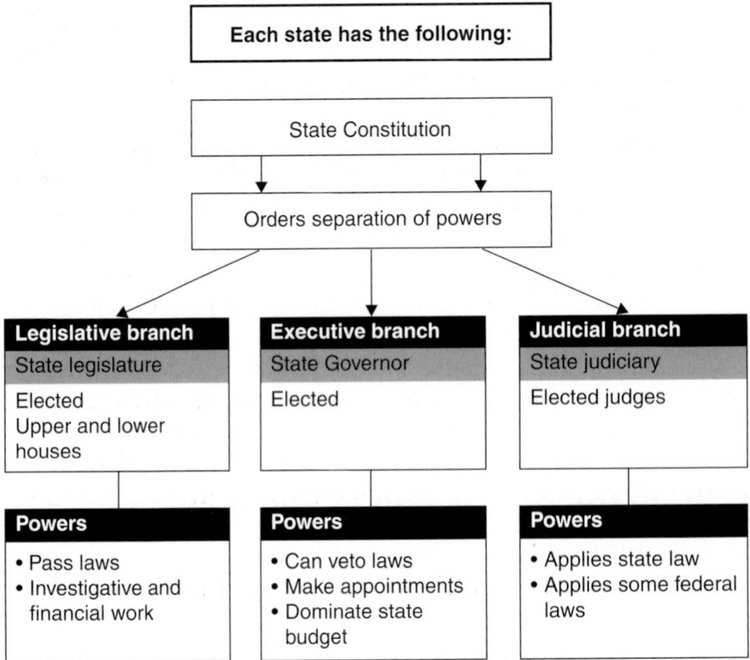

Figure 2.1: The structure of state government in the United States.

(ii) Why were blacks unable to dominate Southern politics?

There were several reasons why blacks were unable to dominate political life in the South:

- Blacks lacked education, organisation and experience.
- Blacks were accustomed to white leadership and domination.
- The black community was divided. Ex-slaves resented free-born blacks who saw themselves as superior.
- Blacks were a minority in most states.
- Sure of the black vote, the Republican Party usually put forward white candidates in the hope of attracting more white votes.
- White Republicans usually considered blacks to be less able to govern than whites.
- Southern black leaders were usually moderates who had no desire to exclude ex-Confederates from office.

(iii) How and why black voting was stopped by the 1890s

Although slavery had been abolished, Southerners still believed in the arguments that had justified it. Southern whites, frightened and resentful of the supposedly racially inferior blacks, depicted Reconstruction as an era of black rule, rape, murder and arson. They made this an excuse to call for the disfranchisement of blacks. Some whites claimed that blacks were immature, irrational, open to corruption, and therefore unfit to possess voting rights. One Mississippi man said that even an educated black like Booker T. Washington (see Chapter 3) was no more fit to vote than 'the coconut-headed, chocolate-coloured, typical little coon' who 'blacks my shoes' and was not 'fit to perform the supreme function of citizenship'.

White supremacist groups such as the Rifle Clubs and the Red Shirts used violence to stop blacks voting. In Louisiana, the White League assassinated several Republican officials in 1874. In the 1890s the Southern state legislatures followed the successful 1890 example of Mississippi and introduced income and literacy qualifications for voting, which penalised more blacks than whites. Illiterate whites were often allowed to vote through notorious 'grandfather clauses', by which a man could vote if it were proved that an ancestor had voted before Reconstruction. White Southern registrars connived at the disqualification of literate blacks by manipulating the literacy test. By 1900, only 3 per cent of Southern blacks could vote. Reconstruction thus failed to bring lasting political gains for blacks.

Key date

Mississippi successfully introduced income and literacy qualifications that stopped blacks voting: 1890

Key question

Did blacks gain social equality during Reconstruction?

(c) Reconstruction and the social position of blacks

(i) Gains

Reconstruction brought some social gains for blacks. Their new freedom of movement enabled those who so desired to move to Southern cities (between 1865 and 1870 the black population of the South's 10 largest cities doubled) or to the North or West. Reconstruction gave some blacks the confidence and opportunity to build and benefit from their own institutions. Black churches and the federal Freedmen's Bureau (1865–72) (see page 23) made education more widely available to blacks, and a few black political leaders, businessmen, teachers, lawyers and doctors emerged. The percentage of illiterate blacks was falling, from 90 per cent in 1860, to 70 per cent in 1880. Some of the educational institutions founded during Reconstruction, including colleges such as Howard (Washington DC) and Fisk (Tennessee), provided some of the leaders of the mid-twentieth-century civil rights movement. Black churches became immensely popular and influential, although naturally they served to perpetuate racial divisions, as whites attended separate churches. In many ways, both blacks and whites preferred to be separate.

(ii) Losses

Although blacks came nowhere near attaining social acceptance and equality after the Civil War, whites remained fearful and hostile. One white Georgian said 'Sambo' should stay in his place, as the United States did not want the 'arrogant, aggressive, school-spoilt African American' who, the Georgian was convinced, 'wants to live without manual labour.' Future President Theodore Roosevelt said, 'A perfectly stupid race [blacks] can never rise to a very high plane'.

A group of white Southern politicians created an anti-Negro crusading group in the 1890s. They depicted blacks as characterised by 'barbarism, voodooism, human sacrifice', and 'contaminated by venereal disease'. Some white politicians advocated deportation, others wanted mass black castration or even, as one Georgian congressman said in 1908, 'utter extermination'.

Social divisions or segregation became enshrined in law. The powers given to individual states under the Constitution facilitated the introduction of **Jim Crow** laws that discriminated against blacks. Individual states controlled not only voting but education, transport and law enforcement. The segregation of schools, housing and public facilities spread quickly after 1865.

Between 1881 and 1915 many Southern states passed laws that insisted upon the separation of white from black in trains, streetcars, stations, theatres, churches, parks, schools, restaurants and cemeteries. Whites were not to use black prostitutes. Textbooks for use in white schools were not to be stored in the same place as those for black schools. Blacks and whites were forbidden to play checkers (draughts) together.

Key question
How and why were black civil rights eroded in the South?

Key term
Jim Crow
An early 1830s' comic, black-faced, minstrel character developed by a white performing artist that proved to be very popular with white audiences. When, after Reconstruction, the Southern states introduced laws that legalised segregation, these were known as 'Jim Crow laws'.

(d) Blacks and the law

The Ku Klux Klan, lynchings and Jim Crow demonstrated black legal inequality.

Key question
Were blacks equal under the law during and after Reconstruction?

(i) The Ku Klux Klan

In 1866 armed white racist groups were set up in most states of the old Confederacy. The most famous was the Ku Klux Klan, established in Tennessee by war hero General Nathan Bedford Forrest. The Klan grew rapidly between 1868 and 1871. Forrest estimated 40,000 members in Tennessee alone, and roughly half a million across the South. Southern Democrats encouraged and colluded in Klan terrorism, which was targeted at black officials, schools and churches. Laws introduced by Republican state governments to try to stop the Ku Klux Klan proved hard to enforce. Klansmen gave each other alibis and were frequently jurors. Governor Holden of North Carolina used the state militia against the Klan. He was condemned by the state legislature for 'subverting [the] personal liberty' of the Klansmen.

In 1870, in response to appeals for help from several state governors, Congress passed three Force Acts, which gave President Grant legal and military power to crush the Klan. These Acts ended most of the Klan violence. However,

Key dates
Establishment of the Ku Klux Klan: 1866
Force Acts gave President Grant powers that successfully crushed the Klan: 1870

Key term

Lynching
Unlawful killing (usually by hanging) of blacks.

ex-Confederate soldiers continued to use violence (particularly **lynching**) and intimidation against Republicans and blacks.

(ii) Lynchings

Lynchings were common. Between 1885 and 1917, 2734 blacks were lynched in the USA. Those responsible for the lynchings were never brought to justice, indicating widespread support for their actions. Blacks had no legal protection.

Key date

PLESSY v. FERGUSON: 1896

(iii) The Supreme Court and blacks

The Supreme Court did nothing about the so-called 'Jim Crow' laws that legalised segregation. Indeed, in PLESSY v. FERGUSON (1896), the Supreme Court said separate but equal facilities were not against the 14th Amendment. The Supreme Court neither prevented Southern states spending 10 times as much on white schools as on black, nor upheld the 15th Amendment, which said blacks should be able to vote. Thus the South ignored the US Constitution with the collusion of the Supreme Court.

Who was Homer Plessy?

Born in New Orleans, Plessy (c1862–1925) was a shoemaker and carpenter who looked white. However, one of his great grandparents was black, which made him 'Negro' in the state of Louisiana. In 1892, Plessy volunteered to be a 'guinea pig' for a group of New Orleans black activists who wanted to test the constitutionality of the 1890 Louisiana Separate Car Law. Plessy bought a first-class railroad ticket and boarded a 'white' carriage. The activists had told the conductor Plessy was legally black, so the conductor asked Plessy to obey the law and get out of the carriage. Plessy refused and the conductor handed him over to the law. Plessy was put in jail, for violating a state racial ordinance. Plessy's lawyers argued that his arrest violated the 13th and 14th Amendments, but the judge ruled in favour of states' rights. The Louisiana Supreme Court upheld the decision approving separate carriages, as did the Supreme Court in PLESSY v. FERGUSON (1896). The remainder of Plessy's life was relatively quiet and trouble-free, but his name, if not his story, remains one of the most famous in American history.

Key question
When and why did the federal government 'abandon' Southern blacks?

(e) The federal government's attitude

Although President Grant ended most of the Klan's violence against blacks, he was keen to end the North's concentration upon the South and to effect a reconciliation with white Southerners. His 1872 Amnesty Act returned voting and office-holding rights to 150,000 ex-Confederates. Also indicative of the loss of Northern interest in Southern blacks was the collapse of the Freedmen's Bureau.

What is black?

Each state's definition of how much 'Negro' blood made a person 'black' varied. In 1910, Virginia switched from the 'single-grandparent' definition that had made Homer Plessy 'black' in 1890s Louisiana, declaring that a black great-great-great grandparent made a person black. In 1930, Virginia said anyone with 'any Negro blood at all' was black – the so-called 'one-drop' measure. Louisiana had become more moderate by then: anyone who *looked* black, *was* black. Ida B. Wells (see page 42) wrote in 1887 about a Tennessee white man who could not get a licence to marry a black woman, so he cut her finger and sucked her blood so he could say he had 'Negro blood'.

The 1875 Civil Rights Act was the last federal attempt to help Southern blacks. The act aimed to prevent discrimination in public places such as railroads, hotels and theatres but had little effect on the South. Several Supreme Court decisions indicated that civil rights were the responsibility of individual states. In 1877 President Hayes (Republican) withdrew all federal troops from the Southern states. While the Republicans concentrated on the North, the South, left to the Democratic Party, became in effect a one-party state. The main unifying factor amongst Southern white Democrats was white supremacy. Democratic politicians such as Ben Tillman of South Carolina and James K. Vardaman of Mississippi specialised in white supremacist rhetoric, and were known as 'demagogues'.

Key dates

Amnesty Act helped to restore political power to ex-Confederates: 1872

Civil Rights Act tried to prevent discrimination in public places: 1875

The end of Reconstruction: 1877

President Hayes withdrew all federal troops from the South: 1877

(f) Erosion of black freedoms in the South

Key question
How and why were Southern black freedoms eroded after 1877?

It proved relatively easy to erode Southern black freedoms after 1877:

- Southern whites used violence and intimidation against blacks.
- Blacks were insufficiently well educated and organised to put up effective opposition.
- The Constitution gave the Southern states power over voting, education, transport and law enforcement, which enabled segregation to spread and work.
- The federal government in Washington wanted to concentrate on the North rather than racial problems in the South.
- Republican voters were predominantly Northerners and Northerners were tired of the South's 'black question'.
- Most Southerners and some Northerners believed that blacks were inferior and did not deserve equality.
- Most Southerners either resented blacks as possible rivals for jobs or wanted to exploit blacks as cheap labour.
- The Supreme Court did nothing to ensure that the 14th and 15th Amendments were made a meaningful reality.

Summary diagram: From Reconstruction to segregation

Black situation	Improvement?
Economic	Free, but without land and good education, stuck in poverty trap
Social	Freedom of movement, more education, growth of black churches, but still considered inferior, and inferiority confirmed in Jim Crow laws
Political	Got the vote, some black officials elected, but then lost the vote
Legal	Supposedly citizens, but Klan violence, lynchings and no Supreme Court aid

4 | Key Debates

Historians are frequently prisoners of their own preconceptions and assumptions, especially where race is concerned. The history of historians on Reconstruction illustrates this.

Early interpretations

President Grant's Vice-President Henry Wilson (1877) naturally exonerated Grant and the Republicans from blame for the failure of Reconstruction. Wilson blamed Southern white racists for the fact that black political participation did not last long. Recent historians have confirmed that Grant was more dedicated to black improvement than was once thought. However, Wilson omitted that most Republican voters were Northern, tired of the black question and the South, which forced President Grant to decrease federal protection for Southern blacks.

In an interesting example of black class divisions, black historian George Washington Williams, who had fought for the North, blamed the failure of Reconstruction on 'an ignorant [black] majority, without competent leaders' who had been unable to rule 'an intelligent Caucasian minority' (1883).

W.E.B. Du Bois and a Marxist interpretation

Between the late 1870s and the mid-1940s, Northern and Southern historians wrote about Reconstruction with the underlying presumption of black racial inferiority, for example, James Ford Rhode (1928). Black historians such as W.E.B. Du Bois (see page 55) naturally disagreed with Rhode's view that Reconstruction represented a foolish attempt to give blacks political power and equality. As a **Marxist historian**, Du Bois saw class struggle as well as racial tension behind white efforts to keep Southern blacks down during and after Reconstruction (1935). Du Bois showed how whites had distorted the history of Reconstruction by selectivity in their use of sources (failing to use black eye witnesses) and events (failing to mention when Congress was supportive of blacks).

Key term

Marxist historian Believes that history has been deeply shaped by economic circumstances. Influenced by the ideology of philosopher Karl Marx.

Contemporary white historians such as William Dunning were contemptuous of Du Bois. Dunning was the leading pro-Southern interpreter of Reconstruction (1907), for whom the 'reckless enfranchisement of the [black] freedmen and their enthronement in power' was a disaster. Later historians writing in the Cold War era disliked the Marxist emphasis in Du Bois' work. However, one of the currently most respected historians of the period, Eric Foner (1982), found Du Bois 'replete with insights', if 'flawed'.

Influence of historical fiction

Sometimes historical fiction has a massive influence on public opinion, and this was the case with Thomas Dixon's *The Clansman: The Historical Romance of the Ku Klux Klan* (1905), which was made into a movie by D.W. Griffith, son of a ruined Confederate colonel. Dixon feared racial mixing, for 'one drop of Negro blood makes a Negro. It kinks the hair, flattens the nose, thickens the lip, puts out the light of intellect, and lights the fire of brutal passions.' President Woodrow Wilson (see page 51) loved the pro-Ku Klux Klan movie. A historian himself, Wilson had written in praise of the Klan (1901).

Changing interpretations

As always, standard interpretations were slowly challenged, and by 1939, Vernon Wharton was giving due credit to black participation in good government in Reconstruction Mississippi. By the 1960s, black historian John Hope Franklin (1961) and Kenneth Stampp rejected the traditional idea that Reconstruction was tragic because greater equality was attempted, and contended that the tragedy of Reconstruction lay in its failure to sustain that promise of equality.

Was Reconstruction successful?

Eric Foner (1988) said yes, because blacks participated in Southern politics. Richard Ranson said yes, because blacks did much better economically than most historians have thought. James McPherson (1998) saw Reconstruction as a worthy experiment by the federal government.

Was Reconstruction a failure?

W.A. Dunning (1907) said yes, because Southern whites suffered at the hands of incompetent black politicians and corrupt, hard Northern politicians. Kenneth Stampp and John Hope Franklin, writing in the 1960s, said yes, but from the black viewpoint, as blacks remained second-class citizens.

Some key books in the debate

W.E.B. Du Bois, *Black Reconstruction in America, 1860–1880* (New York, 1969).
William Dunning, *Reconstruction: Political and Economic, 1865–1877* (New York, 1907).
Eric Foner, *Reconstruction: America's Unfinished Revolution, 1863–1877* (New York, 1988).
Hugh Tulloch, *The Debate on the American Civil War Era* (Manchester, 1999).

Key question
How did Southern blacks respond to their deteriorating situation after 1877?

5 | Blacks' Response to Their Deteriorating Situation

Many blacks never gave up hoping for equality, even as their freedoms were eroded. The black response to the deterioration of their situation varied.

Response 1: co-operation

Blacks responded positively on the rare occasions when white politicians offered co-operation and hope. The People's Party, or Populists, established in 1892, asked blacks to join with them to work in their mutual economic interest. The Populists made electoral pacts with the Republicans in order to oppose the Democrats. This was known as 'Fusion'.

Key date
North Carolina 'experiment in biracial democracy': 1894–8

In North Carolina in 1894, Populist-Republican co-operation got 1000 blacks elected to office. According to the historian Adam Fairclough (2001), this Populist-Republican government of North Carolina between 1894 and 1898 was a revolutionary 'home-grown experiment in biracial democracy', the only such experiment ever attempted in the South. However, in 1898, Red Shirts from the Democratic Party used intimidation and racist slurs to end the Fusion experiment. Blacks were depicted as rapists. Whites rioted in North Carolina's chief city, Wilmington, and ensured that some blacks were expelled and all blacks were disfranchised. President McKinley (Republican) rejected appeals from North Carolina Republicans to send help.

Response 2: emigration and migration

It was hard for blacks to leave the South. Their very basic agricultural skills and illiteracy made migration to Northern cities a frightening prospect, especially as Northern employers and unions excluded black labour. However, Northward migration was popular. Between 1880 and 1900 Chicago's black population rose from 6480 to 30,150.

Some Southern blacks moved West: black migrants founded 25 all-black towns in the new state of Oklahoma.

Other blacks advocated emigration to Africa, to 'establish our own nation', but that was prohibitively expensive and impractical for the vast majority of Southern blacks.

Response 3: political protest

The historian Adam Fairclough describes how throughout the South, blacks held 'indignation meetings', formed equal rights leagues, filed lawsuits to combat discrimination, and boycotted newly-segregated public transport in 25 states. However, Fairclough says the protests were 'sporadic and uncoordinated'.

The elderly Frederick Douglass, ex-slave, abolitionist and universally recognised pre-eminent black leader, urged blacks to stick with the Republican Party. However, campaigning black journalist T. Thomas Fortune said that no white man could be trusted to help blacks, so he established the Afro-American League in 1890. The League had two aims:

- To promote black economic and educational progress.
- To unite blacks in protest against injustice.

The League's inaugural meeting in Chicago attracted 100 delegates from 23 states. Thirty-five-year-old Joseph C. Price, a Bishop of the African Methodist Episcopal Zion Church and President of Livingstone College in North Carolina, was elected president. However, Price's death at 39, divisions within the League, and the establishment of a biracial rival organisation (the National Citizen's Rights Association or NCRA) combined to kill off the League by 1893. NCRA soon followed it.

Not surprisingly, in the face of uncompromising white solidarity, some blacks felt that accommodationism was better than protest.

Profile: Frederick Douglass 1818–95

1818	–	Born in Maryland, the son of a black slave mother and a white father
1830	–	Learnt to read and write, despite laws against slave literacy
1838	–	Escaped from slavery. Settled in the Northern state of Massachusetts
1841	–	Joined and became prominent speaker for anti-slavery movement. White abolitionists told him to speak less intelligently, as people could not believe that he had been a slave
1845	–	Wrote his autobiography, *Narrative of the Life of Frederick Douglass, Written by Himself*, which made him 'the most famous black person in the world' (David Blight, 1993)
1847	–	Edited weekly reform journal, *North Star*
1852	–	Wrote the novel *The Heroic Slave*, which showed his conviction that slaves should rebel for freedom
1856	–	Endorsed the Republican Party
1863	–	Spoke widely in favour of Lincoln's Emancipation Proclamation in 1863, but scolded Lincoln about discrimination against black troops in the Union army
1865	–	Campaigned for equal citizenship for blacks
1877	–	Criticised by other blacks for failing to criticise the Republicans' abandonment of the Reconstruction experiment
1877–81	–	US Marshal for the District of Colombia
1882	–	When his first wife died in 1882, he married a white woman, which antagonised blacks and whites
1890s	–	Denounced lynching, disfranchisement and segregation in the South

Douglass illustrates the changing situation of blacks in the nineteenth century, but his importance lies in the fact that he was the most influential African American of that century. He never stopped agitating for equal rights for blacks.

Key term

Accommodationists Those who favoured initial black concentration upon economic improvement rather than upon social, political and legal equality.

Response 4: accommodationism

Accommodationists believed that the best way for blacks to survive was to accept the status quo and make the most of their economic opportunities. Blacks should develop their educational and vocational skills. The black middle class, especially teachers and ministers, were the strongest supporters of accommodationism. Teachers were motivated by the need for continued white support for black schools and colleges. Black ministers often interpreted white supremacy as God's punishment on blacks for their failure to concentrate upon religion.

The accommodationists and those who favoured protest disagreed with increasing bitterness. Two outstanding black spokespersons of the 1890s stood on these opposing sides. Ida B. Wells favoured protest, while Booker T. Washington championed accommodationism (see Chapter 3).

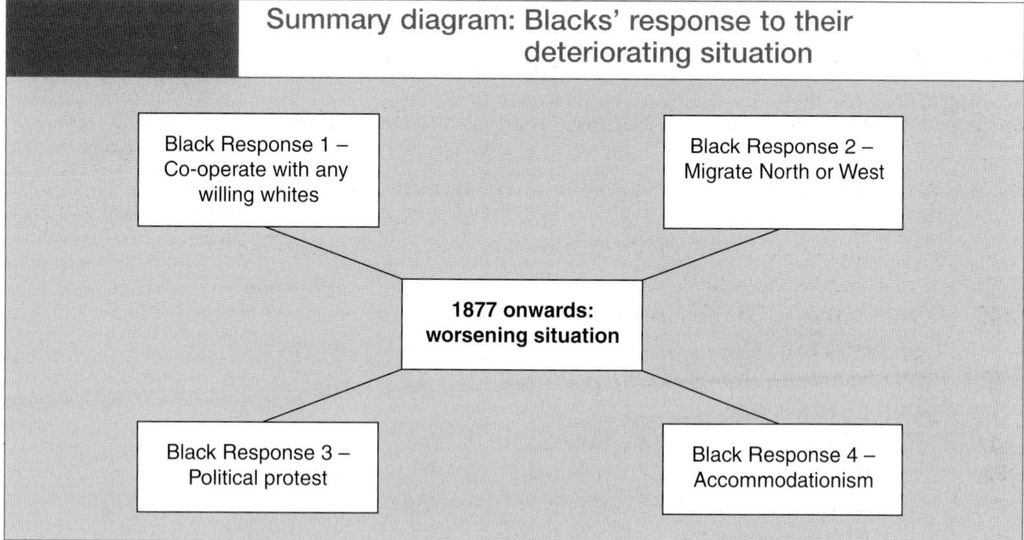

Key question
What was the situation of non-whites in 1900?

6 | American Race Relations in 1900: Summary

The USA thus entered the twentieth century with multiple racial problems. A large black minority and small Indian, Hispanic and Chinese minorities were faced with a white majority who feared racial mixing and were convinced of the supremacy of the white race. Early twentieth century anthropologist Joseph Le Conte asserted that scientific study had 'thoroughly established' that blacks were 'totally incapable of development'.

Fearful whites retreated to segregated educational institutions and residential areas, away from those whose skin was black, red or yellow.

Why did non-whites apparently accept this position of inferiority?

Key terms

De jure Legal, in law.

De facto In fact if not in law.

- Blacks had to overcome ***de jure*** (legal) discrimination in the South, and ***de facto*** (actual) discrimination in the North.

- The end of slavery had left Southern blacks with freedom of movement but without material resources. Most blacks were in a poverty trap. Without good educational opportunities, it was difficult for blacks to better themselves.
- Education for blacks became available in the South only after the Civil War. The new black schools and colleges depended upon Northern white funding.
- With so little and such poor quality education available, it was difficult to organise any mass black movement for equality.
- Indians were divided amongst themselves, because of tribal rivalries and disagreements as to the wisdom of rejecting their traditional culture in favour of the white man's.
- Deprived of their traditional lands, Indians were locked in a poverty trap.
- Most Indians lacked both organisation and understanding of the white man's laws and concepts such as private property.

However, while in the nineteenth century whites had virtually unchallenged domination over other races in America, in the twentieth century there were attempts to alter the balance.

Study Guide: AS Questions

In the style of OCR

1. 'In reality, the position of blacks in the South was little better in 1877 than it had been in 1863.' How far do you agree?

Source: OCR, May 2002

2. To what extent was Lincoln's Emancipation Proclamation (1863) the result of a genuine desire to free blacks?

Source: OCR, January 2003

3. How far were the civil rights of blacks eroded in the period after 1877?

Source: OCR, January 2003

Exam tips

The cross-references are intended to take you to some of the material that will help you to answer the questions.

1. Questions that ask you about the 'position of blacks' can usually be approached through the following paragraphs:

- Their political situation – do blacks have the vote? In theory? In practice? Are there any elected black officials (pages 25–6)?
- Their social situation – are they looked upon/treated as equals? Can they use the same facilities (e.g. schools, transport) as whites (pages 27–8)?
- Their economic situation – are there opportunities for blacks to have as wide a variety of jobs as whites? Are they confined to lower paid jobs (page 25)?
- Their legal situation – do they have equal protection before the law? Are they proportionately represented amongst law enforcement officials and agencies (pages 28–9)?

These topical paragraphs provide you with your essay organisation. Within each paragraph, you need to look first at the position in 1863, then in 1877, mentioning crucial dates in between that brought about change.

'How far' is examiner-speak for 'give arguments for and against this proposition in your answer'.

Take, for example, the economic situation paragraph: in 1863 many blacks were still slaves, despite the Emancipation Proclamation. As slaves, they earned no money for their labour, but their masters provided food and shelter. By 1877, they were theoretically free to do any work in any place they wanted, but in practice, lacking property, education and any experience other than farming and domestic service, most were scraping a living sharecropping on some white-owned land. In terms of material goods, they often remained as poor, if not poorer than in 1863, and just as subject to white landowners. In that sense, things really were not much better, although at least they now had the opportunity to risk moving to seek work elsewhere (perhaps in the city or in the North) and they surely felt better at the end of enslavement.

Within each of these paragraphs, you need some concrete facts to prove your arguments. For example, in your economic paragraph, from page 33, you could use the statistic that between 1865 and 1870, the black population of the South's 10 largest cities doubled – blacks were clearly using their new freedom of movement to seek economic betterment. From page 25, you could mention the cotton glut of the 1870s – falling prices would have hurt black sharecroppers.

2. This is basically a causes question: why did Lincoln issue the Emancipation Proclamation? However, in order to make it less straightforward/more interesting, one of the reasons why he issued the proclamation is picked out for you to concentrate upon. 'To what extent', like 'how far', is examiner-speak for 'look at all the reasons why, but concentrate on comparing their importance with this specified reason' (i.e. that he had a 'genuine desire to free blacks').

Using information about Lincoln's position/words on race, you could do a paragraph on 'yes it was a genuine desire', then another on 'no it was not a genuine desire'. Then in the other paragraphs, you could look at the other reasons, comparing their importance to the 'genuine desire' argument. For example, you could look at the 'military necessity' motive (page 19) and perhaps make the point that if Lincoln genuinely wanted to free blacks, he would have done so long before the defeat at Bull Run showed up the Northern need for black help.

3. This is another question that asks you to look at the situation in two different years. This is like question 1 in style. You could even use similar paragraphs to question 1 if you define civil rights in terms of political, social, economic and legal equality. It is probably best to define what you mean by civil rights in your introduction: that way, so long as your definition is reasonable, you can set the agenda for the rest of your essay. In many race relations questions, you need to note carefully the geographical areas that the examiner expects you to cover. In question 1 you were clearly directed to the South. In this question, you need to mention the North also and you need to be very clear in your essay as to which area of the USA you are talking about – separate paragraphs for the North and the South might help to clarify your location (to you and to the examiner).

3 Protest or Accommodationism 1880–1915

POINTS TO CONSIDER

African Americans have always disagreed amongst themselves over ways in which they should relate to white Americans and how the black situation could be improved. An early example of divisions among leading black spokespersons can be seen with Ida B. Wells, Booker T. Washington and W.E.B. Du Bois. This chapter looks at their lives and careers and invites consideration of two questions:

- How much did Wells, Washington and Du Bois help their fellow blacks?
- Who was right – Washington (accommodationism) or Wells and Du Bois (protest)?

The chapter is divided into the following sections:

- Ida B. Wells and Lynching
- Booker T. Washington and the 'decades of disappointment' 1880–1915

Key dates

1868	Northern whites established Hampton Institute to educate freed blacks
1881	Booker T. Washington appointed Principal of Tuskegee
1883	Booker T. Washington first black to address national education conference
1887	Tennessee Supreme Court decided against Wells in railroad carriage segregation case
1892	Ida B. Wells had to leave the South because of her anti-lynching campaign
1895	Booker T. Washington's 'Atlanta Compromise' speech
1896	Establishment of National Association of Colored Women
1897	W.E.B. Du Bois became a professor at Atlanta University
1900	Booker T. Washington established National Negro Business League
1901	Booker T. Washington dined at the White House
1905	Establishment of the Niagara Movement to end racial inequality

1906 Brownsville (Texas) race riots
1908 Springfield Riot – 2000 blacks driven out
1909 NAACP established
1911 Booker T Washington's unsuccessful suit against assault
Booker T. Washington established National Urban League
1912 President Woodrow Wilson determined to segregate federal bureaucracy
1915 Popular pro-Klan movie, 'Birth of a Nation'

1 | Ida B. Wells and Lynching

Key questions
How and why was Ida B. Wells important?
Why were so many blacks lynched?

(a) The significance of lynching

The erosion of black rights after Reconstruction is well illustrated by the number of lynchings. Between 1880 and 1930, Southern whites lynched over 3000 blacks, usually without trial and without rational reason. Law enforcement officials, politicians, editors and jurors colluded and/or participated in lynchings. Lynching was significant because it demonstrated that blacks had no legal protection and that whites thought black lives worthless and did not consider it a crime to kill them. Blacks who were lynched were usually accused of rape. Southern whites defended lynching as a necessary defence of Southern white women against black rapists. The 'black rapist' myth was also used to justify segregation and economic discrimination.

Most black organisations were fearful of campaigning against lynching in the 1880s, because they were already on the defensive against accusations of the high black crime rate (the judicial system treated white criminals more leniently so statistics suggested that black criminality was greater than white). Southern blacks were reluctant to campaign against lynching because such a campaign could get them killed in the South.

Black criminality
Wells was infuriated by sentencing disparities in the judicial system: 'If a white man steals he often times goes to the legislature or Congress, and the Negro goes to jail.' She cited a white city official who stole $6000 of taxpayers' money, served 15 months, and got pardoned by the Governor. She compared a black man who stole a box of cigars, four bottles of whiskey and two steaks – he got eight years.

Blacks who chose to protest against lynching in the late nineteenth and early twentieth century represent, according to the historian Adam Fairclough, 'the starting point of the modern civil rights struggle – the beginning of the fightback against white supremacy'. The heroines of this early struggle were Ida B. Wells and the black women's clubs; the heroes were the founders (1909) of the National Association for the Advancement of Colored People (NAACP).

Key date
National Association for the Advancement of Colored People (NAACP) established: 1909

Summary diagram: Lynching – why?

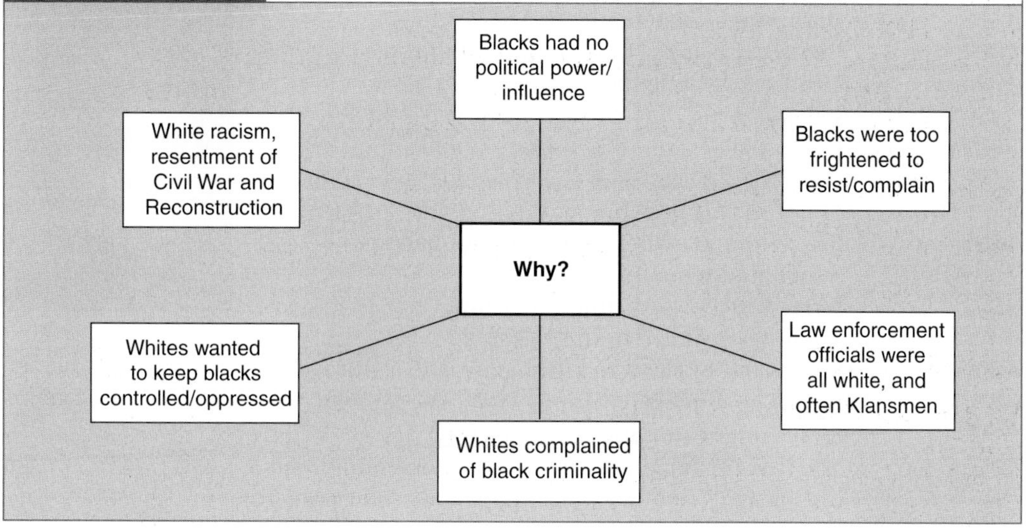

Blacks had no political power/ influence

White racism, resentment of Civil War and Reconstruction

Blacks were too frightened to resist/complain

Why?

Whites wanted to keep blacks controlled/oppressed

Law enforcement officials were all white, and often Klansmen

Whites complained of black criminality

Key question
What does Ida B. Wells' early life tell us about Southern blacks in the second half of the nineteenth century?

(b) The life and work of Ida B. Wells

(i) Early years

Wells' slave parents worked in a Mississippi town. Urban slaves were better equipped to cope with post-Civil War freedom than rural slaves. Wells was born into slavery during the Civil War, but her carpenter father prospered with freedom and sent her to Rust University, one of many schools established by Northern Methodists. Rust taught elementary, high school and trainee teacher pupils. Wells' independence and aggressive personality caused the college's white president to expel her. Nevertheless, she became a teacher, living and working in Memphis, Tennessee, after 1881.

(ii) Teaching

Memphis's black population had rocketed from 3500 in 1860 to over 16,000 in 1865, which worried Memphis whites. Some black Memphians prospered. One-quarter of the city's policemen were black. Black teachers such as Wells received the same salary as white teachers, but had larger classes. The black sense of community was increased by several black Memphis newspapers.

In 1883 a white train conductor tried to drag Wells out of the first-class carriage for which she had paid. She bit his hand, left the train, sued the railroad company and won $200. Following another eviction in 1884 she sued again, winning $500. However, in 1887 the Tennessee Supreme Court decided in favour of the railroad company's appeal. 'Oh God', asked Wells, 'is there no justice in this land for us?'

Key date
Tennessee Supreme Court decided against Wells in railroad carriage segregation case: 1887

Profile: Ida B. Wells 1862–1931

1862	–	Born into a slave family in Mississippi
1884	–	Became a teacher in Memphis, Tennessee
1884–5	–	Unsuccessful litigation against railroad car segregation
1889	–	Wrote articles for several black publications; christened 'Princess of the Press'; became co-owner of a weekly called *Memphis Free Speech*
1891	–	Fired from teaching for criticising inadequate segregated schools
1892	–	Wrote article condemning lynching; forced to leave Memphis and live in the North
1893–4	–	Supported by Frederick Douglass, she campaigned in Britain against lynching, which encouraged more American criticism of lynching
1895	–	Married Ferdinand Barnett, black lawyer, founder of Chicago's first black newspaper, assistant state attorney (1896–1911). Lived in Chicago
1908	–	After riots and lynchings in Springfield, Illinois, called for a national black organisation
1909	–	One of NAACP's' Founding Forty' members
1913	–	Helped to found first black women's suffrage club in Chicago, which assisted the election of Chicago's first black Alderman, Oscar de Priest (1915)
1917	–	Protested about the hanging of 12 black soldiers for participating in a riot in Houston, Texas. Her passport was withdrawn, so could not attend the Paris Peace Conference as the nominated delegate of Marcus Garvey's UNIA (see page 67)
1918–19	-	Publicised post-war race riots, causing federal agencies to label her 'subversive' and to note rumours that she and Oscar de Priest were making bombs and collecting hand grenades
1920s	-	Helped to establish Chicago branch of A. Philip Randolph's Brotherhood of Sleeping Car Porters and Maids (see page 75)
1930	-	Ran unsuccessfully for political office as an independent, saying that Democrats had always been anti-black and Republicans had abandoned the South after Reconstruction
1931	-	Died

Wells was important because of her life-long, wide-ranging activism, particularly her publicising of the evils of lynching. She helped to establish community institutions and local and national organisations that helped both poor and middle class blacks. She empowered women. Her strategies, for example against lynching, were adopted by subsequent activists. Her life illustrates black problems and progress.

Key question
In what ways did Ida B. Wells help blacks?

(iii) 'Princess of the Press'

Wells found teaching children tedious. She began writing for black newspapers. She became part owner in 1889 of the *Memphis Free Speech*. When the school board sacked her for criticising the city's segregated schools in 1891 she became a full-time journalist, nicknamed 'Princess of the Press'. Wells' subject matter of sex and violence assured her of a massive audience.

Wells blamed blacks as well as whites for the post-Reconstruction deterioration in the black situation, describing blacks as a 'disorganised mass'. She criticised passive acceptance of white violence. She applauded the 'true spark of manhood' of blacks in Georgetown, Kentucky, who set fire to white property as retaliation for lynching. Wells believed that it might be necessary 'to burn up whole towns' to stop lynching.

Key date
Wells driven out of Memphis for opposing lynching: 1892

In 1892 the three black owners of a Memphis grocery store were taken from jail by a white mob and shot dead. The basic cause of this lynching was the economic jealousy of a white grocer. Armed black men defended the black-owned store with guns, and shot three Sheriff's deputies. The black grocers were arrested, jailed, then lynched. No-one was ever tried for the lynching. As always, some whites said those lynched were rapists. 'Nobody in this section of the country believes the old threadbare lie that Negro men rape white women', raged Wells in the *Memphis Free Speech*. White Memphis papers called for the lynching of the 'man' who wrote that, but luckily Wells was out of town. She never returned to Memphis. Ironically, driving her out only led her to publicise lynching even more effectively in the North.

Wells believed that one motive of lynching was to 'get rid of Negroes who were acquiring wealth and property and thus keep the race terrorised'. She wrote anti-lynching articles for many newspapers. She lectured on lynching in cities such as Washington, Philadelphia and Boston, and in Britain (1893–4). The consequent international embarrassment made her nearly as famous as Frederick Douglass, although not all blacks approved of her outspokenness. One Memphis minister accused her of 'stirring up', while a black Kansas newspaper called her that 'crazy … animal from Memphis'. Before her marriage, her sexuality and morality were frequently called into question.

(iv) The power of the word

Wells played on basic human emotions. She described how the baby daughter of a man lynched in Memphis,

> too young to express how she misses her father, toddles to the wardrobe, seizes the leg of [his] trousers … hugs and kisses them with evident delight and stretches up her little hands to be taken up into the arms which will never more clasp his daughter.

Wells appealed to white consciences, self-interest and national pride:

> Repeated attacks on the life, liberty and happiness of any citizen … are … imperilling … the freedom of government, law and order … and yet this Christian nation, the flower of the 19th-century civilisation, says it can do nothing to stop this inhuman slaughter.

Wells pointed out that while white Americans sang of the 'Sweet land of liberty', blacks lacked real freedom. Wells did not hold back when talking about the horrors of lynching, describing one in Paris, Texas, where the accused rapist was poked with red-hot irons for 50 minutes, doused with kerosene and set on fire. The accused then tried to get away from the fire and was put back in, twice. Wells described how the 10,000 audience fought for his bones, buttons and teeth as souvenirs, while a little girl proudly said, 'I saw them burn the nigger, didn't I Mama?'.

(v) 'The first step … is organisation'

Wells found all politicians unimpressive. She was particularly scathing about black Mississippi Senator Blanche Bruce: 'What can history say of our Senator Bruce, save that he held the chair of a Senator for six years, drew his salary and left others to champion the Negro's cause in the Senate?'. She was an enthusiastic supporter of T. Thomas Fortune's National Afro-American League. Wells said blacks 'can no longer be passive onlookers … The first step … is organisation.' She wanted the League to boycott the segregated railroads, but was soon critical of League leaders:

> A handful of men, with no report of work accomplished, no one in the field to spread it, no plan of work laid out – no intelligent direction – meet and by their child's play illustrate in their own doings the truth of the saying that Negroes have no capacity for organisation. Meanwhile a whole race is lynched, proscribed, intimidated, deprived of its political and civil rights, herded into boxes (by courtesy called separate cars) … and we sit tamely by without using the only means – that of thorough organisation and earnest work to prevent it. No wonder the world at large spits upon us with impunity.

When Fortune's League quickly collapsed, Wells looked to women for a national organisation.

(vi) The Black Clubwomen's Movement

Key date

National Association of Colored Women established: 1896

Both black and white women formed clubs to do charitable work and to campaign for the cleaning up of cities. The black women's clubs that developed in the 1890s joined together in the National Association of Colored Women (NACW) in 1896. By 1900, NACW had 300 local clubs and 18,000 members. In 1915, it had 50,000. Wells played an important role in the foundation of this movement that initially emphasised lynching and the black lack of civil rights. Always controversial, she soon made enemies within NACW, claiming that it had given up the struggle for equal rights when it changed its focus from protest to home improvement and leaned increasingly toward Booker T. Washington's emphasis on economic improvement (see page 49).

The black clubwomen's movement was very much a middle class movement. Members looked down on the common law marriages and emotional worship habits of lower class blacks. The lack of broad-based support, internal squabbling and snobbery, and the power of white supremacists meant that NACW declined by the second quarter of the twentieth century, but they had raised awareness of social issues and established schools, orphanages, clinics, hospitals and homes for the elderly.

(vii) More organisations

In 1898, Fortune's League was revived as the Afro-American Council, in which Wells tried to work with Booker T. Washington. Washington had inherited Frederick Douglass' position as undisputed African American leader. Wells' disagreements with Washington and her alignment with W.E.B. Du Bois (see page 55) led to her marginalisation in the Council.

Edged out of national organisations, Wells concentrated on the local community, until in 1909 she was one of the founding committee members of a new, national organisation, the white-dominated NAACP. As always, she soon became disillusioned and fell out with her colleagues, one of whom said of her, 'She was a great fighter, but we knew she had to play a lone hand'. Wells decided to concentrate upon local organisations and self-help, for example, in 1913, she founded Illinois' first female suffrage organisation and led a successful campaign to stop legal segregation of public transport in Illinois.

(viii) Ida B. Wells' achievement

By the end of her life, Ida B. Wells was an increasingly isolated crusader. However, W.E.B. Du Bois credited her with beginning 'the awakening of the conscience of the nation', saying her 'work has easily been forgotten because it was taken up on a much larger scale by the NAACP and carried to greater success.' Although Wells failed to get the federal government to legislate against lynching, she put the issue in the public eye. Other factors (such as Southern white fear of the loss of black labour when blacks migrated North) contributed to the post-1892 decrease in lynching, but Wells also deserves credit. She was an activist role model for all blacks, but particularly for women. Her strategies were adapted by subsequent activists.

(ix) Historians and Ida B. Wells

For many years after her death, Wells was virtually forgotten outside Chicago, where she lived from 1895 to 1931. Her daughter struggled for 40 years to get her mother's autobiography published, finally succeeding in 1970. By that date, greater black militancy and feminism led to greater interest in and sympathy with Ida B. Wells. Much has been written about her since.

Summary diagram: The activism of Ida B. Wells

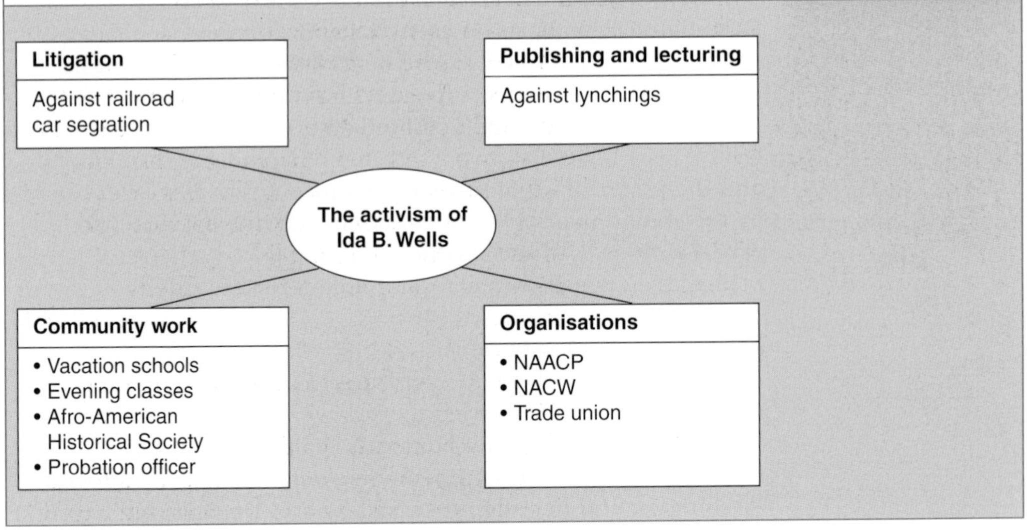

2 | Booker T. Washington and the 'Decades of Disappointment' (1880–1915)

Some historians have described the years 1880–1915 as the 'decades of disappointment' for blacks. Chapter 2 has shown how much of the promise of the 1860s was not fulfilled. Blacks disagreed over whether the career and the achievements of Booker T. Washington illustrated 'decades of disappointment' or decades of progress for blacks.

(a) Booker T. Washington's life up to 1895

Key question
What does Booker T. Washington's life reveal about race relations and opportunities for blacks between 1856 and 1895?

(i) Early years

Born into slavery on a Virginia tobacco plantation, Washington was brought up in a dirt-floored log cabin without windows or beds. His mother was a black slave. His grey eyes and reddish hair were a legacy from a white father who never admitted paternity. Washington subsequently said he was fond of his white owners and worried about their safety in the Civil War. His family rejoiced at the Emancipation Proclamation (see page 18) but were uncertain about coping with freedom. They moved to West Virginia, where Washington worked as a salt packer, coal miner and domestic servant and managed to obtain some schooling.

(ii) Education

Key date
Northern whites established the Hampton Institute to educate freed blacks: 1868

The Hampton Institute was established in 1868 by a group of Northern whites in order to teach trades and industry to freed black slaves. The Virginia state government gave it financial assistance in 1872. Helped by his white employer and black friends, Washington set off for Hampton in 1872. He was forced to spend the first night of the journey outside a hotel that would not accept black guests. His Hampton entrance examination consisted of cleaning a room.

Profile: Booker T. Washington 1856–1915

1856	–	Born into a slave family in Virginia
1865	–	His freed family moved to West Virginia; he worked as a salt packer and coal miner, while attending a local elementary school for blacks
1872	–	Attended Hampton Institute, Virginia. His entrance examination was to clean a room. Worked as a custodian to pay his school fees
1875–8	–	Taught in West Virginia
1879–81	–	Taught at Hampton
1881	–	Appointed principal of Tuskegee, a college with neither lands nor buildings
1884	–	Addressed National Education Association in Wisconsin
Mid-1880s	–	Began secret working relationship with T. Thomas Fortune, editor of *New York Age*, a leading black newspaper, which was militantly anti-lynching and pro-civil rights, and refused to carry advertisements for hair straightening and skin lightening
1887	–	Supported Fortune's Afro-American League, a civil rights organisation
1895	–	'Atlanta Compromise' speech seemed to accept segregation and emphasised economic advancement for blacks
1898	–	President McKinley visited Tuskegee
1900	–	Founded the National Negro Business League
1901	–	President Theodore Roosevelt invited Washington to dine at the White House; outcry caused Roosevelt to admit (privately) a 'mistake' Autobiography, *Up From Slavery*, a bestseller, translated into 18 languages
1903	–	W.E.B. Du Bois' *The Souls of Black Folk* attacked Washington's accommodationist philosophy and emphasis on vocational and industrial education
1906	–	Five-day race riots in Atlanta: Washington helped bring both sides together to reconstruct. Fortune broke with Washington, exasperated by his low-key response to race riots in Atlanta and Brownsville, Texas
1908–11	–	Secretly worked to get Supreme Court to overturn harsh Alabama peonage (virtual slavery) law
1909	–	Anxious that establishment of NAACP might decrease his influence in the black community
1911	–	The white New Yorker who Washington accused of assault was acquitted; jury believed Washington had made advances to the man's wife
1915	–	Died

Unaccustomed to 'luxuries', it took Washington a long time to work out why his bed was provided with two sheets. Initially, he slept on top of both, then underneath both, then finally got it right by observing the other students. Washington was one of Hampton's youngest students; some were in their forties. Extra help was given to poor students. A white New England philanthropist gave Washington financial assistance and his maths teacher Miss Mackie gave him paid jobs. He was surprised that this well-educated white woman from a wealthy family cleaned the school buildings alongside him.

(iii) Teacher

Washington returned to West Virginia to teach in 1875. He was saddened when his old white employer died trying to protect blacks in a clash with the white supremacists of the Ku Klux Klan. From 1879, Hampton employed him to educate Indians. It was a difficult job. Indians considered blacks inferior for having accepted slavery. Many Indians had themselves owned slaves before Emancipation.

(iv) Head of Tuskegee

Washington was such a successful teacher that he was offered the post of founder and head of an institute of higher education for blacks in Tuskegee, Alabama. The idea of a black principal was revolutionary. The task was daunting. The Alabama authorities gave Tuskegee Institute minimal funding. Lacking school buildings, Washington had to teach in an abandoned chicken coop with a leaking roof. A student had to hold an umbrella over his head. Nevertheless, the Institute soon had 70 students. Washington employed black teachers such as Olivia Davidson, whom he married. Born into slavery, Davidson had lost a brother to the Ku Klux Klan. The wife of President Hayes funded her education at Hampton.

Key dates

Booker T. Washington appointed principal of Tuskegee: 1881

Booker T. Washington first black to address national education conference: 1883

In 1882, Washington purchased an old plantation with donations he had solicited from wealthy Northern whites. Washington led the reluctant students in cleaning up the hen house and stable. He felt that the best opportunities for blacks lay in industrial trades, so his curriculum concentrated on practical subjects. Tuskegee taught modern agricultural techniques, trained skilled artisans, and prepared female students to be good housekeepers. Some teachers, students and parents disagreed with Washington's emphasis on the importance of some physical labour for students.

(v) Black spokesman

Washington's reputation grew. He was invited to address a prestigious national education conference in Wisconsin. It was the first time that such a conference discussed black and Indian education. Some of the black delegates were turned away from their pre-booked hotel rooms, but when the conference organisers threatened the hotel with a lawsuit they were allowed in. Washington's speech called for racial harmony. However, he was quick to complain in the press when whites threatened some Tuskegee teachers who had paid for and tried to travel in a first-class railroad car. Railroad officials had forced them to travel some of the way in the far inferior 'Jim Crow' car.

Washington had an increasing number of public-speaking engagements to fulfil. By 1895 he was recognised as America's leading spokesman for black people and their concerns.

Key question
What did Booker T. Washington achieve for blacks?

Key dates
Booker T. Washington established National Negro Business League: 1900
Booker T. Washington's 'Atlanta Compromise' speech: 1895

(b) The achievements of Booker T. Washington

(i) Economic improvement

Through his work at Tuskegee, Washington helped give several generations of blacks vocational education which increased their self-confidence and economic opportunities. In 1900 he established the National Negro Business League, which supported black enterprises. His own struggle for education, and his speeches, books and national fame inspired other blacks to seek education and improvement. It was rarely easy. Washington's daughter graduated from Tuskegee in 1900. She went on to a prestigious Northern women's college, Wellesley. Because of her colour she was forbidden to live on the campus with the other students so she moved to another college.

(ii) 'Atlanta Compromise' speech

Washington was the pre-eminent spokesman for blacks. His most famous speech was at the opening of the Atlanta World Fair. Atlanta's white leadership wanted to project a new image of enlightened racial harmony, so the Fair had a 'Negro Building' to demonstrate black progress at Hampton and Tuskegee. Washington was invited to speak. No black speaker had ever appeared before such an important Southern gathering. The audience included many proud blacks, but also some resentful whites who heckled him. Washington said blacks should not be ashamed of the fact 'that the masses of us are to live by the productions of our hands'. He said it was foolish to agitate for social equality. Equality would come through hard work not force, as no-one of economic importance was ever ostracised for long. Contemporary assessments of the quality of his speech (which became known as the 'Atlanta Compromise') and his ideas differed.

Northern black militants thought that when Washington sought limited economic opportunity and slow progress towards equality, he sought too little. Other blacks felt that limited economic gains were all they could hope for at present and were better than nothing. Washington's willingness to accept social segregation was acceptable to those blacks who had little desire to mix with whites, but other blacks felt that any kind of segregation contributed to the perpetuation of racial inequality. Southern white supremacists thought he sought too much for blacks, even though his speech accepted segregation and emphasised black devotion to whites.

(iii) Role model

In the early twentieth century, Washington began publishing books. The manufacturer of Kodak cameras claimed it was reading Washington's autobiographical *Up From Slavery* that made him donate $10,000 to Tuskegee. The book emphasised racial harmony rather than conflict and gave due credit to any whites who had helped Washington. It was an inspiring story of black achievement.

(iv) Presidential adviser

As the leading black spokesman, Washington met, impressed and befriended a succession of American presidents, starting with President Cleveland.

President Cleveland

Cleveland became a patron of Tuskegee Institute. Presidents had to take notice of Washington. He was becoming an international figure. On a European vacation he was invited to tea with Queen Victoria.

President McKinley

In 1896 Washington became President McKinley's adviser on black affairs. The Southern press was critical of a white president associating closely with Washington, and was particularly hostile when Washington referred to the 'unjust discrimination that law and custom make' against blacks in 'their own country'. When McKinley appointed many blacks to governmental positions, racial tensions increased.

President Roosevelt

In 1901 President Theodore Roosevelt invited Washington to an official dinner at the White House, the first black thus honoured. This was greatly criticised in the white Southern press. 'Afar off', said Senator Ben Tillman of South Carolina, Washington 'sees a vision of equality. The action of President Roosevelt in entertaining that nigger will necessitate our killing a thousand niggers in the South before they will learn their place again'. Despite the controversy, Washington's relationships with presidents successfully raised the black profile and black morale.

Key dates

President Theodore Roosevelt invited Booker T. Washington to dine at the White House: 1901

Brownsville (Texas) race riots: 1906

Washington's presidential contacts did not always help blacks. Although Theodore Roosevelt paid lip service to the advancement of blacks in government, he cut back the number of black political appointments. In 1904 Washington tried, but failed, to get Roosevelt's Republican Party to condemn lynching and disfranchisement. Washington and Roosevelt bitterly disagreed about the 'Brownsville riots'. In 1906 a white man was killed in a shoot-out between blacks and whites outside Fort Brown, Texas. An armed mob from nearby Brownsville marched on the fort demanding that black troops be punished. The black troops denied involvement. Their white officers disbelieved them. The matter was referred to President Roosevelt and raised racial tension nationally. Whites in Atlanta attacked the city's black

Key term

Uncle Tom
The Northern abolitionist Harriet Beecher Stowe wrote the book *Uncle Tom's Cabin* in 1852. Her character was a slave who deferred to whites. Twentieth-century blacks called other blacks 'Uncle Tom' if they seemed too deferential to whites.

business district for five days: 10 blacks died, and many fled the city. Despite Washington's pleas, Roosevelt decided to dismiss all the black soldiers at Fort Brown. In a message to Congress in 1906, Roosevelt justified the lynching of blacks as a lesser crime than blacks raping white women (see page 40). As Roosevelt's advisor on black affairs, Washington had read the speech in advance but failed to get Roosevelt to moderate it. Black militants increasingly regarded Washington as an '**Uncle Tom**' who hung around condescending whites who did nothing for him or his people.

President Taft

In 1908, Washington managed to dissuade President Taft from supporting black disfranchisement laws in his acceptance speech. Although Taft asked Washington to be his unofficial adviser, he stopped appointing blacks in the South and gradually removed those already there. However, Taft appointed a black Assistant Attorney General (the highest rank yet attained by a black official) and several blacks to diplomatic posts in African countries.

Key dates

President Wilson determined to segregate federal bureaucracy: 1912

Booker T. Washington's unsuccessful suit against assault: 1911

President Wilson

In 1912, a Southerner was elected President for the first time since the Civil War. Woodrow Wilson wanted nothing to do with Booker T. Washington. Wilson wanted to introduce Southern-style segregation to the civil service. His officials conducted investigations that concluded that white government workers were suffering. White women were 'forced unnecessarily to sit at desks with coloured women' and sometimes unable to use the same toilet when black users were 'diseased'. Wilson agreed that toilet and eating facilities should be segregated and black men limited to jobs where they would not be in contact with white women. Washington and other black leaders protested but Wilson told them, 'Segregation is not humiliating but a benefit, and ought to be so regarded by you gentlemen.' He felt there was 'nothing to apologise for in the past of the South, including slavery, which had done more for the Negro in 250 years than African freedom had done since the building of the pyramids.' Wilson praised the Ku Klux Klan for helping to save the South from black rule during Reconstruction and removed blacks from government positions. Many of them had been Washington's nominees. However, Washington's mobilisation of opposition stopped the Southern-dominated Congress passing a bill barring foreign-born blacks from immigration into the USA.

(v) White hostility

Like all famous men, Washington aroused hostility as well as admiration. Many whites loathed him. A white chambermaid in an Indianapolis hotel was supposedly fired for refusing to make up Washington's bed, so a Texas newspaper raised funds for this 'self-respecting girl'. Hostile whites grasped any opportunity to damage Washington's reputation, and were particularly keen to 'prove' the supposed excessive sexuality of blacks. In 1911 Washington visited New York. He claimed to have got lost in an area frequented by prostitutes when looking up an old friend. A white drunk attacked him there and accused him of theft. The drunk's 'wife' claimed that Washington had said 'Hello, sweetheart' and tried to molest her. The newspapers believed her. Although Taft and Roosevelt spoke out for Washington, Washington's reputation suffered in the six months of legal wrangling. The court found the white assailant not guilty.

(vi) Black hostility

Some believed that Washington did more harm than good for his fellow blacks. Northern black journalists attacked Washington after the Atlanta Compromise speech. One called him 'the greatest white man's nigger in the world'. Others heckled Washington while he addressed black businessmen in Boston in 1903. A riot ensued. Washington supported the arrest and prosecution of three reporters. That caused tension between Washington and the friend who became his bitter rival, W.E.B. Du Bois.

(c) Booker T. Washington and W.E.B. Du Bois

(i) The aims and methods of Washington and Du Bois

Key question
How and why did Booker T. Washington and Du Bois differ?

In 1904 Du Bois and Washington worked together for the repeal of railroad segregation laws in Tennessee and for a New York conference to discuss black voting rights in the South. While sharing the same ultimate goal (equality for blacks) they advocated different tactics to achieve it. Why?

They had very different backgrounds. Du Bois was born a free man in the North. He experienced relatively little racial prejudice until he attended Fisk, a Southern black university. He gained degrees from Harvard and Berlin, and in 1897 became professor of sociology at Atlanta University. Du Bois typified the élitist Northern black intellectuals, Washington the more pragmatic and lower class Southerners who had to coexist with whites. Washington believed that whites would come around to accepting equal rights if blacks were peaceful, reasonable and made it clear that they meant whites no harm. He wanted blacks to concentrate on improving their economic position, Du Bois believed that civil rights must be obtained first. He thought that without legal and political equality, economic prosperity could not be attained. At this stage, Washington favoured 'separate but equal' while Du Bois sought rapid integration. Washington, frightened by the increasing number of lynchings, felt that Du Bois' more aggressive approach would serve only to alienate whites.

Key date
W.E.B. Du Bois became a professor at Atlanta University: 1897

Key dates

Establishment of the Niagara Movement to end racial inequality: 1905

Establishment of NAACP: 1909

Booker T. Washington established National Urban League: 1911

Springfield riot; 2000 blacks driven out: 1908

Popular pro-Klan movie, 'Birth of a Nation': 1915

(ii) Results of their disagreements

The majority of blacks at the New York Conference supported Washington. In 1905 Du Bois called black leaders to a conference in Buffalo, New York. A racial incident in their Buffalo hotel caused them to move to the Canadian side of Niagara Falls where they established the Niagara Movement. The movement aimed to end inequality. Led by Du Bois, it pointedly excluded Washington. Washington was being superseded as a universally acknowledged black leader. The rivalry between the erstwhile friends became increasingly bitter. Washington employed detectives for protection and he and Du Bois had spies in each other's camp.

Some blacks thought that these divisions damaged the black cause, but Washington stressed that Northern and Southern states required very different handling. His sharp distinction between racial problems in the North and the South made it difficult to sustain his position as a national black leader. He was excluded by Du Bois from the National Negro Committee, which joined with the Niagara Movement in 1909 and became the most famous black organisation of the twentieth century, the National Association for the Advancement of Colored People (NAACP).

NAACP's declared aims were to make America's 11 million blacks economically, intellectually, politically and socially free and equal.

Relations between NAACP and Booker T. Washington were not good. When President Wilson sacked black officials, NAACP did not object because they were Washington's nominees. NAACP concentrated on political and legal matters, while Washington helped to establish the National Urban League to help blacks adjust to urban life and work.

The increasing number of race riots across the USA worried Du Bois. In Springfield, Illinois in 1908, six blacks were killed by a white mob, and around 2000 fled the city. Du Bois therefore became more confrontational. As editor of the NAACP's newspaper *The Crisis*, Du Bois publicised riots and lynchings. He also tried to promote racial change through the law courts. Washington considered Du Bois' tactics provocative. Du Bois thought Washington a self-seeking political in-fighter and master manipulator.

In 1915, the movie 'Birth of a Nation' was a great box-office success. It glorified and revitalised the Ku Klux Klan. Du Bois and the NAACP called for a boycott of the movie, for which they blamed an upsurge in lynching. However, Washington criticised the call as giving the film free publicity. He died soon afterwards. By this time, most articulate blacks favoured Du Bois' social and political activism rather than Washington's accommodationism.

The continuing story of the Ku Klux Klan
After its early successes, the Ku Klux Klan had virtually collapsed due to federal government action and the successful re-assertion of white supremacy after Reconstruction (see pages 28–30). Revitalised in 1915, it claimed four million members by the mid-1920s, when it was a more popular organisation than the Boy Scouts. This 'new' Klan opposed Catholics, Jews and immigrants as much as blacks, and was national rather than Southern: Michigan had more members than any other American state, demonstrating how the Great Migration (see page 64) had spread American racial problems to the North and Midwest. However, by the 1930s, the Ku Klux Klan collapsed because of leadership scandals, laws outlawing the wearing of masks in public, and the $10 membership fee, which was expensive in the Depression (see page 71).

(d) What was the significance of Washington's life and career?

Key question
Did Booker T. Washington pursue the correct strategy for improving life for blacks?

Historians and contemporaries disagree over whether the situation of blacks deteriorated during the lifetime of Booker T. Washington, and whether he contributed to any deterioration.

There was indeed 'disappointment' in the South. After emancipation, blacks had been given political and legal equality, but disfranchisement and legalised social segregation soon followed. Black leaders were divided over how to regain the rights fleetingly held during Reconstruction. Those divisions weakened their cause. Du Bois favoured vociferous campaigning for the full restoration of civil rights. Washington preferred to reassure and conciliate whites, while quietly campaigning against segregation and discrimination through the law courts, and stressing economic advancement.

Key date
W.E.B. Du Bois' *The Souls of Black Folk* advocated protest not accommodationism: 1903

In *The Souls of Black Folk*, Du Bois acknowledged that Washington's rise to the position of 'the one recognised spokesman of his 10 million fellows' was 'the most striking thing in the history of the American Negro' since the end of Reconstruction. Du Bois said that while the elements of Washington's philosophy of 'industrial education, conciliation of the South, and submission and silence as to civil and political rights' were not original, Washington welded them into a coherent and incredibly influential programme. Writing in the 1960s, African American scholar Langston Hughes noted that historians and contemporaries judged that Washington was 'a great accommodator', but 'to create Tuskegee in Alabama in that era he could hardly have been otherwise.'

Hughes gives the key to any assessment of Washington's contribution to black advancement: 'he could hardly have been otherwise'. His private papers reveal that while he gave whites the impression that he favoured segregation, he secretly financed and directed several court suits against segregation in Southern

Profile: W.E.B. Du Bois 1868–1963

1868	–	Born in Massachusetts; attended integrated high school
1884	–	Graduated first in his class but rejected by Harvard
1885	–	At Fisk (black university in Nashville, Tennessee, established 1866), first experienced Southern racism
1888	–	Studied at Harvard, then University of Berlin
1894	–	Taught at a university in Ohio
1896	–	Worked for the University of Pennsylvania
1897–1910	–	Professor at the University of Atlanta, Georgia
1900	–	Attended Pan-African Conference in London (attended such conferences throughout his life)
1903	–	Wrote *The Souls of Black Folk*, which identified the 'color line' as the great problem of the twentieth century
1904	–	Established Niagara Movement, to work for full civil rights and political equality
1909	–	Important in establishment of NAACP, which launched legal suits, lobbied Congress and produced propaganda to help blacks
1909–34	–	Edited NAACP's magazine *Crisis*; wrote inspirational and provocative articles, for example, against lynching, until his controversial advocacy of 'an economic Negro nation within a nation' forced him to resign
1926	–	Visited the Soviet Union, impressed by Marxism
1944	–	Worked for NAACP again, until forced to resign in 1948
1950s	–	Increasingly pro-USSR and anti-USA in Cold War, so federal government confiscated his passport
1961	–	Emigrated to Africa; advocated Pan-Africanism (world black unity); worked on *Encyclopaedia Africana*; joined Communist Party

Key question
Why was Du Bois less influential than Washington?

Du Bois' frequent changes of mind (for example, on integration) and intellectual élitism help to explain why he has been called 'a leader without followers'. However, he helped to establish the most important twentieth-century black organisation, the NAACP. His prestigious posts, publications and assertions that blacks were a chosen people with special cultural and spiritual strengths contributed to the increased black pride manifested in the Harlem Renaissance (see page 67). It was probably because he was unrealistic (he envisaged Africa populated by 'well-bred and courteous children, playing happily and never sniffing or whining'!) and uncompromising that Du Bois had less influence than Booker T. Washington in early twentieth-century America.

railroad facilities, wherein blacks were relegated to the worst carriages and rest rooms. He worked similarly against disfranchisement.

Given the degree, extent and longevity of white hostility to blacks, 'accommodationism' probably stood more chance of consolidating black gains in America than confrontation – in his lifetime at least. He impressed many whites with his achievements and moderation and won important recognition if inconsistent support from presidents and other politicians. He increased the self-confidence of blacks by demonstrating that a black born in slavery could become a nationally and internationally respected figure, mixing with statesmen and monarchs. He helped many individual blacks more directly through the Tuskegee Institute, and encouraged white Southern acceptance of black access to education. His writings and actions artfully, carefully and patiently advertised black and white co-operation. His *Up From Slavery* deliberately avoided any residual bitterness about slavery and emphasised how many whites had helped and befriended him throughout his life. His life and career demonstrated that the situation of black Americans definitely improved after the Civil War.

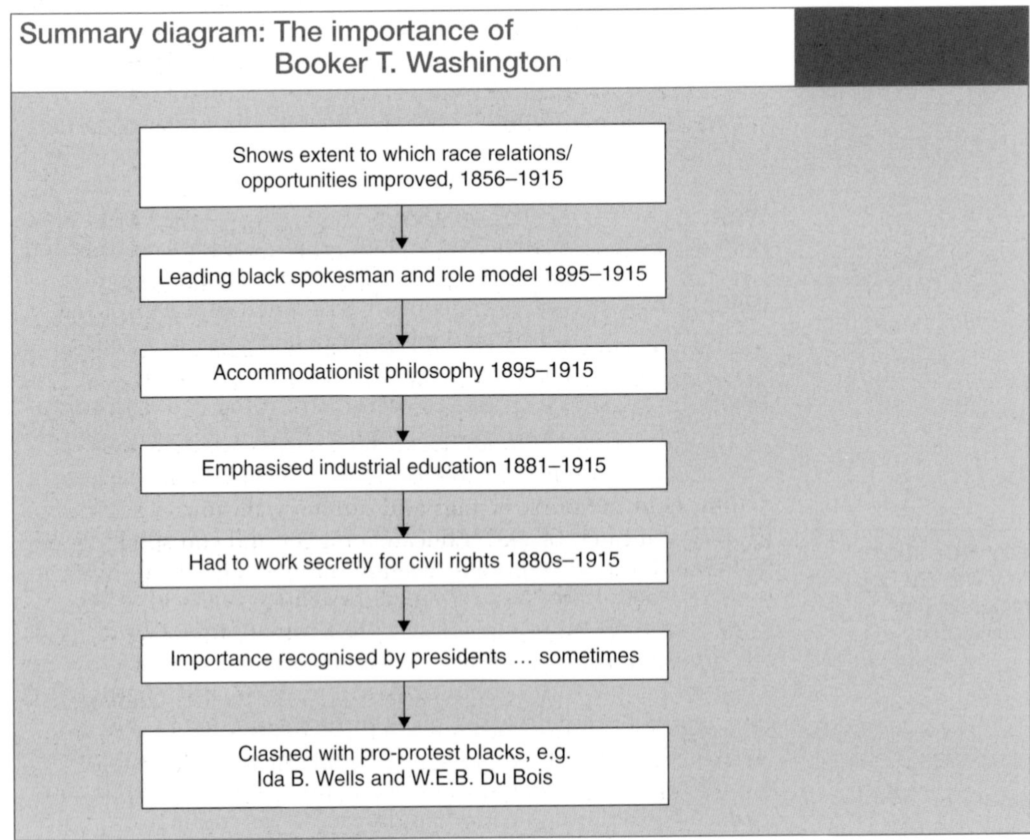

(e) Historians and Booker T. Washington

Booker T. Washington has always provoked very different assessments. W.E.B. Du Bois claimed that Washington's conciliatory approach made Southern whites even worse to blacks.

In the 1960s, historians found evidence of Washington's 'secret life', which demonstrated greater militancy but also greater vanity than had been thought. Donald J. Calista (1964) pointed out that 'beneath his ingratiating manner', Washington 'boiled with contempt for injustices done to his race' but knew that the open protest strategy of Wells and Du Bois would only alienate whites further.

Robert Sherer (1977) pointed out the fate of 'uppity' black college principals in 1887: one was forced to resign for suing against railroad segregation; another had his school closed.

Adam Fairclough (2001) gives an excellent, balanced account of Washington, 'a product of black powerlessness' whose accommodationism psychologically damaged blacks. Fairclough criticised Washington's inability to accept black critics' ideas, insisting that they were motivated by jealousy and political ambition. Washington was loath, says Fairclough, to concede any of his own power.

Washington's most thorough biographer, Louis Harlan (1983), portrayed Washington as a devious, manipulative, power-hungry tyrant and a failure. However, Virginia Denton (1992), using Washington's papers (edited by Harlan!) concluded that he was an unselfish servant and great leader of his race, 'dominated by purpose, not power'.

What was Washington's influence over education?

Many historians lamented Washington's influence over black education, for example, Donald Spivey (1978) believed that industrial education kept blacks in inferior, low-paid jobs. Sherer felt that 'Washington bartered off quality collegiate training for generations of black leaders for the upbuilding of Tuskegee and his own reputation'. Fairclough claimed 'such harsh criticisms ascribe far too much influence to Washington, and failed to appreciate the depth of white opposition to black education'. Whites held the purse strings and did not want to create a class of 'uppity' educated blacks. 'Educate a nigger and you spoil a good field hand' was a common contemporary saying. 'In the 1890s', says Fairclough, 'the question was not so much what kind of education blacks were going to receive, but whether they would receive any education at all'.

In that context, Washington merits praise. He had to neutralise white opposition to education, and the best way to do that was to assure whites that Tuskegee taught practical skills that would contribute to the Southern economy and not threaten educated whites. Quietly, Tuskegee also provided an academic education and produced many black teachers.

Some key books and articles in the debate

Donald Calista, 'Booker T. Washington: another look', *Journal of Negro History*, 1964.

Virginia Denton, *Booker T. Washington and the Adult Education Movement* (Florida, 1992).

W.E.B. Du Bois, *The Souls of Black Folk* (New York, 1903).

Adam Fairclough, *Better Day Coming: Blacks and Equality, 1890–2000* (Penguin, 2001).

Louis Harlan (editor), *The Booker T. Washington Papers* (Illinois, 1972–8).

Louis Harlan, *Booker T. Washington: The Wizard of Tuskegee, 1901–1915* (Oxford University Press, 1983).

Robert Sherer, *Subordination or Liberation: The Development of Conflicting Theories of Education in Nineteenth-century Alabama* (Alabama, 1977).

Donald Spivey, *Schooling for the New Slavery: Black Industrial Education, 1868–1915* (Westport, Connecticut, 1978).

(f) 'Decades of disappointment'? – conclusion

Key question
Were the years 1880–1915 the 'decades of disappointment'?

The early years after the Civil War seemed highly promising for Southern blacks, freed from slavery and supposedly guaranteed the right to vote and equal citizenship. However, during the last 20 years of the nineteenth century, the Jim Crow laws eroded those constitutional rights. From 1880 to 1915, Booker T. Washington was the leading black spokesman, but blacks such as Ida B. Wells and W.E.B. Du Bois felt that he was insufficiently assertive with regard to civil rights. For Wells and Du Bois these years were definitely decades of disappointment, but this was probably also the case for Washington, who worked secretly against Jim Crow. On the one hand, Washington had the ear of successive presidents, but on the other, they usually failed to do what he desired. It could be argued that, even in these 'decades of disappointment', the foundations were laid for future black advancement. Slowly, blacks were developing and organising into a pressure group to which some presidents listened. The black situation was certainly far better than it had been under slavery, although, disappointingly, not as good as had seemed likely during Reconstruction.

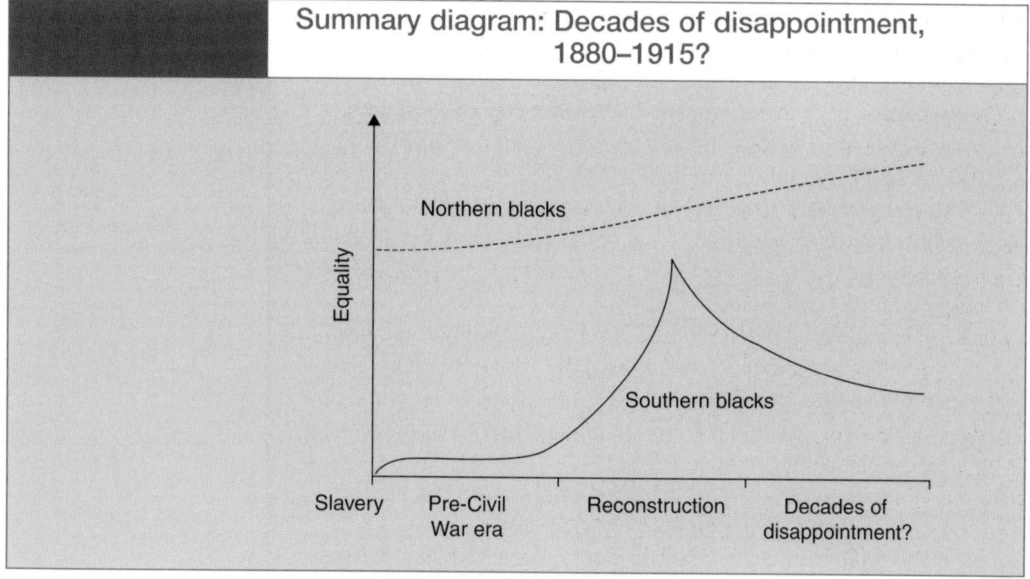

Study Guide: AS Questions

In the style of OCR

1. Compare the position of Booker T. Washington and W.E.B. Du Bois in promoting the position of blacks to 1912.

Source: OCR, June 2003

2. Assess the reasons why blacks suffered from so much prejudice in the South in the period after 1877 (to 1912).

Source: OCR, May 2002

Exam tips

The cross-references are intended to take you straight to the material that will help you to answer the questions.

1. When you are asked to compare two people, you will usually find that there are ways in which they are similar as well as different. Booker T. Washington and W.E.B. Bois often promoted the position of blacks in different ways. Their most famous difference is that Washington emphasised vocational education and Du Bois favoured a more academic education for the 'talented tenth' such as himself. However:
   - Both worked to improve the position of blacks and to encourage whites to change (pages 47–56).
   - The writings of both were designed to inspire blacks and to encourage whites to change (pages 47, 50, 53–5).

   Organising an essay that asks you to 'compare' is best done by a series of paragraphs focused on direct comparisons. For example, in one paragraph, you could say that both worked against segregation, but that Washington kept his support for litigation secret (page 54) while Du Bois attacked segregation more publicly (page 53). Finally, remember to watch the dates in any question. Going outside the dates in a question will usually be a waste of time and marks. Check that you know exactly when your specification begins and take care not to write too much about events prior to that date.

2. This question is a straightforward 'causes question'. In your essay plan (don't spend too long on it in an exam), list all the reasons why, using this chapter and Chapter 2 for your answer. Some of the reasons are:

- The traditional racist attitudes that white Southerners had used to justify slavery, and their bitterness at the loss/cost of the Civil War (page 27).
- White fears that blacks were economic competitors, seeking jobs that whites needed (page 39).
- The federal government abandoned Southern blacks and concentrated on the North (pages 29–30).
- The traditional white élite had deeply resented their loss of power during Reconstruction and had developed the myth of corrupt black/Northern white tyranny during Reconstruction (page 25).
- Black poverty, which seemed to confirm white supremacist ideas (page 25).

Each bullet point could be the focus of a paragraph. In your five paragraphs, you would have the bullet point generalisations, each with some specific facts to prove it. It is often easier to give factual proof by remembering/using biographical details. In your 'racist attitudes' paragraph, you could use the white accusations of rape about which Ida B. Wells complained (page 40). In order to achieve high marks you must assess the relative importance of each reason against each other, and then 'assess' the reason you believe to be most important in your conclusion, giving some factual proof for your choice.

4 Factors Leading to Improvements for Blacks 1900–45

POINTS TO CONSIDER

The great American civil rights movement took place in the 1950s and 1960s. Inevitably, people debate whether and how much the preceding years helped kick-start the civil rights movement. The black situation was certainly improving (slowly) in the first half of the twentieth century and this chapter concentrates upon:

- Factors leading to change between 1900 and 1945
- The extent of change between 1900 and 1945

It looks at these issues through the following sections:

- The black situation in 1900
- The 'Great Migration'
- The First World War
- The increasing sense of community
- The situation in 1930
- The Depression and the New Deal
- Trade unionists and left-wing activists
- NAACP
- The impact of the Second World War

Key dates

1914–18	First World War
1915	NAACP's first successful litigation: Supreme Court outlawed grandfather clause
1919	Race riots in 25 cities
1920s	Harlem Renaissance
1924	All Native Americans given American citizenship
1925	Establishment of A. Philip Randolph's trade union for railroad porters
1925	Garvey's UNIA at its peak
1928	Government report on Indian problems shocked Americans
1930	Walter White became leader of NAACP, replacing W.E.B. Du Bois
1933	Start of President Franklin Roosevelt's New Deal
1934	Indian Reorganisation Act increased tribal powers
1939–45	Second World War

1942	James Farmer established CORE
1943	Race riots in Harlem, Detroit and Alabama Roosevelt set up Fair Employment Practices Commission (FEPC)
1944	SMITH v. ALLWRIGHT: Supreme Court declared exclusion of blacks from state primaries unconstitutional

1 | The Black Situation in 1900

Key question
Did blacks have legal, social, economic and political equality in 1900?

In order to decide how much progress was made in the first half of the twentieth century, we need to recap the situation for blacks around 1900.

(a) Black Americans and the law in 1900

Blacks were frequently the victims of violence in the South. Southern law enforcers, always white, gave blacks little or no protection. Northern blacks were better off, although there were still lynchings that went unpunished. Thus black Americans suffered from legal inequality throughout the USA, but particularly in the South, where their inferior status was made clear in the Jim Crow laws.

(b) Black Americans and social status in 1900

Southern public transport, churches, theatres, parks, beaches and schools were segregated by law. Whites aimed to keep the best work and higher social status for themselves and to ensure no dilution of their race and its culture. Some whites were not totally committed to the status quo but fearful lest alterations caused trouble. Northern blacks were also considered inferior by whites, although this 'inferiority' was not fully enshrined in law.

Blacks in the North suffered segregation, in fact (*de facto*) if not in law (*de jure*). Northern whites had no desire to live near blacks so while blacks had been scattered throughout Northern cities in 1880, by 1900 they were in **ghettos** that were 90 per cent or more homogeneous. Rents were higher within the restricted boundaries of the black ghetto than in white neighbourhoods. In 1910 Chicago, a seven-room apartment for working class whites cost $25 weekly, for blacks, $37.50.

Key term
Ghettos
Areas inhabited mostly or solely by (usually poor) members of a particular ethnicity or nationality.

(c) Black Americans and economic status in 1900

Northern whites feared competition for jobs and housing. Even if a Northern black were more educated and skilled than a white worker, the latter would get priority in the job market. The rural South offered few economic opportunities to black sharecroppers, so increasing numbers were migrating to the North to seek work. By 1900, the number of blacks in Chicago had doubled within the previous decade to over 30,000. These unskilled and uneducated Southern blacks were greatly disadvantaged when they came North. In Boston, 12 per cent of first-generation Irish Americans were white-collar workers, increasing to 24 per cent in the second generation; the increase for blacks was only 7 per cent to 9 per cent. Both Northern and Southern blacks usually had the worst-paid jobs. This was due to poor schooling. Without a good education it was hard to escape the poverty trap.

(d) Black Americans and political status in 1900

Blacks who could vote usually voted Republican, because that was the party of the 'Great Emancipator', Abraham Lincoln. In the North the Republican Party took black votes for granted. Possession of the vote did not bring Northern blacks great gains. The vast majority of Southern blacks could not vote.

Key question
How and why did black people accept their inequality in 1900?

(e) Black acceptance of inequality in 1900

Blacks suffered inequality because:

- The federal government was unhelpful.
- Southern whites dominated local politics.
- Long-standing Southern congressmen exploited seniority rules to maintain a tenacious grip on US Senate committees and used **filibuster** tactics and pragmatic alliances with Republicans to halt bills to help blacks.
- The power of the state governments was vital for the continuation of white supremacy. State governments controlled education, transportation and law enforcement. There was no federal police force to protect blacks from discriminatory state laws in the South.
- As recent migrants from the South, many Northern blacks still feared whites.
- Most Northern blacks were poor. They concentrated upon earning a living. Their poor education left them ill equipped to agitate and to work for a better life.

Key term
Filibuster
Prolonging congressional debates to stop bills being voted upon.

However, things were improving. Blacks had more opportunities, and although the 14th and 15th Amendments were usually ignored, they remained part of the Constitution, to be appealed to in later years. A common black saying summed it up: 'We ain't what we ought to be, we ain't what we going to be. But thank God we ain't what we used to be.'

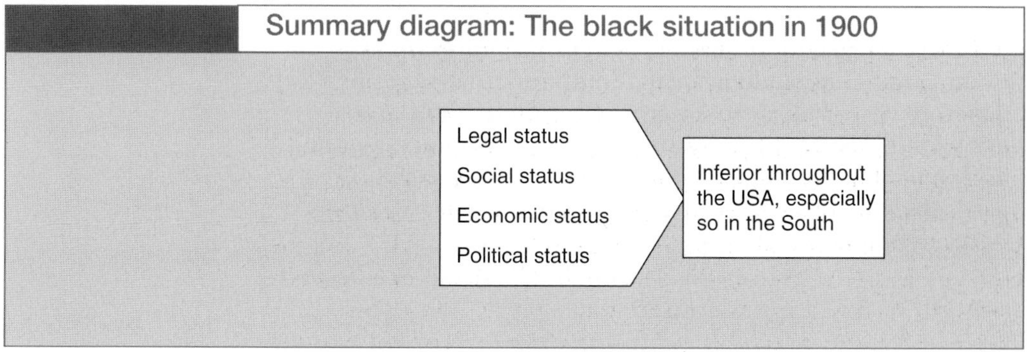

2 | The 'Great Migration'

Key question
How did black movement Northward affect blacks and race relations?

In the South, already one of the poorest parts of America, there were limited opportunities for black economic advancement. One solution was the '**Great Migration**'. Over six million blacks migrated from the rural South to the great cities of the North, Midwest and West between 1910 and 1970. In 1910, 89 per cent of blacks lived in the South; by 1970 it was 53 per cent. The industrial North offered greater economic opportunities, especially when the First World War (1914–18) generated jobs. Southern blacks flocked to Northern cities like New York, Philadelphia, Chicago and the car-manufacturing centre of Detroit (see Table 4.1). A Mississippi black man who migrated to Chicago in the First World War said, 'I should have been here 20 years ago. I just begin to feel like a man.'

Key term
Great Migration
The Northward movement of Southern blacks during the twentieth century.

Table 4.1: Detroit population figures

Year	*Total population*	*Black population*
1910	465,766	5,741
1920	993,675	40,838
1930	1,568,662	120,066

A 300 per cent population increase, but 2400 per cent black population increase.

The other great migration: Hispanics

Hispanics settled in North America before other white Americans. When the USA took over the American Southwest (what is now California, Arizona, New Mexico and Texas), Mexicans were already in residence.

The twentieth century saw a massive influx of Hispanic immigrants seeking economic opportunities. Some of the Hispanic immigrants came from Mexico, some from Puerto Rico (taken over by the USA in 1898). Puerto Ricans settled in New York in particular. In 1910, there were 2000 Puerto Ricans in the USA, rising to 53,000 in 1930. Cheaper air travel after the Second World War led to one and a half million Puerto Ricans in the USA by 1970.

In the early twentieth century, Mexicans arrived by and worked on the railroads. Mexicans were used to living without 'necessities' taken for granted by Americans, for example, running water and indoor toilets. Southwestern Americans therefore viewed Mexican immigrants as undesirable and uncivilised. The Mexicans' customs, poverty, illiteracy, race and lowly paid jobs set them apart from white Americans who, particularly in Texas, used segregation laws to keep Mexicans separate from whites.

When blacks fled the segregated South, their arrival elsewhere caused tension. In 1925, the Western city of Los Angeles suddenly segregated public swimming pools, although by 1931, NAACP-inspired legal action led to their desegregation.

The influx of blacks worsened race relations in Northern cities. Northerners joined the Ku Klux Klan. In 1911 Baltimore passed its first residential segregation law. Other Northern cities followed suit. Competition for jobs and housing and resentment at increasing black political influence in local elections led to serious racial violence in many cities. In Chicago, Irish and Polish workers, supported by the police and the military, committed appalling atrocities as they attacked blacks in the ghetto in 1919. A primarily Southern race relations problem had become a national one. However, urbanisation helped to increase black consciousness and a sense of community.

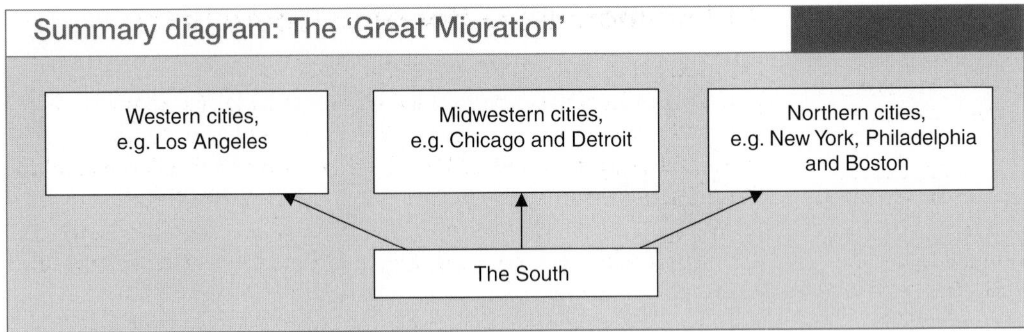

3 | The First World War (1914–18)

Key question
How did the First World War affect blacks?

The First World War generated jobs and gave black soldiers a glimpse of greater equality. Blacks found the French less racist than white Americans, who warned the French to keep their women away from black Americans who would probably rape them. German propaganda targeted blacks, urging them not to believe America's claim that it was fighting for democracy:

> Do you enjoy the same rights as the white people do in America ...? Can you go into a restaurant where white people dine? Can you get a seat in the theatre where white people sit? ... Is lynching ... lawful proceeding in the democratic country?

Key dates
First World War: 1914–18
Race riots (e.g. in Chicago): 1919

When mobilised blacks returned home, white resentment at black competition for jobs and housing led to terrible race riots in 25 American cities in 1919. The Chicago riots lasted for a fortnight. About 50,000 blacks had moved into Chicago between 1910 and 1920. White residents hated blacks moving into white neighbourhoods. When a 15-year-old black boy accidentally crossed the dividing line on a segregated beach that extended into Lake Michigan, whites stoned the boy. When blacks protested, the police arrested them. In the ensuing riots, 38 died and 500 were injured. The governor of Illinois commissioned a report. The report called for desegregation and blamed the riots on unfair treatment of blacks by white law enforcers, ghetto living conditions and increasing black 'race consciousness'.

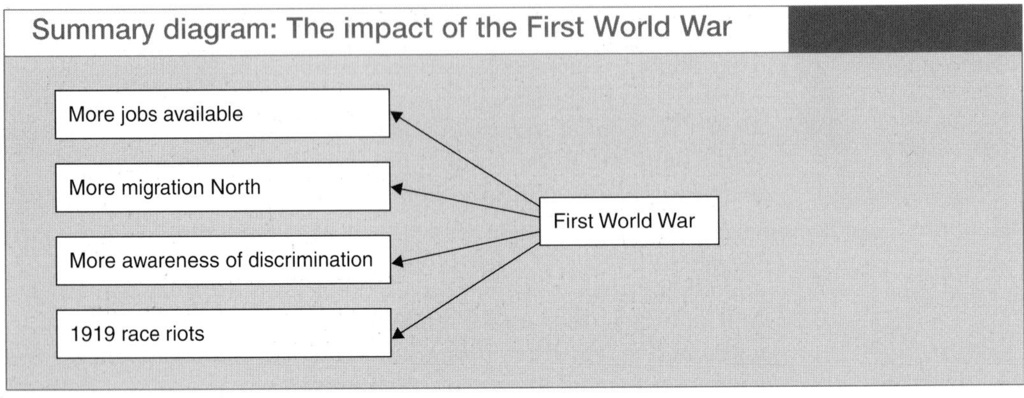

Key question
How and why was black consciousness increased?

Key dates
Harlem Renaissance: 1920s

Establishment of A. Philip Randolph's trade union for railroad porters: 1925

Key terms
Renaissance
A revival or exceptionally productive period for culture.

Trade union
A group of workers united to bargain for better working conditions and pay.

4 | The Increasing Sense of Community

(a) Factors promoting black unity

Black unity increased in the face of unrelenting economic and social discrimination. It increased with shared pride in the Harlem **Renaissance** of 1919–30, wherein black intellectuals like the poet Langston Hughes and jazz musicians like 'Duke' Ellington flourished, and when the 'Brown Bomber' Joe Louis defeated a white heavyweight boxer to become world champion in 1938.

The sense of community was nurtured by black newspapers such as the *Baltimore Afro-American* and *Pittsburgh Courier* and by fraternal organisations, civic clubs and churches. The Abyssinian Baptist Church in Harlem, New York, provided the location, money and leadership for civic clubs wherein politics was discussed. Not all churches were hotbeds of civil rights activity, but most at least helped to promote a spirit of self-help and self-confidence. Blacks could identify with biblical stories of a chosen race who fled enslavement and went to the Promised Land.

(b) Factors hindering the development of black unity

The black community was not always united. There were divisions of class, colour (light or dark skin), creed, location and career opportunities. Differences between the North and South continued to cause black leaders to disagree over how to gain improvements (see page 52).

(c) Methods of fostering unity

Du Bois worked to increase the sense of community through the NAACP, which attracted many middle class blacks in the 1910s and 1920s, even in Southern cities. The black socialist A. Philip Randolph (see page 76) established a black **trade union** for railroad porters in 1925 and urged black workers to co-operate with white trade unionists. However, the individual most responsible for arousing black working class consciousness and awakening organisations such as NAACP to the need for wooing the working classes was West Indian-born Marcus Garvey. Garvey's career illustrates both black divisions and increasing black consciousness.

Key question
What was the significance of Marcus Garvey?

(d) The significance of Marcus Garvey

Between 1890 and 1920, New York City's black population increased from 70,000 to 200,000. Most were born in the South, but about 50,000 were born in the West Indies. Harlem was transformed from an all-white, fashionable upper class area into a densely populated black ghetto. African American and West Indian relations were tense. African Americans resented West Indians as clannish, better-educated, over-ambitious, willing to work for lower wages and unwilling to join black protest organisations. Marcus Garvey's career illustrates the hostility between African Americans and West Indians.

Profile: Marcus Garvey 1887–1940

1887 – Born in Jamaica
1914 – Established Universal Negro Improvement Association (UNIA)
1916 – Moved from Jamaica to Harlem, New York
1920 – UNIA New York City international conference named Garvey provisional President of Republic of Africa
1922 – Trial for business mismanagement
1925 – Jailed
1927 – Deported

Garvey created the first black mass movement in the USA, emphasising racial pride, self-respect and self-reliance. He was the first great black nationalist.

The charismatic Garvey arrived in the USA in 1916. He maintained that God was black and advocated **self-help**, armed self-defence, and separation of races. He appealed to racial pride and (some said excessive) love of pageantry, for example, with his elaborate 'President of Africa' uniform (see the photo in the profile). His *Negro World* newspaper rejected advertisements for 'race-degrading' products that lightened skin and straightened hair. Garvey emphasised 'back to Africa' in the spiritual rather than the physical sense. By 1925, half a million urban blacks, frustrated by the lack of progress after the First World War, swelled his Universal Negro Improvement Association (UNIA) membership way above that of NAACP. However, Garvey frightened and alienated many members of his race. Why?

Key term

Self-help
Booker T. Washington and Marcus Garvey emphasised black-owned businesses as typical of the self-help needed for black progress.

Other black leaders were jealous of this West Indian's appeal to the black American working classes, and, often light-skinned themselves, resented his claims that blacker was better. They particularly disliked his calls for the return of the 'best' (blackest) Americans to Africa (a place Garvey never visited). A light-skinned black Chicago doctor said UNIA really stood for 'Ugliest Negroes in America'. Du Bois called him 'a little, fat black man' and 'the most dangerous enemy of the Negro race' and Randolph's newspaper called him the 'Jamaican Jackass', 'monumental monkey' and 'unquestioned fool and ignoramus'. Garvey was found guilty of mail fraud, jailed in 1923, then deported in 1927, but the impact of UNIA on black consciousness continued for years afterwards.

Key date

Garvey's UNIA at its peak: 1925

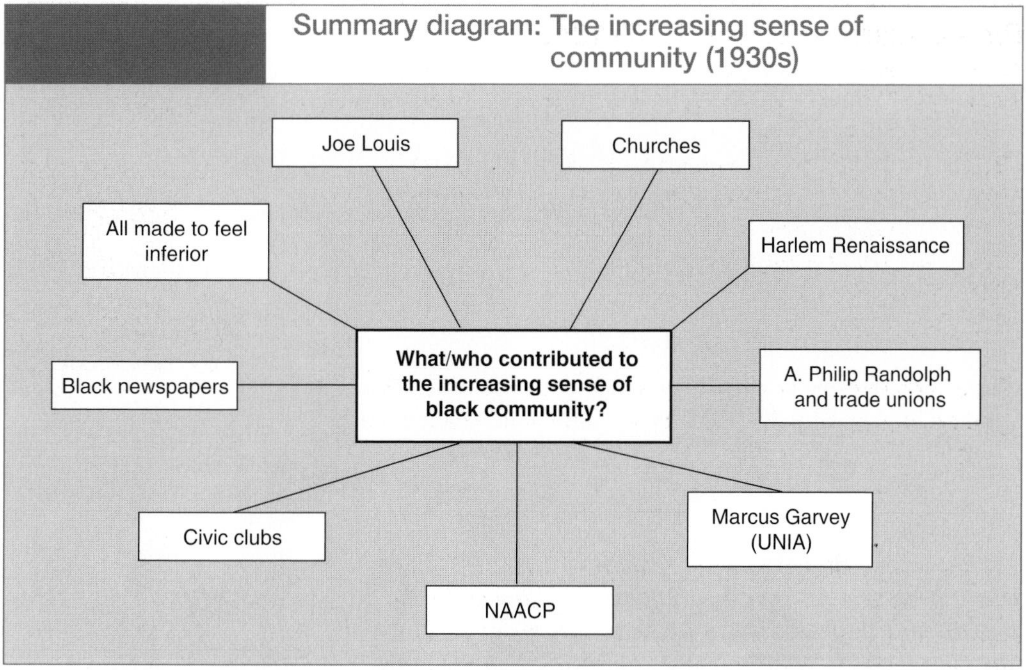

Summary diagram: The increasing sense of community (1930s)

Key question
How much had blacks progressed by 1930?

5 | The Situation in 1930

Individuals such as Garvey had helped raise black consciousness. The NAACP's anti-lynching campaign had publicised the horrors of lynchings and helped decrease their numbers. White supporters helped by claiming that lynchings damaged the South's image and progress. The NAACP had won a few court victories, against the grandfather clause (see page 27), white domination of primaries and mob violence.

However, Jim Crow remained essentially intact in the South. The National Urban League (see page 53) had done little to decrease black urban poverty in the North. Despite Randolph's encouragement, most black workers were not unionised.

Many blacks seemed apathetic. The Southern black middle class usually followed Booker T. Washington's 'accommodationist' ideas (see Chapter 3). A few joined the NAACP but the vast majority remained aloof from the reforming movements because they were preoccupied with earning a living and lacked any great tradition of political consciousness. Perhaps more importantly, Southern blacks knew that opposing white supremacy could mean death.

Northern blacks were in a far better position to improve their status. They could vote and participate more easily in civic affairs, and had more economic opportunities. Despite police harassment and the Ku Klux Klan, Northern blacks lived in a far less violent society. However, most Northern blacks concentrated upon improving their living standards, although some middle class professionals did join the NAACP and working class blacks joined UNIA.

Two blacks are lynched before a satisfied white crowd, in the Northern state of Indiana, 1930.

By 1930 then, black activism was better organised and increasing, but activists remained a minority who had done little to end nation-wide segregation and discrimination. It took the Depression and the New Deal to bring about more dramatic change.

Summary diagram: Comparing 1900 to 1930

1900		1930
Jim Crow in the South	⟶	Same
Lynching	⟶	Decreasing
Black consciousness	⟶	Majority apathetic, but several organisations/individuals contributed to greater awareness
Life in the North	⟶	Slowly increasing economic opportunities

Key question
How did the Depression and New Deal affect blacks?

Key terms

Depression
When a country's economy is nearly ruined. Prices and wages fall, and many people are unemployed, as in the USA after 1929.

New Deal
President Roosevelt's programme to bring the US out of the economic Depression.

Biracial
Black and white together.

Tennessee Valley Authority
A New Deal programme to bring prosperity to rural Tennessee.

Key dates

Start of the Depression: 1929

Start of President Roosevelt's New Deal: 1933

6 | The Depression and the New Deal

(a) The Depression and black Americans

In 1929 the New York stock market collapsed, triggering off several years of economic **depression**.

The Depression probably hit blacks harder than whites. Two million Southern black farmers left the land as crop prices plummeted. Many went to the cities but urban black unemployment was between 30 and 60 per cent and always higher than that of whites. Desperate whites moved into the jobs formerly dominated by blacks, such as domestic service, street cleaning, garbage collection and bellhops. Whites organised vigilante groups such as the Black Shirts of Atlanta to stop blacks getting jobs. As unskilled labour, blacks were usually the last hired and the first fired. There was no effective social security system, so disease and starvation frequently resulted.

(b) The New Deal and black Americans

In 1933, President Franklin Roosevelt began a hitherto unprecedented programme of government intervention to stimulate the economy and help the poor. This programme was called the **New Deal**.

Before 1933 the federal government had appeared uninterested in blacks. Now New Deal programmes helped blacks by providing one million jobs, nearly 50,000 public housing units, and financial assistance and skilled occupations training for half a million black youths. As a result of federal assistance, many black sharecroppers became independent farmers.

The New Deal provided jobs in the world of entertainment and culture, giving some black scholars the opportunity to increase black consciousness by getting black history and contemporary living conditions into the New Deal's state guidebooks. Black songs and oral reminiscences of slavery and hardship were recorded for posterity. Government sponsorship of culture was inevitably controversial, and federal-funded **biracial** theatrical productions were criticised by a congressional committee as encouraging black and white colleagues to date.

The New Deal could not guarantee miracles. Sometimes aid did not reach the people for whom it was intended, particularly in the South where aid was distributed by whites. The federal government refused to guarantee mortgages for houses purchased by blacks in white neighbourhoods. The **Tennessee Valley Authority** (TVA) built all-white towns. Waiters, cooks, janitors, domestic and farm workers were excluded from social security coverage and from the minimum wage provisions of the Fair Labour Standards Act. A 1936 NAACP report said the six million blacks engaged in agriculture received no help from the federal government, although that situation improved.

While it was sometimes hard for blacks to make effective protests about unfairness in the administration of the New Deal, New Dealers were often responsive to criticism and even protest, as with the 1935 Harlem riot. One black died and 200 were

Hispanic Americans – a comparison
The Depression exacerbated racial tensions between Americans and Hispanics. Most Mexican Americans were agricultural labourers, and US agriculture had been in depression since the 1920s. Many Mexicans were therefore on relief. High rates of crime and disease among Mexicans further alienated whites. Mexicans were discriminated against and segregated in public places, such as restaurants and schools. Unlike blacks, Hispanics could be deported. There were large-scale deportations of Mexican immigrants and even Mexican Americans who were US citizens (16,000 in 1931). The Mexican population of the USA, 600,000 in 1930, fell to 400,000 in 1940. Over a million were expelled in 1954. With blacks and Mexicans, white racism was usually due to rivalry over jobs, the belief that the non-whites were economically parasitical, and a dislike of the different style of living of the ethnic minority.

injured in clashes with the police whom they believed to have beaten or possibly killed a young black shoplifter. While the tabloids tried to blame Communist agitators, an investigatory commission blamed Harlem's poverty and discrimination in relief given to blacks. Racist officials were transferred from Harlem and more local blacks were employed to administer relief.

(c) Eleanor Roosevelt

In order to get New Deal legislation through Congress, Roosevelt needed Southern white congressional votes, so he left it to his wife to take a very public interest in black affairs. When a biracial group tried to hold a fully integrated meeting in Birmingham, Alabama in 1938, even Birmingham's racist police chief Eugene 'Bull' Connor could not stop Eleanor Roosevelt sitting between the black and white delegates. The meeting did not condemn Jim Crow outright, but declared support for equality before the law, voter registration for the poor, and funding for black postgraduates. Privately, Eleanor Roosevelt harangued New Deal officials into providing non-discriminatory aid for blacks. She introduced black representatives to her husband. There were nearly 50 blacks with relatively senior positions in the federal bureaucracy. They were nicknamed the 'Black Cabinet' because of their frequent meetings and concerted pressure on the administration.

(d) Conclusions about the New Deal

New Deal agencies often discriminated against blacks, especially in the South, but blacks were getting more help and attention than ever before. Federal aid programmes helped many blacks, inspiring a dramatic change of allegiance amongst black voters. Previously the Democratic Party had been associated in black minds with white supremacy, but now blacks voted for the party of Franklin Roosevelt, even though he introduced no civil rights legislation (he denounced lynching as murder, but never fully supported anti-lynching bills of 1934, 1935 and 1938). The increasing number of Northern black Democrats eventually made blacks a force to be reckoned with in the Party, which proved vital in the future acquisition of civil rights.

Roosevelt's New Deal helped make civil rights a political issue. Not all Democrats were happy. One Southern Democrat said catering to the black vote would lead to the 'depths of degradation' and 'mongrelisation of the American race'. White Southerners noticed increase black assertiveness and blamed Roosevelt: 'You ask any nigger in the street who's the greatest man in the world. Nine out of ten will tell you Franklin Roosevelt. That's why I think he's so dangerous.' Clearly, the New Deal had helped improve the situation of American blacks.

Key question
Was there a New Deal for Indians and how did their situation compare to the blacks?

Key dates
US government report on Indian problems shocked Americans: 1928
All Indians given US citizenship: 1924
Indian Reorganisation Act increased tribal powers: 1934

Key terms
Acculturation
Making Indians live like whites.

Citizenship
Indians were recognised as legally equal to white Americans with all the same rights, for example, voting.

The New Deal and Indians (1889–1914)

After the Indians had been put on reservations (see page 12), successive US governments either lacked interest in Indians, or were actively anti-Indian. A Commissioner of Indian Affairs said in 1889, 'Indians must conform to ... our civilisation or be crushed by it'.

By the early twentieth century, the federal government was more sympathetic. The Indians' situation was clearly and frequently desperate. Their death rate exceeded their birth rate. Some white-dominated organisations publicised the plight of the Indians. However, only one of them opposed '**acculturation**' (see page 11). Then, 24 unsolved murders of Oklahoma 'oil Indians' attracted massive publicity. Indian sympathisers believed whites who wanted the Indians' oil perpetrated the murders. The publicity forced the government to help the Oklahoma tribe. Other similar moves to take land from Indians in the 1920s failed due to publicity. A 1928 report commissioned by the federal government described Indian poverty, disease, and discontent, and shocked Americans. This prompted a Senate investigation.

The impact of war and the Depression

Indians were greatly affected by the First World War and the Depression. In 1924 all Indians were guaranteed **citizenship**, primarily because so many had enlisted eagerly and distinguished themselves in the First World War. Already poor, Indians were particularly affected by the Depression. The Depression led white Americans to accept and expect more federal aid for the unfortunate. John Collier was one of the white intellectuals who were increasingly interested in the preservation of Indian culture. Roosevelt appointed him Commissioner of Indian Affairs. Collier encouraged Congress to pass the Indian Reorganisation Act (1934), which started to restore tribal control over reservation land, and facilitated federal loans to struggling tribes.

Collier continued the process whereby Indian schoolchildren could attend local schools and learn about Indian culture.

Schoolchildren were no longer forced to attend Christian services. Previously forbidden native religious observances were allowed on reservations. Collier influenced Congress to stop trying to halt Indian use of peyote, a hallucinatory substance obtained from a New Mexico cactus. Peyote was not addictive, did not induce violence, and Indians had traditionally used it to produce religious visions. Although some Christian missionaries and exploitative whites opposed the restoration of Indian tribal culture, Collier had Roosevelt's total support.

Did Indians obtain a New Deal?

Although the **Indian Bureau** employed more Indians, its white employees implemented Collier's reforms slowly and reluctantly. Years of cultural persecution and deprivation made it difficult for the Indians to attain the full independence from Bureau control that Collier had envisaged. Much allotted land, for example, had been leased to whites. Nevertheless, the New Deal gave Indians more land, greater farming expertise, better medical services, large money grants, and renewed pride in their traditions and culture.

The New Deal ethos continued for a time under Roosevelt's successor, President Truman. In 1946, Congress created the Indian Claims Commission, which adjudicated all claims arising out of fraud, treaty violations, or other wrongs done to Indians by the government. The 1948 Hoover Commission Task Force's admission that destroying Indian tribal government, organisation, property and culture 'now appears to have been a mistake' seemed to confirm that Indians had benefited from the New Deal. However, like blacks, Indians depended heavily upon federal aid for further improvements.

Key term

Indian Bureau
The federal agency with special responsibility for Indians.

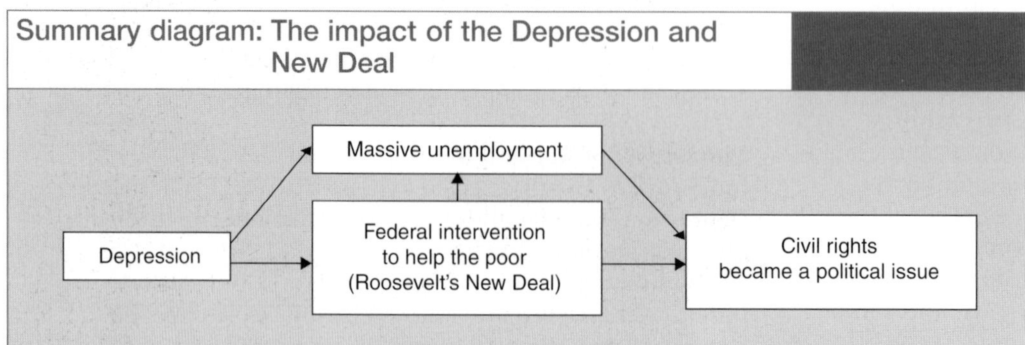

7 | Trade Unionists and Left-wing Activists

Trade unionists, socialists and Communists were important in raising black awareness of potential black political and economic power.

Key question
How did trade unionists and left-wingers help blacks?

(a) Trade unions

US trade unionism, traditionally weak and unsupportive of black workers, grew stronger under pressure of the Depression. Black membership increased dramatically as trade unions for hitherto poorly organised unskilled workers developed. White working class racism still remained a great obstacle to interracial trade unionism, particularly in the South, but the Depression helped to increase black and white working class solidarity.

Key term

Left-wing
Those whose political beliefs included greater economic equality, for example, Communists and socialists.

Usually the more **left-wing** trade unions were the greatest supporters of equal rights, as with the Communist-dominated and 75 per cent black Food, Tobacco, Agricultural and Allied Workers Union (FTA). The FTA promoted mass meetings that discussed voter registration and citizenship, as did other left-led and predominantly black unions such as the United Packinghouse Workers of America.

The first all-black labour union, the Brotherhood of Sleeping Car Porters had been set up by A. Philip Randolph in 1925. At its peak in the 1940s this union had 15,000 members and its New York office was considered, according to the historian J. Anderson, 'the political headquarters of black America', where young black leaders such as Roy Wilkins, James Farmer and later Martin Luther King met.

(b) The CPUSA

Black intellectuals were impressed by the US Communist Party (CPUSA). The CPUSA worked hard to win over blacks working in industry and agriculture in the early 1930s. The party helped Southern black agricultural workers to unionise, as in Lowndes County, Alabama. The unions were not always successful but Lowndes County became a civil rights centre in the 1960s, demonstrating how unionisation contributed to black assertiveness. The CPUSA provided legal help for the nine

A. Philip Randolph (wearing the black and white shoes) is holding the banner of the Brotherhood of Sleeping Car Porters at its 30th anniversary in 1955.

Profile: A. Philip Randolph 1890–1979

Key question
What was the significance of A. Philip Randolph?

1890	–	Born in Jacksonville, Florida. His minister father could not afford to send him to college
1914	–	Married a wealthy widow who was a Howard graduate and beautician trained by Madame C.J. Walker (whose famous hair straightening process had earned her a fortune). Randolph had gone to New York City to become an actor, but had been politicised by attendance at free courses at City College, which was full of socialists and trade unionists
1917	–	Editor of radical black magazine, the *MESSENGER*; attacked US participation in the First World War. Arrested
1925	–	Was asked to organise the long-suffering black porters who worked for the Pullman Railroad Company. The late nineteenth century railroad boom had attracted Black Southern agricultural workers to the less arduous job of porter
1937	–	His Brotherhood of Sleeping Car Porters union was fully organised. Porters who joined often got sacked or mistreated but this, plus Randolph's charisma, kept the union going
1940	–	Randolph threatened a mass march on Washington DC to protest against discrimination in the defence industry. President and Mrs Roosevelt failed to dissuade him, so FDR established FEPC (see page 81)
1940–50	–	Peak membership years of the Brotherhood
1948	–	Randolph used the Cold War situation to pressurise President Truman into desegregating the military (see page 95)
1963	–	Randolph masterminded and dominated the March on Washington (see page 135), which helped pass the 1964 Civil Rights Act (see pages 181–3)
1968	–	Retired from the Union that he had established and then dominated
1979	–	Died

While most black leaders had their roots in religious or educational employment, Randolph derived power and influence from leadership of trade unionists. He was significant in that he was the first black leader to see and use the potential of black workers within a trade union context. He increased black confidence, civil rights militancy and economic opportunities by helping end white trade union discrimination against blacks. He used his trade union power base to make himself an influential voice in the civil rights movement.

It could be argued that what was most significant about A. Philip Randolph was his conception that mass, non-violent protest (or the threat of it) could force the federal government into vitally important measures to help blacks.

Key date
Scottsboro boys: 1931

Scottsboro boys unfairly accused of raping two white women on an Alabama freight train in 1931.

The CPUSA adapted their traditionally atheist message in the South, happily coexisting with black Christianity. In Winston-Salem, North Carolina, the Communist Party met in a black church, sang hymns and prayed.

The Communist-dominated National Negro Congress aimed to promote equal civil and economic rights. A. Philip Randolph was its first elected president. It encouraged protest actions such as economic boycotts of stores that did not employ blacks, but the suspicious black churches and NAACP would not co-operate. The CPUSA often exaggerated the importance of the party in the 1930s and 1940s, claiming that it formed the basis for the civil rights movement of the following decades.

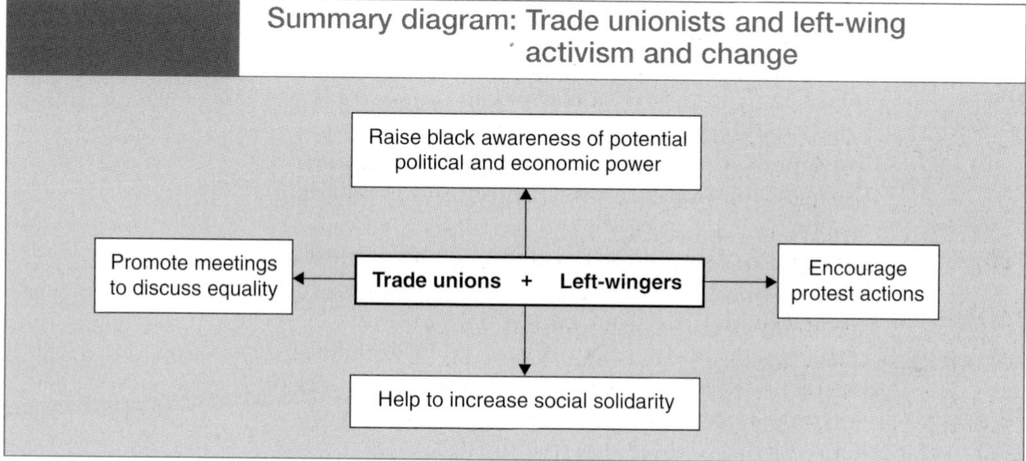

Key question
How did the NAACP help black Americans?

8 | NAACP

(a) Successes and changes

In 1915 the NAACP attained its first success through litigation when the Supreme Court ruled against the grandfather clause (see page 27). After this, NAACP membership grew steadily: by 1919 it had 88,448 members. In 1930 Walter White defeated Du Bois to become leader of the NAACP and in the same year galvanised it into a campaign which helped stop an opponent of black voting become a Supreme Court judge.

White tried to organise a civil rights coalition between trade unions, churches and **liberals**. Sustained pressure from White's NAACP and liberal white allies led the House of Representatives to pass anti-lynching bills in 1937 and 1940, but Southern influence halted the bills in the Senate. The NAACP worked to mobilise Southern blacks. Revitalised Southern urban branches supported voter registration and abolition of the **poll tax**. In 1941 the NAACP, trade unions and the National Negro Congress sponsored a National Committee to Abolish The Poll Tax. Local NAACP branches initiated protests, for example, against

Key terms

Liberals
Generally more sympathetic than most to racial/social/economic equality.

Poll tax
A tax levied on would-be voters, which made it harder for blacks (who were usually poorer) to vote.

Profile: Roy Wilkins 1901–81

1901	–	Born in St Louis, Missouri, son of a brick kiln worker who had fled Mississippi because he had beaten a white man over a racial insult
1905	–	After his mother died, brought up by his uncle, a railroad porter, in St Paul, Minnesota, in a middle class home in a relatively integrated neighbourhood
1923	–	Graduated from the University of Minnesota; during his time at university he was the first black reporter for the college newspaper and an active member of local NAACP branch
	–	Became a reporter in Kansas City, and secretary of Kansas City branch of NAACP
1931	–	NAACP leader Walter White asked Wilkins to become his assistant
1934	–	Became editor of NAACP's magazine *Crisis*
1955	–	After Walter White died, unanimously elected NAACP leader (held post for 22 years)
1960s	–	Increasingly criticised by blacks who opposed his beliefs in integration and his confidence in US institutions. Criticised Presidents Eisenhower and Kennedy, but praised President Johnson for helping blacks
1965–8	–	Young radicals in NAACP within one vote of ousting him
1970s	–	Worked to improve black education, housing, employment, health care, and critical of Republican Presidents Nixon and Ford, for example, over school desegregation
1977	–	Retired from NAACP due to ill-health

As head of the leading national black organisation from 1955 to 1977, Wilkins played a vital part in liaising with the federal government and other black organisations. He helped encourage the former to continue to support blacks and gave vital legal and financial aid to the latter. He always preferred the litigation approach to direct action ('When the headlines are gone, the issues still have to be settled in court ... The other organisations furnish the voice and get the publicity while the NAACP furnishes the manpower and pays the bills') but eventually approved of Montgomery Bus Boycott (see page 105) and the March on Washington (see page 135).

He never got on well with Martin Luther King (he called him a 'self-promoter'), particularly after King attacked the Vietnam War. He also criticised black power (see Chapter 7) as 'the father of hatred and the mother of violence'.

Key date

Walter White became leader of NAACP, replacing W.E.B. Du Bois: 1930

segregated lunch counters (Topeka, Kansas) and against segregated theatres (Council Bluffs, Iowa).

The NAACP was clearly changing. It was becoming increasingly activist and working with other groups to effect change. It was also altering its legal tactics.

(b) Charles Houston and Thurgood Marshall

In the 1920s the NAACP had worked against a wide range of civil rights abuses. From 1931 it concentrated on obtaining a Supreme Court ruling that unequal expenditure on black and white education was against the 14th Amendment. After two white lawyers refused the job, black law professor Charles Houston of Howard University was appointed to direct the NAACP's legal campaign in 1934.

Houston insisted that the NAACP should employ black lawyers. At Howard he had trained a black lawyer élite for this task. In 1936 the NAACP hired his star pupil, Thurgood Marshall ('lean, hard, and Hollywood handsome' according to Roy Wilkins). Houston and Marshall led the fight against segregated education in the 1930s and 1940s, working to involve black communities in litigation at local level. Marshall argued for equal salaries for black teachers in Maryland and Virginia in 1935–40. Most black teachers feared dismissal but a few came forward and gained legal victories. Houston targeted a Supreme Court liberalised by New Deal appointments. He focused first on **graduate schools**, believing they were an easier target than the larger and more high profile **public schools**. In MISSOURI EX REL GAINES v. CANADA (1938), the Supreme Court decreed that blacks had the right to the same quality of graduate education as whites. The NAACP was slowly but successfully encouraging change in the USA.

Key terms

Graduate schools
Universities.

Public schools
Schools financed and run by the government (called state schools in Britain).

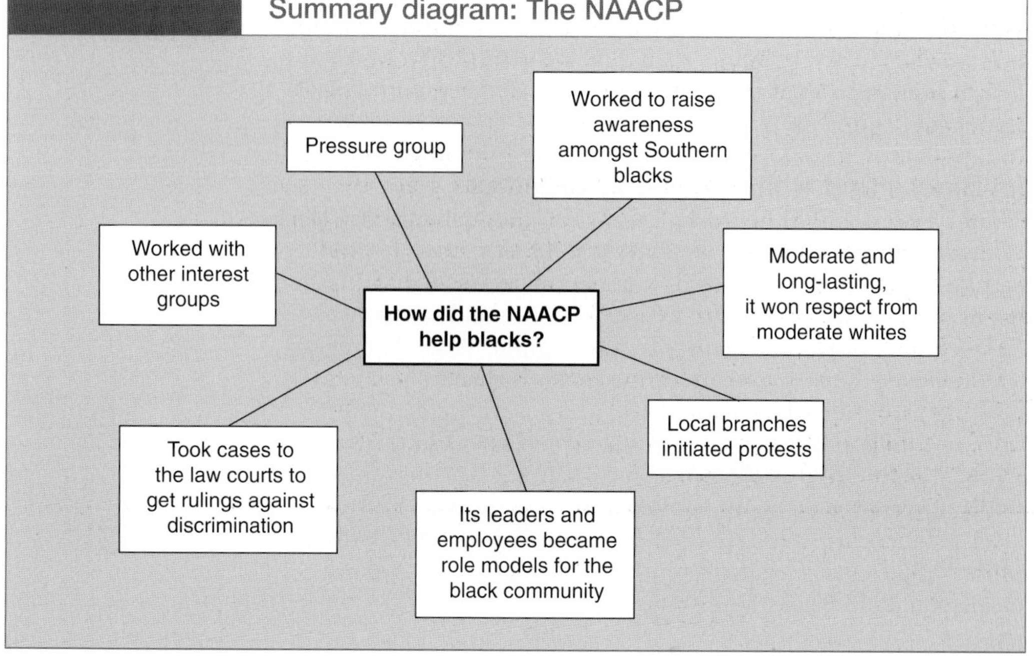

9 | The Impact of the Second World War

Key question
Was the Second World War a turning point for blacks?

The historian Dr Stephen Tuck believes that the Second World War was 'absolutely key' in bringing about change in the black situation. Why?

(a) Migration

Key dates
USA at war against Germany and Japan: 1941–5.
Race riots in Detroit, Harlem and Alabama: 1943

As defence industries became vitally important and Southern farming became more large scale and mechanised, blacks gravitated to the cities. Around four million left Southern farms; two million migrated North and West. Chicago's black population rose from a quarter of a million in 1940 to half a million in 1950. This large-scale migration gave blacks greater economic and political power, and also greater safety. While it was easier for white supremacists to intimidate isolated rural blacks, large numbers of blacks congregated together in a town or city were less vulnerable.

(b) Blacks and whites in overcrowded cities

Urban housing shortages were severe as people crowded into cities such as Detroit, a centre of war industries. Whites saw blacks as rivals for homes. In 1943 there were dozens of race riots across the country. The worst riots were in Detroit, where nine whites and 25 blacks died, and 800 people were injured.

City authorities were unsympathetic to the plight of transplanted Southern blacks. Washington DC's black community suffered as the federal bureaucracy physically expanded. Several hundred black homes were demolished to make way for the War Department's Pentagon building and for the extension of Arlington National Cemetery.

In crowded wartime cities, the unusually close proximity in which blacks and whites found themselves caused tension, especially in the South. There were numerous acts of defiance on overcrowded buses. When in 1943 a New Orleans driver ordered a black soldier to sit at the back of the bus, all 24 resentful black passengers ended up in jail.

(c) Blacks and whites working together

There was tension in the workplace. When the Alabama Dry Dock Company in Mobile finally responded to federal pressure and employed blacks in 1943, white workers (male and female) lashed out at black workers with any 'weapons' they could lay their hands on, including bricks and tools; 50 were injured. Why? There was jealousy over the best jobs and white males disliked black men working alongside white women.

Over a million blacks served in the armed forces in the Second World War. Southern military bases containing Northern black soldiers were trouble spots. In Alexandria, Louisiana, a drunken black soldier's arrest led to a two-hour riot in which black troops, white Military Police, state troopers, local police and civilians participated; 13 blacks were shot.

A white mob in Detroit pulls a black driver from his tram, yelling, 'Here's some fresh meat'. Disputes over housing were the main cause of the 1943 riot.

The number and intensity of these instances of unfairness helped mobilise blacks to try to help themselves.

Key question
Did blacks try to bring about change?

(d) Increased black conciousness and activism

NAACP numbers increased from 50,000 to 450,000 during the Second World War. Most of the new members were Southern professionals (one-third of NAACP members were Southern) but co-operation with trade unions also brought in urban workers. Close co-operation between the NAACP and trade unionists in New Orleans radicalised the NAACP leadership into effective work on equal educational opportunities and voter registration.

Northern blacks cited wartime America's anti-fascist propaganda, which called for freedom and equality, pointing out that the USA itself had not attained true democracy until all Southern blacks could vote. White Americans became increasingly and uneasily aware that American racism was not that different from that of Hitler.

Wartime demand for black labour gave black workers greater bargaining power. Randolph threatened to bring Washington DC to a standstill unless there was equality within the armed forces and the workplace. Impatient at the lack of progress on an anti-lynching law, Walter White was supportive. Advised by his generals, Roosevelt refused to integrate the armed forces. However, he set up a federal agency called the Committee on Fair Employment Practices (FEPC) to promote equality in defence industries, in which two million blacks were employed.

Key date
Roosevelt set up Fair Employment Practices Commission: 1943

Some blacks engaged in boycotts and sit-ins that paved the way for the more famous activities of the 1950s and 1960s (see Chapters 5 and 6).

(e) Sit-ins and boycotts

Some blacks were inspired by Gandhi's confrontational, but non-violent, tactics against the British in India. The Howard-educated Christian socialist James Farmer thought such tactics would be particularly effective in wartime, and advocated non-violent tactics such as **economic boycotts**. In 1942 Farmer established the Congress of Racial Equality (CORE), which organised **sit-ins** at segregated Chicago restaurants and demanded desegregation on interstate transport. In 1941, Reverend Adam Clayton Powell Jr (see page 92), of the Abyssinian Baptist Church of Harlem led a successful bus boycott to force the company to employ more blacks.

However, one black activist said most blacks considered activism as eccentric. Most blacks remained quiescent in the Second World War, not wanting to appear unpatriotic and fearing disorder, especially after violent race riots in Detroit and Harlem in summer 1943. Those riots convinced many blacks that Randolph and the radicals were irresponsible. Wartime prosperity also militated against activism.

Key terms

Economic boycotts
The use of black purchasing power to gain concessions, for example, not shopping at a store that refused to employ blacks.

Sit-ins
An example of economic pressure; black protesters would sit at segregated restaurants until they were served. If they were not served, they would be taking up seats, so white paying customers could not find places. The idea was to force the restaurant to desegregate.

Primaries
When presidential candidates for a particular political party vie to be chosen as that party's candidate.

(f) Federal intervention

A. Philip Randolph had pressured Roosevelt into establishing the Fair Employment Practices Committee (FEPC), to promote equality in defence indistries. However, two-thirds of the 8000 job discrimination cases referred to the FEPC were dismissed and only one-fifth of Southern cases were black victories. Southern congressmen successfully decreased FEPC's funding after it was given greater power in 1943. FEPC accomplished too little to be considered a great success, but enough to show the importance of federal aid. The increasingly sympathetic US Justice Department established a Civil Rights Section, which tried to decrease lynching and police brutality in the South.

Southern black political rights increased thanks to a 1944 Supreme Court decision (SMITH v. ALLWRIGHT). The decision resulted from the NAACP's Texas campaign against white primaries. The Supreme Court declared the exclusion of blacks from the **primaries** unconstitutional under the 15th Amendment. The scholar D.C. Hine described the decision as 'the watershed in the struggle for black rights'. Segregationists resorted to illegality to stop blacks voting, but between 1940 and 1947 the number of black registered voters increased in the South from 3 to 12 per cent.

Key dates

James Farmer established the Congress of Racial Equality: 1942

SMITH v. ALLWRIGHT: 1944

(g) Second World War – conclusions

During the war greater black urbanisation (especially in the North) increased awareness and activism. Inspired by the USA's fight against fascism abroad, direct action was increasing and was

Key question
What had been achieved during the Second World War?

instrumental in the establishment of the FEPC. NAACP litigation was painstakingly eroding 'separate but equal'.

Most of these gains seemed irrelevant as yet to most Southern blacks. They watched the increased activism with interest, but rejected militancy, lest it alienate Southern white liberals. However, things would never be the same again. In a war against a racist German regime, black Americans fought in a segregated US army, frequently led by white officers. As demobilised white servicemen returned, disproportionate numbers of blacks were fired from their wartime jobs. The segregated armed forces damaged the morale of some blacks, while inspiring others to work for change. It was hundreds of ex-servicemen who bravely tried to thwart the election of a racist Mississippi senator in 1946. An ex-corporal from Alabama said, 'I'm hanged if I'm going to let the Alabama version of the Germans kick me around ... I went into the Army a nigger; I'm comin' out a man.' Demobilised soldiers were given government aid for a college education, so black Southerners attended colleges in record numbers. This education increased their economic opportunities and made them more articulate in demanding equality.

Key question
Were Asian Americans treated better or worse than black Americans?

Asian Americans: a comparative study

The USA stopped Chinese immigration in 1882, Japanese immigration in 1907, and immigration by all other Asian Pacific peoples in 1917. Why?

White Americans were suspicious of the different appearance and culture of Asians. For example, Americans disliked it when Japanese or Chinese males in the USA chose a bride from the home country by looking at photographs. Furthermore, the prevalence of single Chinese males in turn-of-the-century USA led to the rise of notorious 'Chinatowns', as in San Francisco. Lurid stories about gang warfare, opium dens and vice districts in Chinatowns turned many Americans against the Chinese. Asian Americans became most unpopular during periods of economic depression.

One of the most famous examples of racial hostility in the USA was the treatment of West Coast Japanese Americans after the Japanese bombing of Pearl Harbor in 1941 brought the USA into the Second World War. About 110,000 Japanese Americans were interned in concentration camps spread across the USA. Two-thirds of them were US citizens, yet they were deprived of property and freedom, and treated as prisoners of war. Although the USA was simultaneously at war with Germany, no such actions were taken against German Americans.

However, despite this treatment, Japanese Americans soon recovered to be one of the most prosperous US ethnic groups, earning on average today far more than Americans of British ancestry do. This led conservative black historian Thomas Sowell to conclude that racism and persecution alone do not explain poverty.

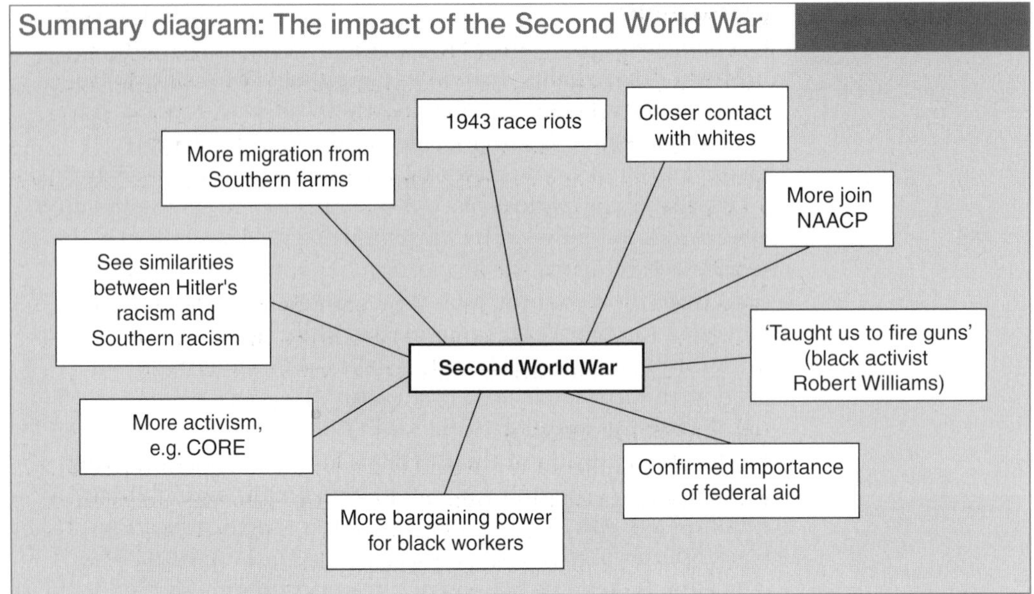

10 | Conclusions

Key question
Why and to what extent had the black situation improved between 1900 and 1945?

In 1900 blacks were economically and socially inferior to whites throughout the USA, but particularly in the South where they lacked any political power. Blacks lacked nationally known and recognised organisations and leaders, apart from Booker T. Washington. By 1945 there had been a clear and dramatic increase in black consciousness and activism. Although segregation and political inequality remained in the South, Southern white supremacy was being slowly and painfully eroded by a series of legal decisions. Now black organisations used a combination of co-operation, coercion and confrontation when dealing with whites. The number of significant black leaders was increasing. These improvements were due to several factors.

(a) Important individuals

The African American situation had improved partly because of the work of individuals such as Booker T. Washington, A. Philip Randolph, W.E.B. Du Bois and Eleanor Roosevelt. Washington had shown what a black person could achieve. He had gained occasionally productive access to successive presidents. As time passed, and there was no marked improvement in the position of blacks, leading spokesmen became more militant. Early twentieth-century blacks had not been ready for Du Bois' calls for greater civil rights activism. Mid-twentieth-century black leaders and organisations initiated a variety of actions help blacks. Randolph used trade unions, and Walter White's NAACP used litigation, negotiation, publicity and boycotts.

(b) NAACP

It was perhaps the organisations, rather than the individuals, which had the greatest potential to mobilise black people. The NAACP worked with quiet tenacity in the first half of the twentieth century, gaining increased membership and respectability over the years. The NAACP increased the awareness and activism of many blacks.

(c) American ideals

Given that white Americans always considered their country the home of freedom, democracy and equality, the position of blacks was inevitably and increasingly perceived as anomalous.

(d) External events

Under the impact of two world wars, blacks moved into the cities where there was greater opportunity for economic gain and for education in political and social inequalities and ways to combat them. The wars and the Depression galvanised the federal government into actions that benefited blacks.

(e) The federal government

Perhaps the involvement of the federal government was the single most important factor in improving the black situation. While Southern states continued to decide the fate of black residents, there was little hope for improvement. However, once the federal government took upon itself clear and consistent responsibility for that improvement, the days of state power would be limited. The increased federal intervention was triggered by the Depression. Federal aid to the poor in the 1930s inevitably meant federal aid to a great many blacks, most of whom were amongst the poorest of Americans.

Thus, due to a combination of factors, the foundations of the great civil rights movement of the mid-twentieth century had been laid.

Summary diagram: Comparing 1900 and 1945

1900	→	**1945**
Jim Crow in the South	→	Same
Discrimination in the North	→	Same
Economic opportunities	→	Slow improvement
Black consciousness	→	Dramatic increase
Black activism	→	Slowly increasing
Federal government uninterested	→	Slightly more interested

11 | Key Debates

(a) Was the 1930s a crucial decade for blacks?

Historians disagree over the extent to which the New Deal helped blacks. Left-wing historian Barton Bernstein (1968) said the New Deal was simply words and symbolic gestures, as far as blacks were concerned. Tony Badger (1989) and Harvard Sitkoff (1978) contend that the New Deal did as much for blacks as was possible given the power of Southern Democrats in Congress, the US tradition of states rights, and the indifference of Northerners.

Meier and Rudwick (1976) saw the Depression years as 'a watershed in Afro-American direct action', unequalled until the 1960s. They argued that non-violent direct action, as practised by Martin Luther King in the 1960s, had a long history in the black community. For example, in the 1930s, blacks boycotted discriminatory retailers in 35 cities, one-third of which were in the South.

(b) Did the civil rights movement start long before King?

Historians disagree over the extent and impact of black militancy during the Second World War. In the 1970s, Harvard Sitkoff contended that blacks were newly militant during the war, which led to violence in 47 cities in 1943, which in turn led to greater moderation. However, by 1997, Sitkoff had changed his mind, emphasising that patriotism led blacks to decrease the direct action that had grown up in the 1930s. While Sitkoff now sees no direct line of continuity between wartime civil rights activism and the 1960s, Mark Newman (2004) disagrees, pointing out that the foundations for the 1960s were laid during the war.

After Martin Luther King's death in 1968, most historians took the classic phase of civil rights activity to be the years of King's ascendancy, from 1955 to 1965, which are covered in Chapter 6. In the 1980s, historians' studies of local community action emphasised that the civil rights movement had its origins in the 1930s and 1940s, owing much to the impact of the New Deal, the Second World War, and the continuing work of NAACP. Adam Fairclough's study of Louisiana (1995) emphasised the importance of pre-King trade unions, schools, teachers, businessmen and organisations such as NAACP. John Kirk's study of Arkansas (1996), John Dittmer's of Mississippi (1994), and many others, confirm that at the very least there was a 'civil rights struggle' if not a 'civil rights movement' long before 1955.

However, Fairclough admits the 'earlier challenges did not seem to have the force of post-1955 protests': the 'undercurrent of discontent' was 'unstructured and ineffective; the countless instances of individual defiance did not add up to collective resistance'. For example, when A. Philip Randolph called for a one-day boycott of segregated transport in 1943, Southern blacks ignored him. E.D. Nixon's biographer, John White, confirms that the 'classic' period had its roots in preceding decades. Probably the main if subsequently unheralded force behind the

Montgomery Bus Boycott (see page 105), Nixon had been inspired by and participated in Randolph's black labour movement in the 1920s and NAACP activities in the 1930s and 1940s. Nixon's actions in 1955–6 clearly did not 'come out of the blue'.

(c) How historians are affected by their situation

The importance of the labour movement and left-wingers in the civil rights struggle 1900–45 was played down during and because of the Cold War (1946–86). American historians were not keen to admit that Communists had played any part in what became the successful civil rights movement.

Some key books in the debate

John Dittmer, *Local People: The Struggle for Civil Rights in Mississippi* (Chicago, 1994).

Adam Fairclough, *Race and Democracy: The Civil Rights Struggle in Louisiana 1915–1972* (University of Georgia, 1999).

Brian Ward and Tony Badger, editors, *The Making of Martin Luther King and the Civil Rights Movement* (New York University Press, 1996).

---

5 The Start of the Civil Rights Movement 1945–60

POINTS TO CONSIDER

Many historians see the 'Martin Luther King years' of 1956–65 as the 'classic' period of the civil rights movement. Others argue that the black activism of those years did not come 'out of the blue', and that black activism and changing federal government attitudes were evident from the end of the Second World War, if not before. This chapter looks at:

- Why consciousness of racial inequalities increased rapidly between 1945 and 1960
- Why some improvements in the legal, political, social and economic position of blacks were made between 1945 and 1960
- Which individuals, organisations, laws and Supreme Court rulings were the most important in helping and hindering change

It does this through the following sections:

- President Truman's early life and career
- How much did Truman help blacks?
- Conclusions about progress under Truman
- The role of Eisenhower
- The Montgomery Bus Boycott
- Little Rock
- Eisenhower's Civil Rights Acts (1957 and 1960)

Key dates

1945 Harry Truman became president
1946 Returning black servicemen attacked in the South
1947 Truman administration report, *To Secure These Rights*
Truman first president to address NAACP
1948 Truman ordered an end to discrimination in the armed forces and civil service
Presidential election (won by Truman)
1950 Supreme Court virtually overturned PLESSY v. FERGUSON
1951 CGCC established
1953 Eisenhower became president

1954	Supreme Court ruled against segregated schools (BROWN)
1955	BROWN II ruled that integration of schools should proceed White Citizens Councils established throughout the South
1956	Montgomery Bus Boycott Supreme Court decision BROWDER v. GAYLE
1957	SCLC established Civil Rights Act Little Rock crisis
1958	Supreme Court declared school segregation unconstitutional (COOPER v. AARON)
1960	Civil Rights Act

1 | President Truman's Early Life and Career

Key question
How do Truman's early life and career illustrate race relations in the first half of the twentieth century?

Key date
Harry Truman became president: 1945

When President Franklin D. Roosevelt died in office in 1945, Vice-President Harry Truman became president. Truman was then elected president in his own right in 1948. Truman illustrates how some racists became increasingly sympathetic to blacks in the twentieth century.

Born and raised in late nineteenth-century Missouri, it would have been unusual if Harry Truman had not been racist. His hometown of Independence, Missouri (population 6000) was nostalgic for the Confederacy. Most of the black residents over 40 had been born in slavery. Blacks lived in the shacks of 'Nigger Neck' in northeast Independence. They were responsible for frequent night-time hold-ups and burglaries. They were unwelcome in most stores, not allowed in the town library, and had a separate school. Words such as 'nigger' and 'coon' were commonly used, and Harry Truman was no exception. The local press reported any lynching in the South in lurid detail, always justifying the event..

Truman's ancestors had owned slaves. His uncle was a thug who shot some blacks 'to see them jump'. Truman told his sweetheart Bess that one man was as good as another, 'so long as he is honest and decent and not a nigger or a Chinaman'. He told her of his Confederate uncle who hated:

> ... Chinks [Chinese] and Japs. So do I. It is race prejudice I guess. But I am strongly of the opinion that Negroes ought to be in Africa, yellow men in Asia, and white men in Europe and America.

When Truman went off to fight to 'make the world safe for democracy' in the First World War, he sailed from New York which he felt had too many Jews (he called it 'Kike [Jew] town') and 'Wops' (Italians). In all this, he was typical of his era. Early in his political career he did what many aspiring politicians did and paid $10 membership dues to the Ku Klux Klan, but apparently got his money back when he insisted on the right to appoint Catholics as well as Protestants to office.

Once in national politics, Truman seemed to change. As president he helped blacks more than any of his recent predecessors had done.

2 | How Much Did Truman Help Blacks?

Key question
How much and why did President Truman help promote racial equality?

(a) Senator Truman

In the Senate in the late 1930s, Truman consistently supported legislation to abolish the poll tax and stop lynching. In his 1940 campaign for re-election to the Senate he made what was a very radical speech for Missouri in that era. He told his predominantly white audience blacks should have equality before the law, civil rights, and better housing.

However, as a Missouri senator, Truman still used the word 'nigger' privately and made racist jokes, even as he favoured legislation to help blacks. Did Truman change his stance because blacks were increasingly important Democratic voters? There were fewer black voters than white voters in Missouri, but any astute politician like Truman had to be aware that race relations were increasingly important in politics. In 1944 President Roosevelt considered Truman as a vice-presidential running mate. Truman's main rival was quite openly racist and complained bitterly that the Negro has come into control of the Democratic party '... Mr President, all I have heard around this White House for the last week is nigger. I wonder if anybody thinks about the white people.'

Roosevelt chose Truman as his vice-president partly because he had 'never made' any such 'racial remarks' – at least, not publicly.

(b) President Truman and the FEPC (1945)

When Roosevelt died, Vice-President Truman became president. At first he did nothing significant to help blacks. In 1945, the FEPC (see page 81), which had succeeded in 16 other Northern and Western cities, tried to end discriminatory hiring policies by a Washington DC transportation company. Truman gave them no real help in Washington. He did try to get Congress to continue funding the FEPC but they refused. Does his personal ambivalence on race relations explain his half-hearted commitment to FEPC? More probably he felt that as the voters had not elected him president he needed to be cautious over controversial issues.

(c) Truman and Adam Clayton Powell (1945)

The sensitivity of the race issue was demonstrated in 1945. The **Daughters of the American Revolution** (DAR) refused to allow black **Representative** Adam Clayton Powell's black musician wife to perform in their hall. Powell asked Mrs Bess Truman to boycott a DAR tea. Bess said she deplored the treatment of Mrs Powell but would attend the tea. Powell described the First Lady as 'the last lady of the land'. This infuriated ultra-loyal Harry Truman,

Key terms

Daughters of the American Revolution
A prestigious middle class society whose members could claim US ancestry back to the revolutionary war era, distinguishing them from newer immigrants.

Representative
Member of the House of Representatives, the lower chamber in Congress.

Adam Clayton Powell introducing presidential candidate John Kennedy to a crowd in Harlem, New York, in 1960.

who privately christened Powell 'a smart aleck and a rabble rouser', saying he would not receive 'that damned nigger preacher' at the White House. The whole affair showed how racial discrimination increasingly made headlines, what a struggle it was to reject racist traditions, and how difficult it was to keep everyone happy.

(d) Post-war attacks on black servicemen (1945–6)

Truman was racist but he tried to be fair. He said legal equality for blacks was the black man's basic right, 'because he is a human being and a natural-born American.' Like many contemporaries, he was horrified by attacks on black servicemen returning from the Second World War. The worst attacks were in the deep South. In 1946 Truman described how his stomach

> turned over when I learned that Negro soldiers, just back from overseas, were being dumped out of army trucks in Missouri and beaten. Whatever my inclinations as a native of Missouri might have been, as President I know this is bad. I shall fight to end evils

Profile: Adam Clayton Powell 1908–72

Key question
In what way was Adam Clayton Powell significant and what did he achieve?

1908 – Born in New York City where his upper middle class father was minister at Abyssinian Baptist Church

1933 – Despite parental opposition, married an ex-Cotton Club (Harlem's famous night-spot) show-girl and divorcee. All three of his marriages failed, but he said it was never his fault

1934–5 – Involved in Harlem's 'Don't buy where you can't work' campaign (similar campaigns in Chicago and Detroit)

1937–71 – Powell succeeded his father at Abyssinian Baptist Church

1938 – After Supreme Court ruling said anti-discrimination boycotts acceptable, Powell led successful boycott against New York bus companies that employed only whites

1941 – Powell won a seat on the New York City Council

1942 – Founded newspaper *People's Voice*, which campaigned against discriminatory employers (such as Macy's, and the city's colleges, all of whose 2282 professors were whites) and the Red Cross (it segregated blood donations). Compared American racism to Nazi racism

1944 – Elected to Congress by newly created congressional district dominated by Harlem's quarter of a million blacks

1945–69 – Re-elected 12 times to House of Representatives

1961 – Due to Congress' seniority system, became chairman of the powerful House Committee on Education and Labour – the most influential position any black had ever obtained within the government

1965 – Libel case – Powell tried and convicted by an all-white jury in Manhattan, where 50 per cent of population black or Puerto Rican

Mid-1960s – Powell aligned with black power movement (see Chapter 7). Claimed to have originated the phrase 'black power'. Defined black power as black dignity and pride

1970 – Harlem blacks finally rejected Powell due to scandals: indictment for income tax fraud, improper use of congressional funds, abuse of privileges, increased rejection of non-violence, excessive absences from Congress ('part-time Powell', said one black opponent)

Powell was a highly significant figure, partly because elected black representatives were so rare at that time, and partly because of his incessant and sometimes successful agitation for racial equality in

Congress. He 'taught us pride in ourselves', said David Dinkins, New York City's first black mayor. When Powell was temporarily excluded from Congress by his colleagues (many of whom were equally corrupt), he said it was because he was black. Perhaps, but he was also incredibly arrogant, outspoken, dishonest, and a self-publicist. Arthur Spingarn, NAACP president for 26 years, said, 'he's a tragedy. If he had character, he'd be a great man.'

He worked hard in Congress on behalf of civil rights, fairer employment practices, anti-lynching legislation and desegregation in interstate travel. He won black access to the press gallery and segregated cafeterias and barbershops in Congress. He helped in the passage of Johnson's Great Society legislation (see page 181) and 1964 Civil Rights Act (the section that denied federal funds to schools refusing to desegregate was basically the 'Powell Amendment' for which Powell had long lobbied).

> like this … I am not asking for social equality, because no such things exist, but I am asking for equality of opportunity for all human beings … When a mayor and a City Marshal can take a Negro Sergeant off a bus in South Carolina, beat him up and put out one of his eyes, and nothing is done about it by the State Authorities, something is radically wrong with the system.

Key dates

Returning black servicemen attacked in the South: 1946

To Secure These Rights (anti-segregation report of Truman-appointed committee): 1947

Truman recognised that, regardless of race, the general principle of respect for the law was at stake. Privately he still spoke of 'niggers' and his sister claimed that 'Harry is no more for nigger equality than any of us'. Publicly he told Southern friends they were 'living 80 years behind the time' and for the good of the USA they had better change.

(e) *To Secure These Rights* (1947)

In September 1946, President Truman established a liberal civil rights committee to investigate increasing violence against blacks. He deliberately chose liberals to be on the committee, ensuring that their report would draw national attention to unacceptable situations. Although Walter White and Truman's advisers felt the committee 'was nothing short of political suicide' Truman told his aide to 'push it with everything you have'.

In October 1947 the committee gave Truman their report, entitled *To Secure These Rights*. It said the USA could not claim to lead the free world while blacks were not equal. The report advocated eliminating segregation from US life by using federal power. It called for:

- anti-lynching legislation
- abolition of the poll tax
- voting rights laws
- a permanent FEPC
- an end to discrimination in interstate travel
- an end to discrimination in the armed forces

- a civil rights division in the **Justice Department**
- **administration** support for civil rights suits in the federal courts
- the establishment of the United States Commission on Civil Rights.

These were revolutionary recommendations in a country where relations between blacks and whites were so tense that segregation was still legally enforced in all the former states of the Confederacy, and, in slightly less extreme form, in Maryland, West Virginia, Kentucky and Truman's home state of Missouri. In the North and West, while not legally enshrined, segregation was a social fact. New York's Brooklyn Dodgers had just introduced the first black baseball player to the major league. Jackie Robinson's presence caused antagonism amongst fans and players throughout the North. Southerners and even some Northerners referred to grown black males as 'boy'. In the movies, black characters were often wide-eyed, slow-witted buffoons. Nevertheless Truman went ahead, implementing the changes that were within his power and calling for the changes the report recommended in his **State of the Union addresses** in 1947 and 1948.

Key terms

Justice Department
Branch of the federal government in Washington DC with special responsibility for justice.

Administration
When Americans talk of 'the Truman administration' they mean the government as led by that particular president.

State of the Union Address
Annual presidential speech that sums up the situation in the USA and/or advertises the president's achievements.

Cold War
From about 1946 to 1989, hostility between the USA and the USSR was known as the Cold War.

(f) Speeches (1947–8)

The distance travelled by the racist from Missouri could be seen in June 1947 when he told his sister:

> I have got to make a speech to the Society for the Advancement of Coloured People tomorrow, and I wish I didn't have to make it. Mrs Roosevelt [who was also speaking] has spent her public life stirring up trouble between white and black – and I am in the middle. Mamma won't like what I say because I wind up by quoting old Abe [Abraham Lincoln]. But I believe what I say and I am hopeful we may implement it.

On the steps of Washington DC's Lincoln Memorial and before 10,000 people, he made the first presidential speech to the NAACP, saying all Americans were entitled to full civil rights and freedom. He urged an end to lynching, the poll tax, and inequality in education and employment. Walter White felt that for its bravery and in the context of the time, it ranked as one of the greatest presidential speeches. It had been the strongest presidential statement on civil rights since Lincoln himself.

Key date

Truman first president to address NAACP: 1947

In his 1947 and 1948 State of the Union addresses, Truman urged the civil rights legislation recommended by the committee. Truman said 'our first goal' must be 'to secure fully the essential human rights of our citizens'. He pointed out the disparity between the words of America's Founding Fathers ('all men are created equal') and the actions of their descendants. He said it was important to set a good example to a **Cold War** world faced with the choice between US-style freedom and Soviet-style enslavement. This risked splitting his party and damaging his chances of getting elected in 1948.

Key terms

Korean War
From 1950 to 1953, the USA, South Korea and the United Nations fought against Communist North Korea and China in Korea.

National Guard and reserves
Each state has its own 'army', the National Guard, ready to deal with state problems, but also available to be federalised if the federal government needs extra manpower. The reserves are federally controlled, trained and ready to supplement the regular armed forces in an emergency.

Key dates

Truman ordered an end to discrimination in armed forces and civil service: 1948

Supreme Court ruled against discrimination in housing, in SHELLEY v. KRAEMER: 1948

(g) Ending discrimination among federal employees (1948)

In the presidential election year of 1948, despite dissent within his own party and Republican antagonism, Truman suddenly issued executive orders to end discrimination in the armed forces and guarantee fair employment in the civil service. The army top brass resisted for as long as they dared (over two years). There were few black officers until shortage of manpower in the **Korean War** speeded up the desegregation. However, the **National Guard and reserves** remained segregated.

Similarly, although his Fair Employment Board (established in 1948) was designed to give minorities equal treatment in federal hiring, it was handicapped by a shortage of funds, and conservative employees. However, its mere existence affirmed federal commitment to the principle of equality and set an example to other employers.

Truman probably calculated that as he had already lost the extremist white vote, he might as well ensure the liberal and black vote. He was also under pressure from A. Philip Randolph's call for a black draft-resistance movement (a frightening prospect in the Cold War). Also, these reforms could be done on the president's authority, which helped to show up the uncooperative Republican Congress.

(h) Pressure on the Supreme Court (1948)

In 1948, the Truman administration supported the NAACP in SHELLEY v. KRAEMER, wherein the Supreme Court ruled against restrictive covenants that were used to stop blacks purchasing homes in white areas. The ruling proved ineffective, despite Truman's efforts.

(i) The advantages and disadvantages of liberalism on civil rights

There was political advantage to Truman's liberalism on civil rights. Some Democrats such as New York's 'Boss' Ed Flynn wanted the black vote. Truman's advisers told him many believed 'the Northern Negro vote today holds the balance of power in presidential elections' because the blacks voted as a block and were geographically concentrated in pivotal large and closely-contested electoral states such as New York, Illinois and Michigan.

However, there were political disadvantages in seeking civil rights legislation. Although Truman reminded them that his Missouri background led him to sympathise with them, Southern Democrats were furious. One refused to attend a dinner with Truman in case he was seated alongside a 'Nigra'. Polls showed that only six per cent of voters supported a civil rights programme. Not surprisingly, Truman made only one civil rights speech during the 1948 presidential campaign – in Harlem!

(j) The Dixiecrats and the 1948 presidential election

Controversy erupted during the 1948 **Democratic Convention**. Minneapolis Mayor Hubert Humphrey rejected the party's 1944 civil rights plank, designed to appease Southern whites. Humphrey advocated adopting Truman's new programme, saying:

> There are those who say to you – we are rushing this issue of civil rights. I say we are 172 years too late … The time has arrived for the Democratic Party to get out of the shadow of states rights and walk forthrightly into the bright sunshine of human rights.

Northerners and Westerners cheered in the aisles, but Southerners stayed glumly seated. While Humphrey probably contributed greatly to Truman's election by ensuring a large black vote, Truman criticised Humphrey's group as 'crackpots' who split the party. Southern Democrats nominated Strom Thurmond as their candidate for president. Thurmond's '**Dixiecrat**' platform advocated segregation and the 'racial integrity of each race'. Strom Thurmond thought it was 'un-American to force us to admit the Negro into our homes, our eating places, our swimming pools and our theatres'. One Alabama Dixiecrat said that Truman's civil rights programme aimed 'to reduce us to the status of a mongrel, inferior race'.

Truman's stance required considerable courage. In the face of Dixiecrat threats that 'they would shoot Truman, that no-good son-of-a-bitch and his civil rights', Truman campaigned in frequently racist Texas. He was booed in Waco when he shook hands with a black woman, although segregation was abolished for the day in Dallas Rebel Stadium where blacks and whites cheered him. It was a political gamble to show support for blacks in the South especially as Truman's ideas were deliberately misrepresented. His call for equality of opportunity was interpreted as calling for miscegenation. Integrated political meetings in Southern states sometimes led to serious violence. In Memphis the local political 'Boss' tried to stop the black singer and actor Paul Robeson addressing an integrated political rally. The Ku Klux Klan surrounded the several thousand-strong crowd, but dared not attack because 100 armed blacks stood alongside them.

The first president ever to campaign in Harlem, Truman carried an unprecedented two-thirds of the black vote in the 1948 presidential election. This played a big part in getting him elected, especially in crucial states like California and Illinois. So was that why Truman had apparently changed his position on blacks? Surely not. After all, the South was traditionally and solidly Democrat, and Truman's civil rights advocacy cost him the 'Dixiecrat vote', which was probably as numerically significant as the black vote. Furthermore, once elected, he continued to prod the USA towards a fairer society. As he told his racist sister, he really believed that such changes were essential for the USA's national well-being, in respect of law and order, economic

Key terms

Democratic Convention
Democrats and Republicans each have a national convention in a presidential election year, to choose/confirm their presidential candidate.

Dixiecrat
A racist political party established in 1948.

Key date

Presidential election (won by Truman): 1948

advancement and its proclaimed leadership of the free world against **Communism**. Truman's motivation was not purely political.

Key term

Communism
The ideology of the USSR and its allied states. Emphasised economic equality and state control of the economy. As the Communist Party was supposed to be the party of the people, Communist states were usually one-party states on the grounds that no other party was needed.

(k) Symbolic actions, appointments and expenditure

Truman wanted to give greater federal aid to impoverished blacks. He tried to open more public housing to blacks after 1948. However, the administration's urban renewal programme often left blacks homeless. There were usually fewer homes available in the new and more spacious public housing units than in the slums they replaced.

Truman appointed a black judge to the federal courts and a black Governor of the Virgin Isles. He tried to use federal purchasing power to prompt other employers to work towards equality. By Executive Order 10308 (December 1951) he established a Committee on Government Contract Compliance (CGCC). Federal defence contracts were not supposed to be given to companies that discriminated against minorities. However, as the CGCC could only recommend, not enforce, it was even less effective than FEPC. This angered black activists, but Truman could not afford to antagonise Congress during the Korean War. The *Pittsburgh Courier* recognised CGCC was the best Truman could do 'under the circumstances'. It was the forerunner of more effective committees under subsequent presidents.

Key date

Committee on Government Contract Compliance established, to encourage companies to halt job discrimination: 1951

Perhaps the most important thing Truman had done was to awaken the USA's conscience to civil rights issues, through his speeches and symbolic actions. Small steps, such as integrated inauguration celebrations in January 1949 and the desegregation of Washington DC Airport, served collectively to make an important point.

Key question
Did Truman help blacks just in order to get their votes?

(l) Truman's motivation – conclusions

Harry Truman appeared to modify his views on non-whites during his life and career. Were his motives purely political? Or did events, age and responsibility make him more sympathetic to ethnic minorities? Possibly, while Truman remained a racist at heart, he knew racism was wrong and should be combated by those in power. Harry Truman could be as cynical as any man when votes were at stake but he was also a genuine patriot. He wanted to do what was best for the USA. He wanted US society to retain respect for the law. He felt equality was vital to maintain America's moral standing in the Cold War world. He told black Democrats that better education for blacks would benefit the economy and thereby help all Americans. It was a combination of the black vote, respect for the law, humane revulsion at racist attacks, personal integrity and his perception of what was best for his country that served to turn Truman towards advocacy of greater equality for blacks.

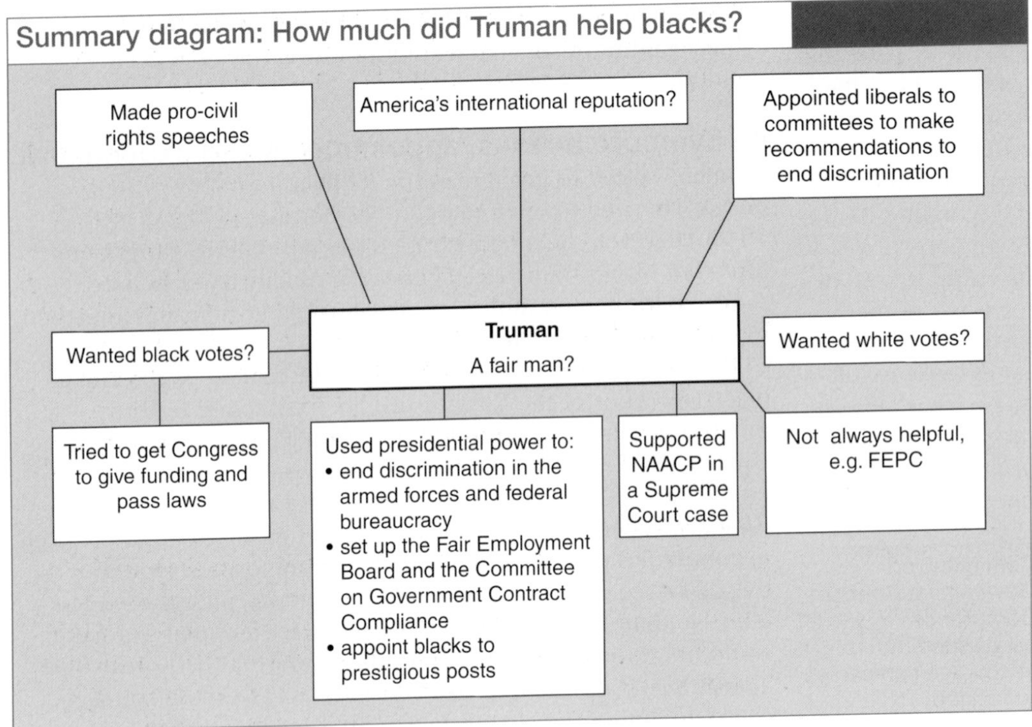

3 | Conclusions about Progress under Truman

(a) Progress

Some progress had been made during Truman's presidency: awareness of the need for greater equality had increased and there had been a few concrete advances, such as the CGCC and decreased discrimination in federal employment and contracts.

Was it all due to Truman? No. There were other forces and factors at work. Democrats such as Flynn, individuals such as Randolph and organisations such as the NAACP and CORE all put pressure on Truman to act. CORE organised sit-ins and '**Freedom Rides**' such as the 1947 'Journey of Reconciliation' through the border states, which tried to ensure the enforcement of the 1946 Supreme Court ruling against segregation on interstate bus transportation.

NAACP used a variety of tactics, such as economic boycotts. For example, in New Orleans in 1947, NAACP activists picketed stores that refused to allow black women to try on hats.

The NAACP lawyers were working against 'separate but equal' (see page 29) in the law courts and gained some successes. In 1950 the Supreme Court made three civil rights decisions that set important precedents for future years. It held that:

- Segregation on railway dining cars was illegal under the Interstate Commerce Act (HENDERSON v. US).
- A black student could not be physically separated from white students in the University of Oklahoma (McLAURIN v. OKLAHOMA STATE REGENTS).

Key question
Who or what was most responsible for progress in civil rights in the Truman years?

Key term
Freedom Rides
When integrated groups of civil rights activists rode on interstate buses to defy segregation and monitor whether Supreme Court rulings against segregation were being ignored.

Key date
Three Supreme Court decisions effectively overturned PLESSY v. FERGUSON: 1950

- A separate black Texan law school was not equal to the University of Texas Law School to which the black petitioner had therefore to be admitted (SWEATT v. PAINTER).

PLESSY v. FERGUSON (see page 29) was thus almost overturned. In the dying days of Truman's presidency, the administration intervened pro-Brown in BROWN v. BOARD OF EDUCATION OF TOPEKA, which proved vital in the Supreme Court reversal of the separate but equal doctrine in 1954 (see page 102).

Local government also played its part. By 1952, 11 states and 20 cities had fair employment laws, 19 states had legislation against some form of racial discrimination, and only five states retained the poll tax.

Truman had led by example and his support played a part in attaining all this.

(b) Lack of progress

Organisations, institutions, and individuals were also responsible for the lack of progress. Congress, dominated by Republicans, refused to pass meaningful civil rights legislation, and hampered a fairer distribution of federal funds to black schools. Truman usually had to resort to **Executive Orders** to make progress on equality. Public opinion slowed down progress on civil rights. Things could not and would not be changed overnight. Congress resisted Truman's civil rights legislative programme. Polls in 1949–50 showed that while many voters favoured abolition of the poll tax, only 33 per cent favoured the fair employment bill.

Given the degree of opposition amongst the white electorate and politicians, one must conclude that Truman played a brave and crucial individual role in precipitating change. Americans needed the presidential authority and prestige to move more quickly on the road to racial equality. Responsibility for the raising of awareness that precipitated presidential and legal actions also lay with the black activists themselves, particularly the trade unionist Randolph and the NAACP.

Key term

Executive Orders The constitution reserved certain powers to the executive (the president). For example, the president could issue executive orders regarding the armed forces in his constitutional capacity as commander-in-chief.

Summary diagram: Conclusions about progress under Truman

Progress	Lack of progress
CORE activism	Some whites remained in racist organisations
NAACP litigation	Jim Crow laws remained in South
Supreme Court rulings	Congress refused to pass civil rights legislation
Some states legislated against discrimination	Some states retained discrimination
President Truman urged reform	White opinion slowed down progress

4 | The Role of Eisenhower (1953–61)

Key question
To what extent was Eisenhower committed to racial equality?

Key date
Eisenhower became president: 1953

In his first State of the Union address (February 1953) the Republican President Eisenhower called for a combination of publicity, persuasion and conscience to help end racial discrimination. He reaffirmed Truman's commitment to desegregation of the military, although blacks still did not get equality in promotions or assignments. He also worked against discrimination in federal facilities in Washington and federal hiring, but his President's Committee on Government Contracts lacked teeth. When forced into action (see page 112) he could be helpful to blacks but for the most part he was far less inclined than Truman was to propel the USA towards racial equality. Why?

- Eisenhower often reminded people he was born in an all-white town in the South and spent much of his life in Southern states and in the segregated armed forces (in 1948 he told Congress of his belief that the armed services should not be fully desegregated).
- He shared the typical white fears of miscegenation, assuring his speech writer that his public calls for equality of opportunity did not mean black and white had 'to mingle socially – or that a Negro could court my daughter'.
- He said he feared the 'great emotional strains' which would arise from desegregating schools.
- He was ideologically opposed to large-scale federal intervention in any great issue, which was why he rejected the re-establishment of the wartime FEPC.
- There were good political reasons for inactivity. His Republican Party had seen the damage inflicted on the Democrats by disagreements over civil rights. The Republicans had done unusually well in the Southern states as a result. The Republican Party could only lose by adopting a firm civil rights policy.

The sole black on Eisenhower's staff, ex-NAACP worker E. Frederic Morrow, was employed in 1955 with the black vote in the presidential election in mind. Initially he arranged parking spaces for staffers, then he answered correspondence from blacks. White House clerks and typists refused to file or type for him and Eisenhower never consulted him on civil rights. Morrow was shocked by the administration's ignorance and concluded that Eisenhower never understood how blacks felt.

Eisenhower only met black leaders (King, Wilkins and Randolph) once. Randolph criticised Eisenhower's inactivity and called for more presidential leadership. Eisenhower avoided talking to Congressman Adam Clayton Powell, whom he considered to be a rabble-rousing extremist. When Powell tried to make federal aid for school-building contingent upon desegregation, that lost the federal aid, which infuriated Eisenhower. Eisenhower's staff felt that black organisations over-dramatised incidents of racial injustice, demanded too much time and attention, and were insufficiently grateful for the administration's deeds on their behalf. One presidential aide felt that black demands were made with 'ugliness and surliness'.

Key question
How important was the BROWN decision?

5 | BROWN (1954)

(a) Oliver Brown and the NAACP

Kansas was one of the 17 states in which schools were legally segregated schools. Church minister Oliver Brown decided to challenge segregated schools in Topeka, Kansas. Brown could not send his daughter to a whites-only school five blocks away, only to an all-black school 20 blocks away. The NAACP had been working against segregated schools in the law courts, slowly eroding the 'separate but equal' decision of the Supreme Court (PLESSY v. FERGUSON). Now, the NAACP decided to support Brown in his appeal to the Supreme Court. The organisation felt that it had a good chance of success, because Kansas was not a Southern state.

Exterior and interior views of a school for black children in Ruleville, Sunflower County, Mississippi, in 1949: 'separate' but clearly not 'equal'.

(b) The Supreme Court BROWN decision (1954)

The leading NAACP lawyer Thurgood Marshall represented Brown before the Supreme Court. Marshall argued that segregation was against the 14th Amendment. In BROWN v. THE BOARD OF EDUCATION, TOPEKA, KANSAS (1954), Chief Justice Earl Warren adjudged that even if facilities were equal (they never were), separate education was psychologically harmful to black children. The Supreme Court agreed, in defiance of President Eisenhower's wishes.

Key dates

Supreme Court's BROWN decision opposed segregated education: 1954

BROWN II ruled that integration of schools should proceed: 1955

White Citizens Councils established throughout the South to combat integration: 1955

(c) Results and significance of the BROWN ruling

The BROWN ruling was highly significant.

- It was a great triumph for the NAACP's long legal campaign against segregated education. Brown seemed to remove all constitutional sanction for racial segregation by overturning PLESSY v. FERGUSON.
- The victory was not total: the Supreme Court gave no date by which desegregation had to be achieved and said nothing about *de facto* segregation.
- The NAACP returned to the Supreme Court in BROWN II (1955) to obtain the ruling that integration be accomplished 'with all deliberate speed', but there was still no date for compliance. Warren believed schools and administrators needed time to adjust. The white reaction suggests that Warren was right.
- White Citizens Councils were quickly formed throughout the South to defend segregation. By 1956 they boasted around a quarter of a million members. The Councils challenged desegregation plans in the law courts. The Ku Klux Klan was revitalised once more.
- Acceptance of the BROWN ruling varied. In the peripheral and urban South desegregation was introduced quite quickly: 70 per cent of school districts in Washington DC and in the border states of Delaware, Kentucky, Maryland, Missouri, Oklahoma and West Virginia desegregated schools within a year. However, in the heart of the old Confederacy (Georgia, South Carolina, Alabama, Mississippi, and Louisiana) schools remain segregated. Some school boards maintained white-only schools by manipulating entry criteria. From 1956 to 1959, there was a 'massive resistance' campaign in Virginia: whites closed some schools rather than desegregate. Virginia labour unions financed segregated schools when the public schools were closed.
- BROWN now became a central issue in Southern politics. Most Southern politicians signed the Southern Manifesto. The signatories committed themselves to fight against the BROWN decision, and thereby the Supreme Court. President Eisenhower said the federal government had no power to intervene when his political ally the governor of Texas used state troopers to prevent school integration. Events at Little Rock, Arkansas, precipitated by the Supreme Court decision, forced Eisenhower's hand (see pages 111–12).

(d) Eisenhower and the BROWN ruling

(i) The appointment of Earl Warren

Eisenhower inadvertently helped blacks with his appointment of the liberal Southern Republican Earl Warren to the Supreme Court as a reward for his support in the 1952 campaign. Eisenhower told Warren that Southerners were not 'bad people':

> All they are concerned about is to see that their sweet little girls are not required to sit in school alongside some big overgrown Negroes.

Despite Eisenhower's opposition, Warren's Supreme Court struck a great blow against segregated schools with BROWN.

(ii) The reluctance to use federal power

Eisenhower refused to use federal power to enforce the BROWN decision, until forced by events at Little Rock, Arkansas (see pages 111–12). His initial silence over BROWN owed much to his belief in the separation of the powers of the president and the judiciary. He disliked federal intrusion into private lives and he feared that some schools would close rather than let in blacks:

> It is all very well to talk about school integration, but you may also be talking about social disintegration. We cannot demand perfection in these moral questions. All we can do is keep working toward a goal.

His public silence was widely interpreted as signifying his lack of support for BROWN. He refused to condemn the pro-segregation Southern Manifesto, saying change would have to be gradual.

(iii) Results and significance

Chief Justice Warren thought that a word of approval from Eisenhower on BROWN would have helped stop the mob violence that kept blacks out of white schools throughout the South.

Eisenhower's speechwriter Arthur Larsen came to the 'inescapable conclusion' that President Eisenhower 'was neither emotionally nor intellectually in favour of combating segregation'.

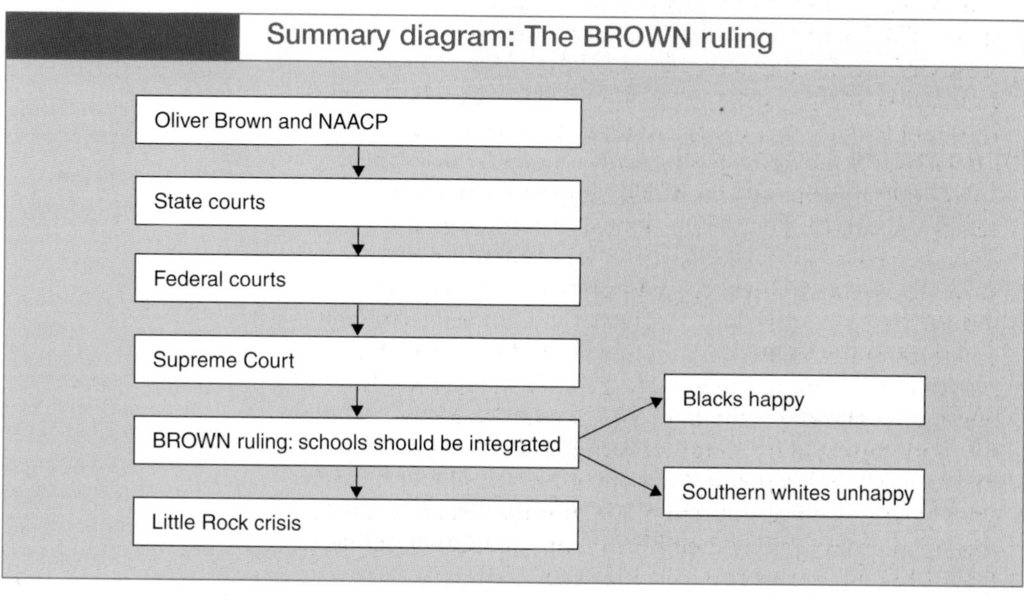

6 | Emmett Till and Autherine Lucy

Key question
Why were these two teenagers so significant?

(a) Emmett Till (1955)

Emmett Till wolf-whistled at a white woman. In August 1955, his mutilated body was dragged out of a Mississippi river. Till's mother had an open casket funeral service to demonstrate 'what they did to my boy'. In his appeal to the jurors the lawyer defending the men accused of the murder said he was 'sure that every last Anglo-Saxon one of us has the courage to free' them. The defence argued that Till was really alive and well in Chicago and that this was all an NAACP plot! The defence lawyer and his congressman brother were leading Democrats in the county. This was the first time white men were charged with murdering a black man in Mississippi, but the verdict was 'not guilty'. Eisenhower made no comment, in sharp contrast to Truman's brave and just condemnation of the murder of black soldiers. The murder of Till encouraged many blacks to become civil rights activists.

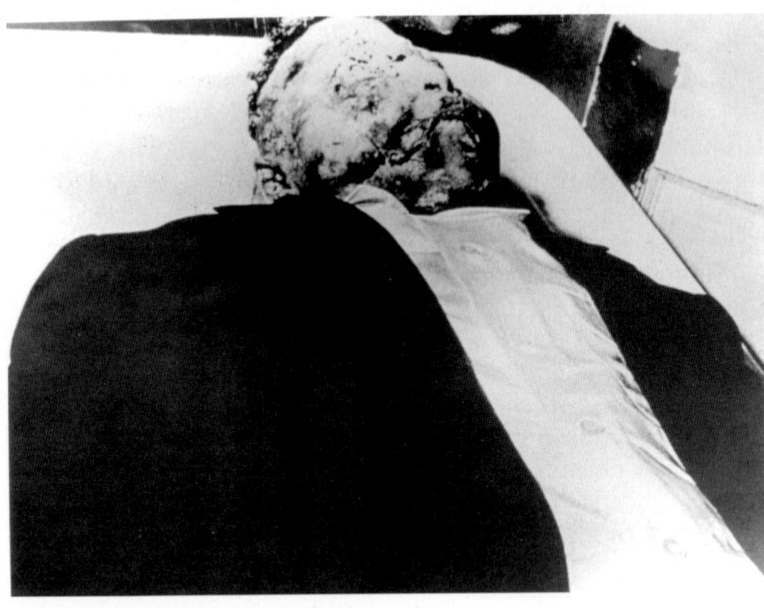

Emmett Till's mother wanted his coffin open so that everyone could see his battered body.

(b) Autherine Lucy (1955)

Although Eisenhower said he would always support federal court orders, he also kept quiet about the expulsion of the first black student from the University of Alabama. Autherine Lucy successfully took the University to a federal court to obtain admission, but the University then expelled her. They said she had lied when she claimed she had been excluded because of her race.

Eisenhower seemed to hope that race relations would somehow gradually improve of their own accord. He feared that 'if we attempt merely by passing a lot of laws to force someone to like someone else, we are just going to get into trouble'. Eisenhower also refused to give federal support for the Montgomery Bus Boycott.

Key question
Why did the Montgomery Bus Boycott take place?

7 | The Montgomery Bus Boycott (1956)

The Montgomery Bus Boycott is seen by many as the real start of the US **civil rights movement**.

Key term
Civil rights movement
Aimed at legal, social, political and economic equality for blacks. Black and white activists campaigned, particularly in the 1960s, with some success. Historians disagree over the exact dates of the movement.

(a) The trigger event

In December 1955, Mrs Rosa Parks returned home by bus after a hard day's work as a seamstress in a department store in Montgomery, Alabama. The bus soon filled up. A white man was left standing. The bus driver ordered her and three other blacks to move because of the city ordinance that said no black could sit parallel with a white passenger. The others moved, but Mrs Parks refused. She was arrested, and charged with a violation of the Montgomery city bus segregation ordinance.

(b) Rosa Parks and the NAACP

Many writers portray 42-year-old Rosa Parks as a tired old lady who had been exhausted by the day at work and could not take any more. But her defiance was not unpremeditated. She had joined the NAACP in 1943. She soon became Montgomery branch secretary. The branch had been looking to challenge Montgomery's bus segregation laws. They had contemplated using Claudette Colvin who had been arrested in March 1955 for refusing to give up a seat to a white passenger, but Colvin was a pregnant, unmarried teenager who was also accused of assault. As the challenge would cost NAACP half a million dollars, 'respectable' Rosa Parks was a safer test case.

Key date
Black lecturers in Alabama State College established Women's Political Council and campaigned for bus desegregation: 1945

(c) The mobilisation of the black community

Weeks before the Rosa Parks incident, a black mother had boarded a Montgomery bus, two babies in her arms. She placed the babies on the front 'white' seats in order to free her hands to pay her fare. The driver yelled, 'Take the black dirty brats off the seats', then hit the accelerator. The babies fell into the aisle. Many of the Montgomery black community had had enough.

Once Rosa Parks had been arrested, the NAACP and (black) Alabama State College helped her. Encouraged by lecturer Jo Ann Robinson and the Women's Political Council, students copied and distributed propaganda leaflets to elicit total support from the black community. Believing that church involvement would increase working class black participation and decrease the possibility of disorder, NAACP worked with local church leaders, especially Dr Martin Luther King Jr. The 26-year-old Baptist minister had already rejected an offer to lead the local NAACP branch, but he let his church be used as a meeting place to plan a bus boycott to protest at Parks' arrest. The church would thus provide the organisation, location, inspiration, and some financial aid.

(d) The boycott

Boycotts hit white pockets and were a traditional and effective mass weapon. Blacks had boycotted streetcars throughout the South between 1900 and 1906. In March 1953, blacks in Baton

Rouge, Louisiana, used their economic power (most bus passengers were black) to gain bus seating on a **first-come, first-served** basis. These Baton Rouge tactics were now adopted by Montgomery black activists.

Thus the Montgomery bus boycott had its origins in grassroots black activism and in two well-established black organisations, the NAACP and the church. Blacks successfully boycotted Montgomery buses on the day of Rosa Parks' trial. Blacks demanded the bus company use a first-come, first-served system, that drivers should be polite to blacks, and that black drivers be employed. No-one as yet demanded an end to segregation on the buses. The city commissioners rejected the proposed changes so the one-day boycott became a year-long one.

Key dates

Baton Rouge bus boycott: 1953

Montgomery Bus Boycott: 1956

Supreme Court decision BROWDER v. GAYLE – segregation of Alabama buses unconstitutional: 1956

Key terms

First-come, first-served
Southern buses were divided into black and white sections. Sometimes blacks would be standing while the white section was empty. Blacks therefore wanted seating on a first-come, first-served basis.

Passive resistance
Gandhi's sit-down protests against British imperialism in India were called 'passive resistance'. King felt 'passive' sounded negative.

(e) The choice of leader: Martin Luther King

The community agreed that King would be a good leader of the boycott. Some historians say he was a compromise candidate. Others say there was no better alternative: the national NAACP did not want to get involved and also lacked the influence of the church, while Alabama State College employees risked dismissal. King therefore headed the new umbrella organisation, the Montgomery Improvement Association (MIA).

(f) Black unanimity

A successful long-term boycott required unanimity amongst Montgomery's 50,000 black population. For the most part, it was achieved. On one occasion during the boycott, a black man used the bus. As he got off, an elderly black woman with a stick raced toward the bus. 'You don't have to rush, auntie,' said the white driver, 'I'll wait for you'. 'In the first place, I ain't your auntie', she said. 'In the second place, I ain't rushing to get on your bus. I'm jus' trying to catch up with that nigger who jus' got off, so I can hit him with this here stick.'

(g) Black vs white

The Montgomery White Citizen's Council organised the opposition. Its membership doubled from 6000 in February 1956 to 12,000 by March. The Council was dominated by leading city officials who ordered harassment of blacks. King was arrested for the first time (January 1956). He had driven at 30 mph in a 25 mph zone. On 30 January his house was bombed. His family urged him to quit. He said later he was tempted but felt called by God to continue. King's speeches were inspirational and even appealed to some whites:

> If we are wrong, the Supreme Court of this nation is wrong. If we are wrong, the Constitution of the United States is wrong. If we are wrong, Jesus of Nazareth was merely a … dreamer.

King stressed the boycott was 'non-violent protest', but it was not '**passive resistance**', it was 'active non-violent resistance to evil'.

Montgomery whites used Alabama's anti-boycott law against the black community, and their mass indictments attracted national media coverage. Northerners made collections for Montgomery blacks. King was the first boycott leader to be tried. He was found guilty, and given the choice of a fine or 368 days in jail.

This white hostility made the MIA up the stakes. In a case partly funded by the NAACP the federal district court said segregation on buses was unconstitutional (BROWDER v. GAYLE) (June 1956). It cited BROWN (see page 102). Montgomery city commissioners appealed to the Supreme Court but the Supreme Court (November 1956) backed the federal district court. The boycott was called off when desegregated buses began operating (December 1956). The Ku Klux Klan responded by sending 40 carloads of robed and hooded members through Montgomery's 'nigger town'. Blacks did not retreat behind closed doors as usual, but came out and waved at the motorcade!

(h) Results and significance of the Montgomery Bus Boycott

Key question
How important was the Montgomery Bus Boycott?

- Bus boycotts were not new: Montgomery blacks used tactics used at Baton Rouge in 1953. However, there had never been a boycott as long and as well organised as the Montgomery one.
- The boycott did not just come out of the blue: it was a result of black organisations (the Church and NAACP) that had been developing for years.
- It demonstrated the power of a whole black community using direct but non-violent action. Montgomery whites could not believe local blacks had started and sustained the movement: 'We know the niggers are not that smart'. 'Our leaders', responded Claudette Colvin, 'is just we ourselves'.
- It showed the importance and potential of black economic power. Black shoppers could not get downtown without the buses, so businesses lost $1 million. White businessmen began to work against segregation.
- It demonstrated how white extremism frequently helped to increase black unity and determination.
- It revealed the hatred and determined racism of many white Southerners, but also the idealism of a handful of Southern whites like Reverend Robert Graetz, minister at a black Lutheran church in Montgomery, who supported the boycott. His house was bombed.
- It demonstrated the importance of the churches in the fight for equality.
- It showed the continuing effectiveness of the NAACP strategy of working through the law courts and the importance of dedicated individuals such as Rosa Parks.
- It inspired more Northern white support and more co-operation between Northern and Southern blacks. A. Philip Randolph gave financial support.
- In Montgomery itself, the boycott was a limited victory. Apart from the buses, the city remained segregated.
- The black reaction to the Ku Klux Klan showed morale had been boosted.
- It inspired similar successful bus boycotts in 20 Southern cities.

- The boycott inspired others, including Melba Pattillo (page 111).
- It brought King, with all his inspirational rhetorical gifts, to the forefront of the movement (see Chapter 6). In 1957 he helped establish a new organisation, the Southern Christian Leadership Conference (SCLC) (see page 126). This proved particularly important as the NAACP had been persecuted in the Deep South since BROWN.

Key date: Southern Christian Leadership Conference established: 1957

(i) Rosa Parks (1913–2005)

Key question: To what extent were Parks' actions influenced and initiated by others?

Rosa Parks is the best remembered *female* participant in the civil rights movement. Her contemporaries and historians disagree over the extent to which her action was influenced and initiated by others and whether she deserves the status of greatest heroine of the civil rights movement. Her life illustrates black problems and achievements in the twentieth century.

(i) Youth

Born in 1913 in Alabama of mixed race descent, Rosa considered herself black. Her pale-skinned, slave-born grandfather enjoyed seeing whites embarrassed upon discovering he was black. As a child, Rosa went to bed clothed, ready to flee if the Klan attacked the house. Rosa belonged to the politically active African Methodist Episcopal Church.

(ii) Education

It was hard for Montgomery's 50,000 blacks to get an education. They had no public high schools until 1946. Rosa went to 'Miss Whites's Montgomery Industrial School for Girls' until 1928 when whites forced the old, blind and infirm Miss White and the other 'Yankee nigger lover' teachers out of Montgomery.

(iii) Raymond Parks

In 1931, 18-year-old Rosa married light-skinned Raymond Parks. He encouraged Rosa's successful return to high school to obtain her diploma – a rare achievement for Montgomery blacks. Raymond helped found Montgomery's NAACP, sold papers such as *The Crisis* in his barbershop, and helped raise funds for the lawyers who kept the Scottsboro youths out of the electric chair (see page 77). Raymond worked at a military base that had been integrated by order of President Roosevelt.

(iv) NAACP

In 1942, Parks joined NAACP, which she said 'was about empowerment through the ballot box. With a vote would come economic improvements.' She resented her brother Sylvester being drafted by a democracy in which he could not vote. In NAACP she worked closely with railroad porter E.D. Nixon, who helped Randolph plan the march on Washington (1941) that resulted in FEPC (see page 81).

(v) Trying to vote

Parks 'failed' the literacy test in 1943 but in 1945 successfully registered to vote. Paying the $16.50 poll tax was expensive for a part-time seamstress. She voted for 'Big Jim' Folsom for governor. He denounced the Klan and racial and sexual inequality, but won!

(vi) Detroit

Sylvester moved to Detroit, where, despite frequent 'White workers preferred' notices, Parks noted, 'you could find a seat anywhere on a bus' and 'get better accommodation'. However, when the 1943 Detroit race riots made her realise 'racism was almost as widespread in Detroit as in Montgomery', she dropped the idea of moving North.

(vii) Challenging Jim Crow

In 1943, Parks clashed with bus driver James Blake when she tried to board his bus at the front. Blake ordered her off. She vowed never to board Blake's bus again. At an NAACP leadership training seminar in Florida in 1946 Parks was inspired by Ella Baker (page 128), NAACP's top female worker. Parks was increasingly ready for activism. 'Every day in the early 1950s we were looking for ways to challenge Jim Crow laws.' She was particularly excited by the bus boycott in Baton Rouge in 1953, but disappointed when the Baptist Church called it off. In August 1955, Parks was one of only 30 people (mostly women) who turned up to hear exciting new preacher, Martin Luther King, address an NAACP meeting on BROWN. Parks recalled, 'You can't imagine the rejoicing [over BROWN] among black people, and some white people'.

(viii) Activist friends

During 1954–5, Parks worked for white couple, Clifford and Virginia Durr, whose friends included Lyndon Johnson and (black) educationalist Mary McLeod Bethune, anti-poll tax campaigner and friend of Eleanor Roosevelt. Virginia introduced Parks to Highlander Folk School, established in Tennessee in 1932, as a centre for the study of worker and black rights. Activists such as Martin Luther King, John Lewis of SNCC, and future Washington DC Mayor Marion Barry, received training there. Parks found Highlander inspirational. The Durrs knew the black women lecturers at Alabama State University, such as Jo Ann Robinson who helped organise the Montgomery bus boycott.

Rosa Parks sitting in the front of a bus in Montgomery, Alabama in a photo taken after the famous incident. The man sitting behind her is Nicholas C. Chriss, a reporter for United Press International out of Atlanta.

(ix) Montgomery Bus Boycott

Claudette Colvin, a 15-year-old NAACP youth member whose NAACP mentor was Rosa Parks, wrote a school essay denouncing the law that prohibited blacks from trying on clothes in white department stores as they would 'smell or grease up the merchandise'. NAACP nearly made Colvin a test case for bus segregation but, as Parks said, the white press would have depicted the pregnant teenager as 'a bad girl'. In December 1955 Parks boarded James Blake's bus by mistake. He told four blacks to give up their seats so that a white man would not have to sit by them. Parks refused. After her arrest, she was allowed neither water nor phone calls for several hours. The police would only respond to white lawyer Clifford Durr. Nixon decided to make her an NAACP test case. Parks ignored her husband's warnings: 'Rosa, the white folks will kill you'.

(x) Life after fame

Key question
After looking at the role of other women covered in this book, does Rosa *deserve* to be the best remembered female participant in the civil rights struggle?

Because of the activism, Rosa lost her job in a Montgomery department store. Raymond stopped working at the base, because any discussion of 'Rosa' became a sacking offence. The Parks' white landlord raised their rent. They received phoned death threats. Raymond began to drink and smoke heavily. 'Rosie, get the hell out of Montgomery', advised her cousin. 'Whitey is going to kill you'. After countless death threats, the inability to get work (they were 'troublemakers') and jealousy from within the Montgomery civil rights movement (especially from men), the Parks moved to Detroit. She had no sympathy for ghetto rioters: when they looted Raymond's barbershop in the 1967 Detroit riots, Rosa called them 'hooligans' (see Chapter 7).

Parks frequently returned to Southern civil rights gatherings. She admitted great 'admiration' for Malcolm X (especially when his racism became muted), sympathising with Malcolm's inability to 'turn the other cheek' as King urged. The black power movement (see Chapter 7) inspired Parks to wear 'African' clothes. In 1975, city officials invited Rosa to Montgomery to celebrate the twentieth anniversary of the bus boycott. There had been no elected black official in Alabama in 1955; in 1975, there were 200.

When South African freedom fighter Nelson Mandela visited Detroit in 1990, it was primarily to see Rosa Parks.

Summary diagram: The Montgomery Bus Boycott

When?	1955–6
Why?	Segregated buses
Where?	Montgomery, state capital of Albama – Deep South, heart of the old Confederacy
Who?	NAACP, Rosa Parks, Martin Luther King, local black community
What?	All blacks refused to use buses
With what result?	Montgomery buses desegregated – Jim Crow slowly coming to an end

Key question
What caused the Little Rock crisis?

8 | Little Rock (1957)

(a) Causes of the crisis

Governor Orval Faubus of Arkansas was struggling to get re-elected. He decided to exploit white racism to ensure re-election. The city of Little Rock's plans for compliance with BROWN were scheduled to come to slow completion in 1963: Central High School was to be the first integrated school. Nine black students reported to Central High in September 1957. Faubus declared that it was his duty to prevent the disorder that would arise from integration. He ordered the Arkansas National Guard to surround the school and to keep black students out.

Key date
Little Rock crisis: 1957

(b) Melba Pattillo

One of the nine students, Melba Pattillo, wrote about her experiences years later. She had volunteered to be a 'guinea-pig' when asked by the NAACP and church leaders. Her mother was initially against it, saying it endangered her job. A white man violently assaulted her crying, 'I'll show you niggers the Supreme Court cannot run my life'. Others cried 'Two, four, six, eight, we ain't gonna integrate', 'Keep away from our school', 'Go back to the jungle', 'Lynch the niggers'. She was inspired by the 'self-assured air' of Thurgood Marshall, and had the backing of her mother and grandmother, many blacks and a few whites. A white boy, whom she trusted despite the warnings of her family,

One of the nine black students, Elizabeth Eckford, tries to enter Central High School in Little Rock, Arkansas, despite the hostility shown by the white crowd.

befriended Melba at Central High. However, inside the building she was frequently spat on, tripped, punched, kicked and pushed downstairs. She suffered obscenities and flaming paper wads and acid were thrown at her. Once, only a held-up book prevented her being knifed. Others in the black community resented the 'meddling' nine who had tried to leave the all-black schools. Subsequently. she wondered 'what possessed my parents and the adults of the NAACP to allow us to go to school in the face of such violence'.

(c) Eisenhower's intervention

Eisenhower had said before the crisis that he could never envisage sending in federal troops to enforce the federal court ruling (which had doubtless encouraged Faubus). However, Little Rock's mayor now told Eisenhower the mob was out of hand, so Eisenhower sent in troops to protect the black children. While Southerners cried 'Invasion!', Eisenhower's radio speech to the nation tried to restore harmony. He said he had acted because of his 'inescapable' responsibility for enforcing the law. He made no mention of integration. He blamed 'disorderly mobs' and 'demagogic extremists'. He again refused to endorse BROWN, and tried to rally the nation by saying its Soviet enemies were making propaganda capital out of Little Rock. He stressed that most Southerners were law-abiding.

Why had the great opponent of federal intervention intervened?

- Eisenhower had tried but failed to negotiate a settlement with Faubus.
- Eisenhower's public appeals to the rioters had been ignored.
- Local officials had begged the president to act
- The Constitution and federal law seemed threatened.
- Eisenhower was concerned about the US's international 'prestige and influence'.

(d) Results and significance of Little Rock

Key question
How important was Little Rock?

- It showed that Supreme Court rulings like BROWN met tremendous grassroots resistance in practice. Blacks tried to push things along more quickly at Little Rock, and still there was no dramatic immediate improvement. Faubus got re-elected four times!
- Neither local nor national authorities were keen to enforce BROWN. Faubus did what Eisenhower had always feared and closed the schools rather than integrate. Eisenhower did not respond. It was 1960 before Central High was integrated and 1972 before Little Rock's schools were fully integrated. In contrast, some cities, such as Atlanta, desegregated to avoid Little Rock-style violence and publicity.
- As late as 1964, only two to three per cent of the US's black children attended de-segregated schools.
- The image of black children being harassed and spat at by aggressive white adults in Little Rock helped to influence

moderate white opinion throughout the USA, a testimony of the increasing importance of the new television age to the civil rights movement. Little Rock had drawn national television crews; on-site television reporting was pioneered here.

Key date
COOPER v. AARON ruling – any law that tried to keep schools segregated was unconstitutional: 1958.

- The Supreme Court ploughed ahead. In COOPER v. AARON (1958) it said that any law that sought to keep public schools segregated was unconstitutional.
- Finally, and perhaps most significantly, blacks realised that they probably needed to do more than rely on court decisions.

Summary diagram: Little Rock

When?	1957
Where?	Little Rock, state capital of Arkansas, upper South
What?	Nine black children tried to enter Central High School; a white mob tried to stop them
Why?	White schools were better and in BROWN, the Supreme Court had ruled pro-integration. Many blacks wanted integrated schools, most whites did not
With what result?	Slowly, Central High and other schools were integrated

Key question
How helpful were Eisenhower's Civil Rights Acts?

9 | Eisenhower's Civil Rights Acts (1957 and 1960)

(a) 1957 Civil Rights Act

In order to win the black vote in the 1956 election year, the Eisenhower administration drew up a civil rights bill that aimed to ensure that all citizens could exercise the right to vote. Eighty per cent of Southern blacks were not yet registered to vote, including the professors at Tuskegee.

Key date
Civil Rights Act: 1957

In his State of the Union address in January 1957, Eisenhower praised the bill. He expressed 'shock' that only 7000 of Mississippi's 900,000 blacks were allowed to vote, and that registrars were setting impossible questions (such as 'How many bubbles are there in a bar of soap?') for blacks trying to register.

Democratic senators worked to weaken the bill. They thought it would damage national and party unity. They claimed it sought to use federal power 'to force a co-mingling of white and Negro children'. Eisenhower then cravenly claimed that he did not really know what was in the bill ('there were certain phrases I did not completely understand') and did not fight to keep it intact. Strom Thurmond filibustered for 24 hours to try to kill the bill. It passed as a much-weakened act that did little to help blacks exercise the vote, as any public official indicted for obstructing a black voter would be tried by an all-white jury. The act established a Civil Rights Division in the Justice Department and a federal Civil Rights Commission to monitor race relations. As the first such act since Reconstruction, it pleased some black leaders. Others felt that it was a nauseating sham.

(b) 1960 Civil Rights Act

Key date: Civil Rights Act: 1960

In late 1958, Eisenhower introduced another bill because he was concerned about bombings of black schools and churches. While Eisenhower considered the bill to be moderate, Southern Democrats again diluted its provisions. It finally became law because both parties sought the black vote in the presidential election year. The act made it a federal crime to obstruct court-ordered school desegregation and established penalties for obstructing black voting. These Civil Rights Acts of 1957 and 1960 added only three per cent of black voters to the electoral roles during 1960. Contemporaries were unimpressed, but at least the acts acknowledged federal responsibilities, which encouraged civil rights activists to work for more legislation.

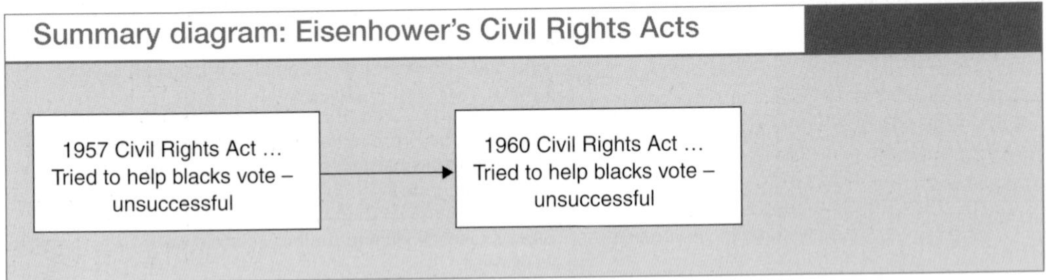

10 | The Cold War and Decolonisation

Key question
How did the Cold War and decolonisation impact upon the progress of racial equality?

(a) Cold War

The need for national unity during the Cold War helps explain Eisenhower's frequent inactivity on civil rights. He did not want to antagonise the white majority. Black civil rights activists with Communist sympathies became very unpopular, especially amongst trade unionists who wanted to prove their patriotism. The Cold War thus damaged the civil rights–labour axis (see pages 74–5). However, the Cold War helped as well as hindered the civil rights movement. It was difficult for both Truman and Eisenhower to try to rally the free world against Communism when blacks in the American South were so clearly unfree.

(b) Decolonisation

African Americans were fascinated by the emergence of independent African nations. **Decolonisation** inspired black Americans such as Melba Pattillo, whose grandmother told her to read about Gandhi's struggle for independence from British colonialism. There were frequent contacts between black Americans and Africans. Thurgood Marshall acted as legal adviser to Kenyan nationalists seeking independence from Britain. Among the American guests at Ghana's independence day were Vice-President Richard Nixon, Adam Clayton Powell, A. Philip Randolph and Martin Luther King. W.E.B. Du Bois and Paul Robeson were invited but the US government barred them from foreign travel due to 'Communist sympathies'.

Key term
Decolonisation
After the Second World War, countries such as Britain allowed their colonies to become independent.

The newly emerging African nations, the embarrassment caused by the number of non-white foreign dignitaries exposed to segregation in Washington DC, and the Cold War combined to persuade the Eisenhower administration to act. It is probably no coincidence that the 1956 Hungarian uprising against Soviet oppression and Britain's granting of independence to Ghana were followed by the Civil Rights Act in the USA.

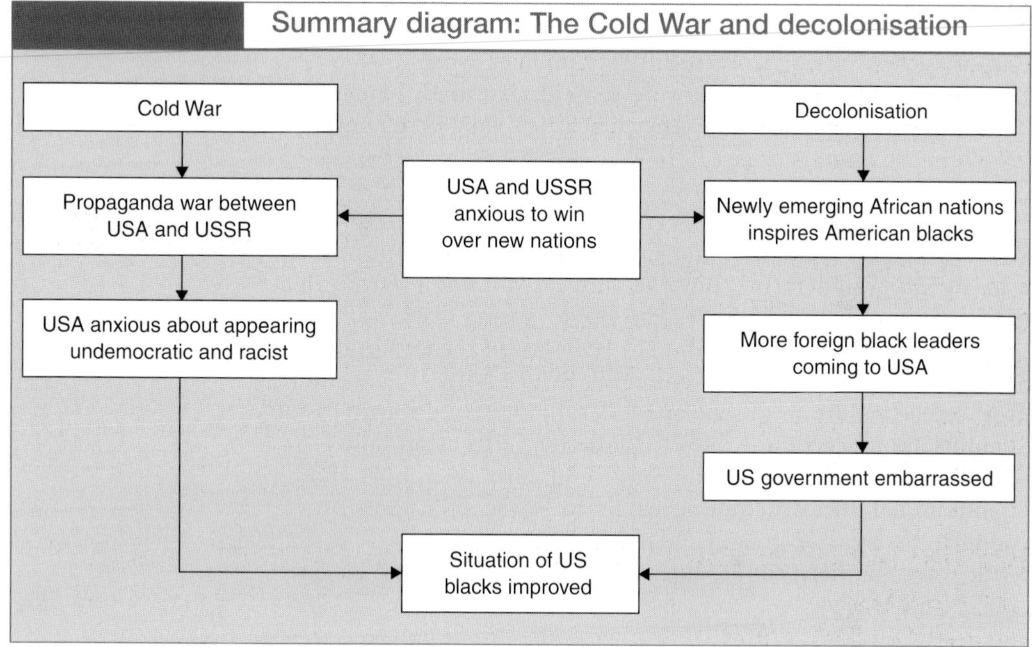

Key question
What progress was made toward racial equality in the Eisenhower years? Who or what contributed most to that progress?

11 | The Eisenhower Years – Conclusions

Unlike Truman, Eisenhower did not seem keen to help the black movement toward equality.

Eisenhower's biographer Stephen Ambrose concluded that until his hand was forced at Little Rock, in 1957, Eisenhower provided 'almost no leadership at all' on the most fundamental social and moral problem of his time. On the other hand, Eisenhower supporters claim that his evolutionary approach to civil rights was best for national unity. Eisenhower loved to quote a story he heard while golfing in Augusta, Georgia. An agricultural worker supposedly said, 'If someone does not shut up around here, particularly those Negroes from the North, they are going to get a lot of us niggers killed!'.

The historian Robert Cook sees 'relative federal inactivity' and 'limited organisational goals' as the main reason why the civil rights movement stood relatively still in the late 1950s. It was blacks themselves who bore greatest responsibility for precipitating such change as there was in the Eisenhower years. Activists, especially the NAACP, were the moving force behind the Supreme Court decisions, Little Rock and the Montgomery bus boycott. This incessant black pressure along with the international situation and the black vote, forced the Eisenhower administration to propose civil rights legislation.

Although the Supreme Court had declared segregated schools unconstitutional (BROWN), desegregation proved painfully slow. This was due to a powerful white backlash. In 1960, only 6.4 per cent of blacks went to integrated schools in the South, and only two per cent in the Deep South. On the other hand, BROWN could be considered as the first breach in the dam, which ensured further progress. Many historians talk of a 20-year 'Second Reconstruction' dating from BROWN. Similarly, while Eisenhower's Civil Rights Acts were so weak that many blacks dismissed them as irrelevant, other blacks felt they were another breach in the dam.

The civil rights movement was acquiring 'heroes', such as Rosa Parks. However, there were also victims such as Emmett Till. While there were signs that mass action could bring about results, as in the Montgomery Bus Boycott, this was still not a universal, organised movement. There was no single, strong black organisation. After BROWN the NAACP was persecuted in the South, and was jealous of the emerging SCLC. NAACP met some great setbacks, such as obstructive federal judges and unsuccessful attempts at mass action. King's Crusade for Citizenship failed because as yet SCLC lacked the massive grassroots support and organisational infrastructure necessary for success. Progress on voting rights awaited greater federal assistance against recalcitrant Southern states, and the mobilisation of rural blacks.

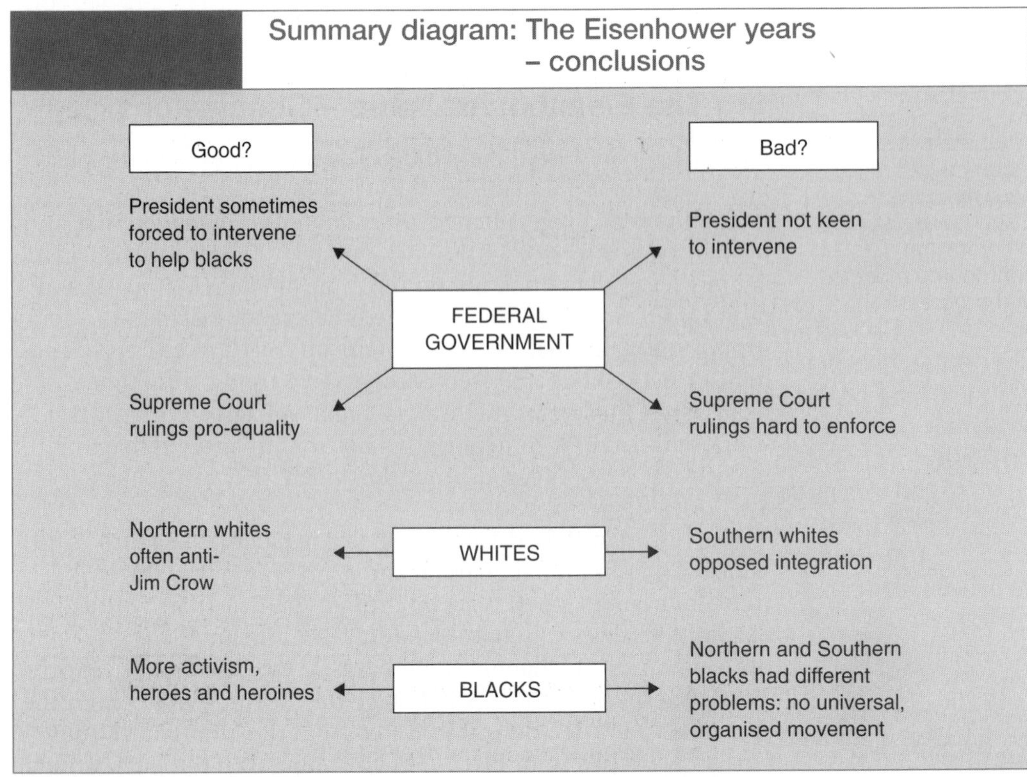

Key question
How and why were there similarities and differences in the experiences of blacks and Indians in the 1950s?

Indians – a comparative study

The historian Angie Debo described the 1950s as 'back to the bad old days'. Commissioner Dillon Myer reversed Collier's policies (see pages 73–4). Myer intervened in tribal affairs in dictatorial fashion, for example, selling Pueblo Indian land without their consent. He wanted to break-up Indian reservations and scatter the people. Myer's relocation programme aimed to get Indians jobs in the cities, but one-third of Indians returned to their reservations, and those who remained in the cities often ended up on welfare. Indians felt Myer was trying to destroy Indian civilisation. They wanted jobs to be brought to reservations.

Congress also disliked tribal self-government. They 'terminated' some reservations, usually where the Indians were few, poor, and on land that might prove valuable to white men. Scattered bands of poor, illiterate Utah Paiutes were 'terminated' because it was believed there was oil and uranium on their land. Congress aimed to save the white taxpayer subsidising Indians, and to release Indian lands for white economic development. In 1953 Congress increased state government jurisdiction over reservations. A good example of the unsympathetic attitude of state authorities is the state of Vermont's sterilisation of disproportionate numbers of Indians because they were supposedly 'immoral', 'criminal', or 'suspected feeble-minded'.

Thus Indians, like blacks, found federal and state government unsympathetic in the 1950s. However, while blacks still made some progress toward equality, Indians did not. Why?

Blacks had more contact with whites, so they used white traditions such as national organisation and litigation. Indians were fewer in number, less urbanised, and culturally disorientated. Separate tribes and geographical segregation militated against national and effective organisations. Therefore, Indians were easier prey for an administration that preached the virtues of self-help and minimal federal intervention.

12 | Key Debate

When did the civil rights movement start?

Many historians date the start of the civil rights movement in the Eisenhower years, although they disagree over the crucial events. Sociologist Aldon Morris (1984) dated it to the Baton Rouge bus boycott (1953). Harvard Sitkoff (1993) sees the BROWN decision (1954) as the start of the struggle. However, law professor Michael Klarman concluded (1992) that BROWN 'was a relatively unimportant motivating factor for the civil rights movement', and that its real significance was to generate a vicious white backlash.

David Garrow (1994) disagreed, saying BROWN inspired the Montgomery Bus Boycott. Studies of Georgia and Louisiana suggest BROWN did not generate civil rights activism immediately, although many activists have attested the inspirational importance of BROWN. While Garrow thought the Montgomery Bus Boycott signalled the start of the civil rights movement, Mark Newman (2004) says it 'did not spark a mass movement', and cites SCLC's early ineffectiveness as proof.

Recently, historians have emphasised the significance of the federal government's anxieties about America's image in the Cold War world. Mary Dudziak (2000) talks of 'the Cold War imperative' which encouraged the federal government to try to make blacks more equal, while pointing out on the other hand how anti-communism made criticism of the status quo difficult.

Study Guide: AS Questions

In the style of Edexcel

1. In what ways did black Americans feel themselves discriminated against in 1945? (20 marks)
2. Account for the black protests that occurred in the South in the 1950s. (40 marks)

Exam tips

The cross-references are intended to take you to some of the material that will help you to answer the questions.

1. Questions that ask you to plant yourself in a particular year are quite difficult – they require you to know a great deal about what has gone before. You need to be very careful to ensure that your points are relevant for that particular year, so the examples with which you prove your generalisations can be taken either from 1945 itself or from several years before so long as there has been no change between that time and 1945. 'In what ways' invites you to categorise the ways. You could say that blacks felt that they were discriminated against socially (page 98), politically (page 93), economically (page 90) and legally (page 91). When you are discussing discrimination in the USA, take care to cover the different areas. Discrimination in the North was different from discrimination in the South. For example, in the South, there was *de jure* segregation of schools (page 101), while in the North's ghettos there was *de facto* segregation of schools. Occasionally, you might make a point about the shades of difference in border states such as Maryland (page 79).

2. Questions that begin with 'account for' are 'causes' questions. Before you start to think of several 'reasons why', establish what the 'black protests' were and what the Southern situation was. Then think about 'why the 1950s' – why then? Why not earlier? Had some decisive event(s) occurred before or during the 1950s? The main black protests were the Montgomery Bus Boycott (page 105) and Little Rock (page 111), but do not forget to mention others, such as the 1953 bus boycott in Baton Rouge, Louisiana (page 106). Take care not to make your answer a mere narrative account of these events. For example, explain how the Montgomery Bus Boycott did not come out of nowhere, but through:

- long-term organisational activity (the Montgomery NAACP and the local Women's Political Council, page 105)
- recent events unrelated to buses that both encouraged (BROWN, page 102) and infuriated (Emmett Till, page 104) the local community
- recent events on the buses (Colvin, page 105) and NAACP and WPC discussions about the desirability of a bus boycott (page 109)
- a particular individual (Parks) with her long-term involvement in activist organisations and the unexpected events of the day she mistakenly boarded Blake's bus (page 110).

When you know that there is controversy as to whether events in Montgomery reflected the 'new Negro' (page 148) or not, you could use that controversy to make an interesting introduction.

6 The 1960s – I: King of the Civil Rights Movement?

POINTS TO CONSIDER

The 1960s were a vital decade for America's black population. The decade will be covered from three interlinked perspectives in the next three chapters:

- This chapter (I) covers Martin Luther King and the civil rights movement
- Chapter 7 (II) covers the black power movement
- Chapter 8 (III) covers the federal government – the presidencies of John Kennedy and Lyndon Johnson.

Some of Martin Luther King's contemporaries and some historians consider him the crucial figure in the civil rights movement. Others regret the emphasis upon King and stress the contribution of other individuals and organisations. King's organisational abilities and his personal reputation are also controversial. This chapter looks at:

- The extent to which Martin Luther King bore responsibility for civil rights activity and black advancement, 1956–68
- King's organisational and campaigning skills, saintly reputation and achievements

Key dates

1956	Montgomery Bus Boycott
1957	Southern Christian Leadership Conference (SCLC) formed
1960	Sit-ins in the South
1961	Freedom Riders travelled the South
	Albany Movement
1963	Birmingham riots
	March on Washington
1964	Mississippi Freedom Summer
	Civil Rights Act
1965	Selma to Montgomery march
	Voting Rights Act
	Watts riots
1966	Meredith March
1968	King assassinated

1 | Martin Luther King

Profile: Martin Luther King Jr 1929–68

1929	–	Born in Atlanta, Georgia
1944–8	–	Studied at Morehouse College, Atlanta; ordained as a minister
1948–51	–	Attended Crozer Theological Seminary in Pennsylvania
1951–4	–	Doctorate at Boston University's School of Theology; married Coretta Scott
1954	–	Pastor of Dexter Avenue Baptist Church, Montgomery, Alabama
1955	–	Headed Montgomery Improvement Association during Montgomery Bus Boycott
1957	–	Founded Southern Christian Leadership Conference (SCLC); spoke at Prayer Pilgrimage for Freedom in Washington DC
1959	–	Moved to Atlanta, headquarters of SCLC; co-pastor with father of Ebenezer Baptist Church
1960	–	Sent SCLC's Ella Baker to organise students who had started sit-ins in Greensboro, North Carolina; arrested for participating in Atlanta sit-in, but phone call from presidential candidate John Kennedy speeded up his release
1961–2	–	Involved in unsuccessful Albany Movement
1963	–	Initiated Birmingham campaign; 'I have a dream' speech during march on Washington; *Time* magazine's man of the year
1964	–	Nobel Peace Prize
1965	–	Leading figure in Selma, Alabama, campaign
1966	–	Chicago ghetto campaign
1967	–	Published *Where Do We Go From Here?*, rejecting black power; spoke out against Vietnam war; initiated Poor People's Campaign
1968	–	Assassinated in Memphis, Tennessee

Key question
How do King's life and career illustrate mid-twentieth century US race relations?

(a) Childhood, youth and education

King was born into a well-educated and relatively prosperous family that gained strength from the church and NAACP. His grandfather and father were pastors of a Baptist church in Atlanta, Georgia, and NAACP activists.

As a small child, King had a white friend. Then, King recalled:

> He told me that one day his father had demanded that he would play with me no more. I never will forget what a great shock this was to me … For the first time, I was made aware of the existence of a race problem.

If young Martin wanted 'a day out' downtown, he would have to travel from 'nigger town' at the back of the bus. He could not buy a soda or hot dog at a downtown store lunch counter. If a white drugstore served him, they would hand him his ice cream through a side window and in a paper cup so no white would have to use any plate that he had used. He had to drink from the 'colored' water fountain, and use the 'colored' restroom. He had to sit in the 'colored' section at the back of the balcony in the cinema. King said it made him 'determined to hate every white person'.

King received poor-quality education in Atlanta's segregated schools. When he went North to college, he experienced further racial prejudice. When he demanded service in a Philadelphia restaurant, his plate arrived filled with sand. A New Jersey restaurant owner drew a gun on King when he refused to leave. King had problems getting student accommodation in Boston in 1951:

> I went into place after place where there were signs that rooms were for rent. They were for rent until they found out I was a Negro and suddenly they had just been rented.

However, his attitude towards whites changed. He particularly liked white women. Devastated when friends convinced him that marriage to a white sweetheart would not work, he married fellow black student Coretta Scott. She hated the segregated South, but King insisted on returning there, 'because that's where I'm needed'.

(b) Minister in Montgomery

Initially King rejected a church career, believing the church concentrated on life in the next world instead of working to improve life in this world. However, he felt called by God and became pastor of a 'rich folks' church' in Montgomery, Alabama in 1954. King urged his congregation to register to vote and join the NAACP. His involvement in the black boycott of Montgomery's segregated buses (see pages 105–10) resulted in many threats on his life and family. His family urged him to give up activism. He wavered, but:

> it seemed at that moment that I could hear an inner voice saying to me, 'Martin Luther, stand-up for righteousness. Stand-up for justice. Stand-up for truth. And lo I will be with you, even until the end of the world' … I heard the voice of Jesus … He promised never to leave me.

King lacked reliable legal protection down South. After the bus boycott, two whites who had confessed to trying to blow up King's home were adjudged innocent by an all-white Alabama jury. He was nearly killed on a 1958 visit to Harlem. A deranged black woman stabbed him. It took hours for surgeons to remove the blade, which was millimetres from his aorta. Had King sneezed while awaiting the blade's removal, he would have died. The dangers did not deter King: 'My cause, my race, is worth dying for.'

By 1957, King was recognised as one of black America's leading spokesmen. In 1960 he moved to Atlanta, Georgia, headquarters of Southern Christian Leadership Conference (SCLC) (see page 120). The restaurant in SCLC's office building refused to serve King: his small daughter found it hard to understand why she could not have an ice cream there.

(c) Protest and publicity

As few blacks were registered to vote in the segregated South, they lacked the political power to change the situation. King therefore became increasingly involved in demonstrations to draw attention to black problems. He wanted demonstrations to be peaceful and non-violent but was frequently arrested while participating in them. The resultant publicity drew national and international attention to black problems and helped procure civil rights legislation. King then concentrated on the problems of Northern black ghettos: one hot July weekend in Chicago in 1965, he made 20 speeches in less than 48 hours. The workload, the constant fear for his life, the slow rate of progress, ghetto riots and increasing numbers of black and white extremists, all made him increasingly pessimistic. His close friend Reverend Ralph Abernathy said, 'He was just a different person ... sad and depressed'.

(d) Disillusionment

Increasingly pessimistic, King concluded he had overestimated the successes of 1955–65. He said the 'vast majority' of whites were racist, 'hypocritical', and had committed a kind of 'psychological and spiritual genocide' against blacks. King also felt he had underestimated black rage. He was exasperated by militant black racists such as Stokely Carmichael. 'Many people who would otherwise be ashamed of their anti-Negro feeling now have an excuse.' However, 'Stokely is not the problem. The problem is white people and their attitude.'

Whites and blacks became increasingly critical of him. When he toured riot-stricken Cleveland, Ohio, black teenagers mocked and ignored him. He knew he had raised their hopes but failed to fulfil them. Many blacks thought him too moderate, an 'Uncle Tom', in awe of white authority figures. Many whites considered him an extremist. The *Washington Post* accused King of inciting anarchy because he had urged non-violent disruption of Washington DC to 'create the crisis that will force the nation to look at the situation'. He called that 'massive civil disobedience'.

In spring 1968 King went to support black strikers in Memphis, Tennessee. There, he was assassinated by a social misfit who called him Martin 'Lucifer' King or Martin Luther 'Coon'.

King's early life illustrates black problems and opportunities in mid-twentieth century USA. The story of his activism reads like a history of the civil rights movement. He was involved in most of its significant events. The hostility he faced shows how difficult it was to bring about change at a universally acceptable speed. Some blacks thought he moved too slowly. Some whites thought him too extreme.

2 | Martin Luther King – Saint or Sinner?

Key question
Does King deserve his saint-like reputation?

King's campaign depended greatly upon convincing people of the morality of the racial equality he sought. Therefore, many people believed that his campaign and his behaviour should be above reproach. His enemies and critics were quick to say that they were not.

(a) Glory seeker?

King worked hard to counter criticisms that he was a glory seeker. In 1958 a friend criticised his account of the Montgomery Bus Boycott for giving the impression 'that everything depended on you', King revised it to emphasise the contributions of others. King's actions could be interpreted as either helpful to the black cause or as attention seeking: NAACP leader Roy Wilkins described King as presumptuous and self-promoting, but King's friend said that while King felt God had called him to leadership, he craved a more normal existence. The problem was that King had to publicise the cause. In 1958, for example, he chose a jail sentence in preference to a $10 fine. Initially he denied it was a 'publicity stunt' but then admitted, 'sometimes it is necessary to dramatise an issue because many people are not aware of what is happening.'

(b) Hypocrite?

Coretta King described her husband as 'a guilt-ridden man', whose awareness of his own faults made him feel unworthy of the adulation he received. Under pressure of events, he was not always truthful: during the troubles in Birmingham, local businessmen and King both gave distorted versions of their agreement.

King preached the importance of monogamy and declared sex outside marriage sinful. However, one SCLC worker said all of King's intimates had trouble dealing with King's sexuality – 'a saint with clay feet'. The FBI believed King was a national security threat, so they monitored his phone calls and bugged his hotel rooms. The FBI chief, a homosexual with a fondness for young boys, described King as a 'tom cat' with 'obsessive degenerate sexual urges'. The FBI were thrilled to hear King and several SCLC colleagues involved in a drunken party in Washington with two women from Philadelphia, but disappointed when King and a colleague, on a Hawaiian holiday with two Californian lady friends, produced nothing but the sound of the television set playing loudly – King had guessed he was being bugged. SCLC colleagues worried that King's sex life could be used to discredit him and the civil rights movement itself. King was depressed about his romantic affairs, which he considered to be sinful, but could not bring himself to stop. 'I was away from home 25–27 days a month,' said King. 'Fucking is a form of anxiety reduction'. Some friends considered it just standard pastoral care, common in black churches. 'Everybody was out getting laid', recalled one activist. King's fame gave him more opportunities than most. One fascinated observer:

> watched women making passes at Martin Luther King. *I could not believe* what I was seeing in white Westchester [a wealthy commuter area] women … It was unbelievable … They would walk up to him and they would sort of lick their lips and hint and [hand him] notes … After I saw that thing that evening, I didn't blame him.

(c) Betrayer of his people?

King was willing to compromise his popularity for what he believed in. He was more than a black civil rights spokesman: 'I am interested in rights for Negroes, but I am just as interested in Appalachian whites and Mexican Americans and other minorities.' Some SCLC workers disliked this. One said, 'I don't think I am at the point where a Mexican can sit in and call strategy.'

Some blacks disliked King's anti-Vietnam War stance because it alienated President Johnson. King tried to maintain silence on the war but pictures of young Vietnamese children wounded by US firepower, and the knowledge that the war was diverting money from social reform programmes, made him speak out: 'I know it can hurt SCLC, but I feel better … I was politically unwise, but morally wise'. Opinion polls showed 73% of Americans and 48% of blacks disagreed with his opposition to the war and 60% believed his opposition had hurt the civil rights movement.

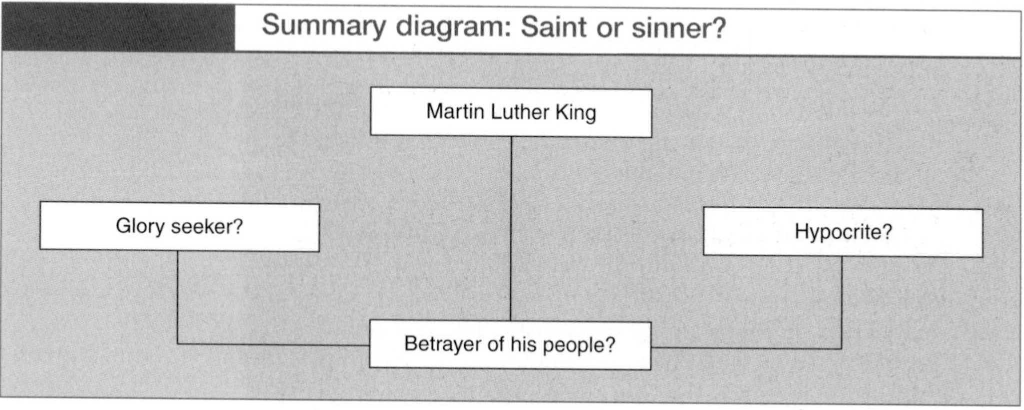

3 | The Leadership of the Civil Rights Movement

In order to decide who or what was responsible for protest and progress from 1956 to 1968, it is necessary to look at the main events of those years.

(a) The Montgomery Bus Boycott (1956)

We have seen (page 106–10) how local NAACP activists started the protest and how King and other churchmen took up the leadership. The feeling developed that King was the focal point of the boycott, but he said:

> I just happened to be here ... If M.L. King had never been born this movement would have taken place ... there comes a time when time itself is ready for change. That time has come in Montgomery, and I had nothing to do with it.

Key question
To what extent was King the leader of the Montgomery Bus Boycott?

Key dates
Montgomery Bus Boycott: 1956
Establishment of the SCLC: 1957

One local activist agreed: it was 'a protest of the people ... not a one-man show ... the leaders couldn't stop it if they wanted to'.

King's prominence upset many others, including NAACP's Roy Wilkins. A friend noted that:

> King's colleagues felt that he was taking too many bows and enjoying them ... he was forgetting that victory ... had been the result of collective thought and collective action.

Wilkins and King disagreed over tactics. Wilkins and NAACP favoured litigation; King preferred mass action. Relations deteriorated further when King set up his own organisation.

(b) SCLC (1957–60)

Key question
How useful was the SCLC?

King set up SCLC in 1957. SCLC aimed to improve the black situation in the South. Early SCLC rallies were effectively sabotaged by NAACP which considered SCLC a superfluous rival. Was it wise of King to set up a new organisation?

NAACP was a national organisation. SCLC concentrated on the South, which had very specific problems that needed addressing. Furthermore, Southern NAACP members suffered great persecution after BROWN. It was harder for Southern racists to attack a Church-dominated organisation such as SCLC. SCLC wanted to offer an alternative (direct non-violent action) to NAACP's litigation strategy. CORE had tried that, mostly in the North, but CORE currently lacked dynamism. The National Urban League concentrated on improving life in the Northern cities. Perhaps the time was ripe for a new organisation. Studying SCLC's achievements enables us to decide whether the new organisation was necessary.

King's main strategy was to attract national attention to racial inequality. He began with one of his favourite tactics, a march in Washington, in support of Eisenhower's civil rights bill (see page 113). King demanded the vote for all blacks before a crowd of around 20,000 outside the Lincoln Memorial in May 1957.

One-off events such as marches were relatively easy to organise and gained maximum publicity for minimum work. Sustained local campaigns proved more difficult for SCLC. Poor organisation and the lack of salaried staff and of mass support hampered SCLC's 'Crusade for Citizenship', which aimed to encourage Southern blacks to vote.

In 1959, King admitted that the SCLC had achieved little in its first 36 months. He therefore gave up his Montgomery ministry and moved to Atlanta to concentrate on SCLC. As always, one of the greatest organisational problems he faced was local and national black divisions. 'Jealousy among [national] black leaders is so thick it can be cut with a knife', said the *Pittsburgh Courier*. For example, King wanted to gain publicity for the cause by picketing the Democratic and Republican conventions. Adam Clayton Powell opposed the idea and said that if King did that, he would 'go public' with the accusation that King had a physical relationship with an associate who had been prosecuted for homosexual activity with two other men in a parked car. The picketing in Los Angeles and Chicago went ahead, but failed to attract much support or attention.

Most historians consider organisation one of King's great weaknesses. SCLC's early disorganisation and lack of inspiration seem to prove that.

Key question
Was King's role in the sit-ins of any importance?

(c) Sit-ins

(i) Who was responsible for the sit-ins?

King admitted that the SCLC achieved little in the three years after Montgomery. Then the civil rights movement exploded into life again in February 1960. Initially, King had nothing to do with it.

Whites pour food on a black and white student 'sit-in' at a Woolworth's lunch counter in Jackson, Mississippi in May 1963.

Key date
Sit-ins: 1960s

In Greensboro, North Carolina, four black college students spontaneously refused to leave the all-white Woolworth's cafeteria when asked. Other students took up and retained the seats, day after day, forcing the cafeteria to close. NAACP was unenthusiastic about helping the students and disgruntled SCLC employee Ella Baker warned them not to let adults like King take over their protest.

As many as 70,000 students joined these sit-ins across the South. These students were better educated than their parents and more impatient with the slow progress toward equality. Responsibility for this mass action can be attributed to the original four, or the students who joined them, or the other black protesters who had pioneered the same technique in Oklahoma and Kansas in 1957–8, or the press, which covered Greensboro extensively. While King's talk of non-violent protest was surely inspirational, King had his own ideas as to who was responsible for the movement. When a Greensboro SCLC member contacted him, King quickly arrived to encourage the students and assure them of full SCLC support, saying, 'What is new in your fight is the fact that it was initiated, fed, and sustained by students.' Atlanta students persuaded King to join them in sit-ins. As in Montgomery, King was led rather than leading.

Key question
Why was Ella Baker so important?

Profile: Ella Baker 1903–86

1903 – Born in Virginia, daughter of a teacher: 'We did not come into contact with whites too much'

1918–27 – Attended then worked at Shaw University, Raleigh, North Carolina; rejected teaching as a 'demeaning' career, because schools were largely white controlled

1927 – Went to live in Harlem, 'a hotbed of radical thinking' in the Depression years. Worked as a waitress and librarian. Published political articles, such as 'The Bronx Slave Market' (described black women selling themselves for either house work or sex). Became increasingly socialist: favoured mutual aid and wealth redistribution

1936 – Employed by a New Deal agency as a teacher

1940 – Married, but rarely at home and rarely mentioned her husband

1940 – Joined staff of NAACP; felt unappreciated. Travelled to help set up and stimulate NAACP branches, for example, Birmingham, Alabama. Frequently defied segregation rules on trains. Constantly monitored by the FBI, which considered her a dangerous subversive. Described NAACP leader Walter White as 'very much in love with himself'. Disliked NAACP's reliance upon litigation, preferring mobilisation of ordinary blacks

1946 – Left NAACP employment

1952 – Elected first female president of the New York City NAACP branch; concentrated on combating the segregated educational system that remained even after BROWN (1954), and on police brutality. Fundraised, for example, for the Montgomery Bus Boycott, which confirmed her belief that ordinary people could make a difference. Never had much money herself, saying if she ever wrote an autobiography it would be called *Making a Life, Not Making a Living*

1956 – Inspired to return South by the Montgomery Bus Boycott. Helped organise the founding meeting of SCLC. Never felt valued by Martin Luther King: 'After all, who was I? I was female, I was old. I didn't have any PhD ... [and was] not loathe to raise questions.' Worked for SCLC. Helped organise the 1957 'Prayer Pilgrimage for Freedom' in Washington DC. She used old NAACP contacts in SCLC's Crusade for Citizenship. Let King know how she disapproved of hero worship of him: 'Strong people do not need strong leaders.' Disagreed with King on non-violence: she preferred self-defence.

1960 – Left SCLC. Joined SNCC, the organisation willing to take on the impossible, for example, voter registration in Mississippi. Baker shaped SNCC's goal, the politicisation of local communities and empowerment of ordinary people.

1964 – Helped set up Mississippi Freedom Democratic Party (see page 136)

1966 – Although sympathetic to black power, drifted away from SNCC when it became more radical (see page 160)

1970 – Campaigned for the (probably unfairly) imprisoned Black Panther radical and Communist Party member Angela Davies

1970s – Age, asthma and arthritis slowed her down, but helped many different organisations

1986 – Died

Ella Baker was significant because she worked tirelessly and often effectively to empower ordinary people into an activism that could be sustained independently of any leader or organisation. She empowered black women, through her example and encouragement. She reminds historians of the civil rights movement that to give an accurate account of the black struggle for freedom they cannot ignore the role of women and grassroots protest. Her co-workers at SNCC recognised her importance, although some historians have missed it.

(ii) The significance of the sit-ins

Key question
What was the significance of the sit-ins?

The sit-ins helped erode Jim Crow: loss of business made Woolworth's desegregate all its lunch counters by the end of 1961. One hundred and fifty cities soon desegregated various public places. Black students had been mobilised, although when they set up the Student Non-Violent Co-ordinating Committee (SNCC), inter-organisational strife increased. SNCC accused SCLC of keeping donations intended for SNCC, NAACP lawyer Thurgood Marshall refused to represent 'a bunch of crazy colored students', while King's public acknowledgement of NAACP/SCLC divisions infuriated Roy Wilkins. Blacks desperately needed a single leader who could unite all activists. King never managed to fulfil that role, but others such as the prickly Wilkins were equally if not more culpable.

The sit-ins shifted the focus of black activism from litigation to mass direct action. Encouraged by Ella Baker, the students felt their actions had rendered King's cautious programme and 'top-down' leadership obsolete. SNCC was more egalitarian and more appreciative of women workers than any other black organisation. From 1961 to 1964, SNCC organised grassroots struggles in places like Danville, Virginia, Lowndes County, Alabama, Albany, Georgia, Pine Bluff, Arkansas, and the Mississippi Delta. SNCC workers became known as the 'shock troops' of the civil rights movement: wherever there was activism or the need for activism, SNCC workers and volunteers were there, as in the Freedom Rides.

(d) Freedom Rides (1961)

(i) Aims and methods of the Freedom Riders

Key question
Did King play an important role in the Freedom Rides?

Key date
Freedom Rides: 1961

While King seemed unable to think up new tactics for gaining attention, CORE's 'Freedom Ride' of May 1961 electrified the civil rights movement. A small, integrated group travelled the South testing Supreme Court rulings against segregation on interstate transport (MORGAN v. VIRGINIA, 1946) and on interstate bus facilities (BOYNTON v. VIRGINIA, 1960). The tactic had been used before in 1947 without success. Now CORE's director James Farmer explained that:

> We planned the Freedom Ride with the specific intention of creating a crisis. We were counting on the bigots in the South to do our work for us. We figured that the government would have to respond if we created a situation that was headline news all over the world, and affected the nation's image abroad.

As expected, Alabama racists attacked black passengers with clubs and chains and burned their buses. King quickly made contact with the riders. Students criticised King for not going on the rides himself, but as he was on probation for a minor traffic offence he feared arrest.

(ii) The significance of the Freedom Rides

Although CORE initiated the Freedom Rides, King used them to get CORE, SCLC and SNCC to work together – or to ensure

Key term

Interstate
Between states, for example, between Alabama and Georgia.

SCLC domination, his critics said. All agreed that the aim was publicity. It worked. Attorney General Bobby Kennedy enforced the Supreme Court rulings on desegregated **interstate** travel in November 1961, demonstrating yet again the importance of federal intervention. However, black divisions remained. CORE insisted SCLC announce that CORE had originated the Freedom Rides!

(iii) How well had King done by 1961?

King's first 18 months in Atlanta had been productive. SCLC was better organised, better financed, and more united. It was agreed that some members could concentrate on protests, others on voter registration. King's leadership was characterised by a willingness to be led by others when their methods were effective. Despite tensions, SCLC, CORE, NAACP, the National Urban League, and the SNCC all agreed to work together on voter registration in Mississippi. King was also learning how to use the media.

Key question
What was King's role in the Albany movement?

(e) Albany (1961–2)

(i) Initiators and aims

In November 1961 others led the way again. SNCC organised students from (black) Albany State College, Georgia, in sit-ins in Albany bus station, which had ignored the Interstate Commerce Commission's order to desegregate. Hundreds of freedom riders were arrested. Blacks boycotted white businesses but the city authorities refused to desegregate, despite pressure from Attorney General Kennedy.

Key date

Albany Movement: 1961–2

(ii) The role of Martin Luther King

Once again King followed rather than led. Older leaders of the 'Albany Movement' invited him to join them. This angered SNCC leaders who stressed that the Albany Movement was 'by and for local Negroes'. King told a reporter, 'The people wanted to do something they would have done with or without me.'

King led a march and came to a promising agreement with the city authorities. However, after King left, the authorities reneged on the agreement. The Albany Movement petered out in a series of decreasingly supported protests. King recognised Albany as a major defeat. The interstate terminal facilities were desegregated, and more black voters were allowed to register, but the city closed the parks, sold the swimming pool, integrated the library only after removing all the seats, and refused to desegregate the schools.

(iii) Why had the Albany Movement failed?

The Albany Movement had failed because some black violence achieved bad publicity. The local police chief had carefully avoided violence, so the federal government had not had to intervene. 'The key to everything is federal commitment,' said King. Also, black divisions were crucial: some were paid informants of the white city leadership; local black leaders resented 'outsiders'; NAACP, SNCC and SCLC failed to co-operate. King was criticised by some blacks for indecision over black divisions, and by others for choosing a fine rather than remaining in Albany jail for Christmas as he had promised.

(iv) What had been achieved by the Albany Movement?

The Albany Movement was not without some success.

- Local black leaders claimed the black community had lost a lot of its fear of white power.
- The entire black community had been mobilised.
- SNCC's 'jail not bail' strategy could fill the jails with protesters and bring the courts and jails to a standstill.
- National attention had been gained.
- King learned it was unwise for the SCLC to intervene in an area without a strong SCLC presence and that it was probably more effective to focus upon one particular aspect of segregation.
- King said that as blacks had little political power, it was unwise to concentrate upon negotiations with the white authorities; it made more sense to boycott white businesses so businessmen would advocate negotiations.
- All of these lessons showed the best way forward in Birmingham, Alabama.

(f) Birmingham (1963)

Key question
How effectively did Martin Luther King lead in Birmingham?

In 1963, King concentrated upon segregation and unequal opportunities in Birmingham, Alabama.

(i) Why Birmingham?

King chose Birmingham for several reasons. Faced with competing civil rights organisations and the increasing attractiveness of black nationalism (see Chapter 7), the SCLC had to demonstrate it could be dynamic and successful. The SNCC and NAACP were relatively inactive in Birmingham, where the local black leader was affiliated to SCLC and King's own brother was a pastor. While King expected fewer crippling black divisions, white divisions looked promising. White businessmen felt racism held the city back, while white extremists had recently castrated a Negro, prohibited sale of a book that featured black and white rabbits, and campaigned to stop 'Negro music' being played on white radio stations. Birmingham could be expected to produce the kind of violent white opposition that won national sympathy.

Key date
Birmingham campaign: April–May 1963

King described Birmingham as 'by far' America's 'worst big city' for racism. Birmingham's Public Safety Commissioner 'Bull' Connor was a hot-tempered, determined segregationist who had dared to clash with Eleanor Roosevelt years before. Connor had ensured that Freedom Riders under attack from a racist Birmingham mob had not received protection from his police, whom he gave the day off because it was Mother's Day! Bull and Birmingham would show the media segregation at its worst. Finally, King was impatient with the Kennedy administration's

A black demonstrator attacked by Bull Connor's police dogs in Birmingham, Alabama, 1963. An SCLC worker said the demonstrator was trying to stop other blacks responding to police violence.

inactivity. The Freedom Riders had shown that violence forced federal intervention. 'To cure injustices,' said King, 'you must expose them before the light of human conscience and the bar of public opinion.'

(ii) Events in Birmingham

The SCLC's Birmingham actions were carefully planned. King was leading rather than led. However, he made miscalculations. SCLC failed to recruit enough local demonstrators, because the local SCLC leader was unpopular. Many blacks felt the recent electoral defeat and imminent retirement of Connor made action unnecessary. King admitted there was 'tremendous resistance' amongst blacks to his planned demonstrations. SCLC had to use demonstrators in areas where there were lots of blacks to give the impression of mass action and to encourage onlookers to participate.

Then, as expected, Connor attracted national attention. His police and their dogs turned on black demonstrators. King defied an injunction and marched, knowing his arrest would gain national attention and perhaps inspire others. He was kept in solitary confinement and not allowed private meetings with his lawyer. He wrote an inspirational 'Letter from Birmingham Jail', partly on prison toilet paper. Coretta called President Kennedy, who got King released.

It remained difficult to mobilise sufficient demonstrators. 'You know, we've got to get something going,' said King. 'The press is leaving.' Despite considerable local opposition and King's doubts about the morality of the policy, the SCLC enlisted black school children, some as young as six. It was very successful. Five hundred young marchers were soon in custody. Birmingham was headlines again. Connor's high-pressure water hoses tore clothes off students' backs. SCLC succeeded in its aim of 'filling the jails'. A leading SCLC official 'thanked' Bull Connor for his violent response, without which there would have been no publicity.

As whites and blacks used violence, Birmingham degenerated into chaos, which President Kennedy said was 'damaging the reputation' of Birmingham and the USA. A deal was reached to improve the situation of Birmingham blacks, but Connor's Ku Klux Klan friends tried to sabotage the agreement. Bombs hit King's brother's house and King's motel room. State troopers (commanded by a friend of both Connor and of Alabama's racist Governor George Wallace) disappeared from guarding the motel just before the explosion. Blacks began to riot. A policeman was stabbed. Bobby Kennedy feared this could trigger off national violence, and urged his brother to protect the Birmingham agreement: 'If King loses, worse leaders are going to take his place'. When conservatives in the Birmingham educational establishment tried to derail the settlement by expelling 1100 students for having skipped classes to demonstrate, King persuaded local black leaders not to call for a total boycott of all schools and businesses, but to take the cases to court. They did so, and a federal judge obtained the students' reinstatement.

(iii) Results and significance of Birmingham

Key question
Did Birmingham contribute to the 1964 Civil Rights Act?

Birmingham was the first time that King had really led the movement. Had he got it right? The SCLC had correctly assessed how Connor would react and how the media would depict his reactions. 'There never was any more skilful manipulation of the news media than there was in Birmingham,' said a leading SCLC staffer. While little changed in Birmingham, the SCLC had shown America that Southern segregation was very unpleasant. Extra donations poured into the SCLC. The Kennedy administration admitted that Birmingham was crucial in persuading them to push the bill that eventually became the 1964 Civil Rights Act. 'We are on the threshold of a significant breakthrough,' said King, 'and the greatest weapon is the mass demonstration.' In the summer of 1963 protests throughout the South owed inspiration to Birmingham. King had shown that he could lead from the front and force desegregation, if through rather artificially engineered violence. He recognised that non-violent demonstrations 'make people inflict violence on you, so you precipitate violence'. However, he excused it: 'We are merely bringing to the surface the tension that has always been at the heart of the problem'. Critics accused him of hypocrisy:

> He marches for peace on one day, and then the very next day threatens actions we think are coldly calculated to bring violent responses from otherwise peaceful neighbourhoods.

Key question
Why was the March on Washington so important?

Key date
March on Washington: 1963

(g) The March on Washington, August 1963

(i) Organisation and aims

Marches were a favourite tactic of civil rights activists, and Washington DC a favourite location. The March on Washington of August 1963 aimed to encourage passage of a civil rights bill and executive action to increase black employment. Initially, neither Roy Wilkins nor President Kennedy were supportive, which worried King, who felt the March would maintain black morale and advertise the effectiveness of non-violent protest. He feared non-violence was decreasingly popular amongst blacks, many of whom were embittered by the slow pace of change.

(ii) The March

The March was a great success. The predominantly middle class crowd was around a quarter of a million. A quarter of them were white. King's memorable speech made a powerful appeal to white America, with his references to the Declaration of Independence, and to the Bible, with his typically black emphasis on the Old Testament God who freed his enslaved people:

> I have a dream. It is a dream deeply rooted in the American dream. I have a dream that one day this nation will rise up and live out the true meaning of its creed – we hold these truths to be self-evident, that all men are created equal …
>
> I have a dream that my four little children will one day live in a nation where they will not be judged by the colour of their skin but by the content of their character. I have a dream today! …
>
> Let freedom ring … When we allow freedom to ring, when we let it ring from every village and every hamlet, from every state and every city, we will be able to speed up that day when all of God's children – black men and white men, Jews and Gentiles, Protestants and Catholics – will be able to join hands and sing in the words of the old Negro spiritual, 'Free at last, free at last; thank God Almighty, we are free at last.'

This was King the leader at his best, involved in an action the morality of which could not be doubted, and the quality of which he raised immeasurably by helping to persuade Wilkins to participate and by making a superb speech.

(iii) The significance of the March

The March on Washington was the first time the major civil rights leaders collaborated on a national undertaking, although the co-operation did not extend beyond this single march. The March impressed television audiences across the world. Historians disagree over the extent to which its emotional impact helped the passage of civil rights legislation. While many contemporaries were thrilled by the March, the *New York Times* described Congress as unmoved by it.

(h) SNCC and Mississippi (1961–4)

Key question
What was the significance of the Mississippi Freedom Summer?

The SNCC's finest hour was the Black Freedom Movement in Mississippi.

(i) The problems in Mississippi

Key date
Mississippi Freedom Summer: 1964

By 1960, only 5.2 per cent of Mississippi blacks could vote (the Southern average was over 30 per cent). White voter registrars set impossible questions and opened offices at inconvenient hours to stop blacks registering to vote. Although half of Mississippians were black, there had been no elected black official since 1877. With blacks politically powerless, Mississippi whites spent three times more on white students than on black. Seventy per cent of Mississippi blacks were illiterate. With only six black doctors in Mississippi, a black baby was twice as likely to die as a white baby. Half a million black Mississippians had migrated North to escape. Andrew Young confessed that the SCLC 'knew better than to try to take on Mississippi'. In 1961, NAACP activists, increasingly victimised, called for help from the SNCC, knowing that SNCC's white volunteers would attract media attention to Mississippi's racist horrors.

(ii) SNCC activities and achievements in Mississippi

The SNCC worked at local community level, establishing Freedom Schools to educate would-be voters and get them registered. It was the local, poorer black population, people such as Fannie Lou Hamer (see page 183), not the black middle class, who responded to the SNCC in Mississippi. SNCC workers lived in fear of white extremists and were unprotected by the federal government.

In November 1963, the SNCC organised the 'Freedom Vote', a mock election for disfranchised blacks. SNCC then promoted another voter registration drive, the Mississippi Summer Project, or Freedom Summer, in 1964. Predominantly white Northern volunteers poured into Mississippi to help. All America took notice of 'Mississippi Freedom Summer' after three young activists (two of whom were white) were murdered by segregationists. SNCC also helped to organise the Mississippi Freedom Democratic Party (MFDP) delegation to the Democratic National Convention in autumn 1964 (see page 183). While the delegation's experience there was disappointing, the MFDP successfully politicised many poor black Mississippians (especially women), developed new grassroots leaders, and brought black Mississippi suffering to national attention. However, disillusioned with the lack of federal protection, SNCC became far more militant, which contributed to the disintegration of the civil rights coalition.

Key question
How effective a leader was Martin Luther King in the winter of 1963–4?

(i) King's problem: what to do next?

(i) Revolution?

Despite the successful publicity of Birmingham and the March on Washington, King's leadership was still criticised. He was disappointed by the conservatism of some of his black and white supporters. He admitted his was a 'social revolution', a 'movement to bring about certain basic structural changes in the architecture of American society' and while he hoped it would remain a non-violent revolution, he rejected 'allies who are more devoted to *order* than to *justice*'.

(ii) Ghettos

King was indecisive during tense SCLC debates over whether to concentrate on the Citizenship Education Programme or upon the more glamorous and emotionally satisfying direct action. The SCLC believed that a limited focus on one city gave a greater chance for success. But which city? And what to do there?

King publicised his increasing concern over the ghettos of the North. However, when New York City's mayor asked King to help stop the black rioting triggered by a white policeman shooting a black youth, King's visit proved unproductive. The mayor was uncompromising, while some Harlem blacks called King an 'Uncle Tom'.

(iii) Birmingham

Meanwhile, little had changed in Birmingham. A bomb killed four young black girls attending Sunday School in September 1963. The three whites arrested were freed for lack of evidence. Blacks rioted on the streets, and pelted police with rocks and rubbish. Policemen fired over the heads of the crowd and shot a black youth. King felt it vital to 'emerge with a clear-cut victory' in Birmingham, 'the symbol, the beginning of the revolution' where the SCLC's reputation was at stake. However, Birmingham's black leaders no longer wanted 'outside help' or 'outside interference'.

(iv) St Augustine

Key date
St Augustine: 1964

The SCLC moved into St Augustine, Florida in spring 1964. King received Klan death threats, and said SCLC had never worked in a city 'as lawless as this'. St Augustine's white leadership refused to negotiate. In spring 1964, an integrated group of seven protesters tried a new tactic – a 'swim-in' in a motel pool. The motel owner poured gallons of pool cleaning chemicals into the pool in vain. A policeman had to drag them out. Klansmen attacked police who tried to protect marchers. When the Klan picketed and fire-bombed places that had reluctantly desegregated, most of St Augustine re-segregated. King was keen to get out of the St Augustine impasse. SCLC had failed to get much support from local black leaders, but those who had supported King were embittered by his departure. On the other hand, some historians believe that although President Johnson refused to send in federal forces, the violent scenes of St Augustine helped get the civil rights bill through.

King had thus temporarily reverted to a reactive rather than a proactive policy. There is no doubt that the demonstrations and protests in which he played such a large part had helped ensure the passage of the July 1964 Civil Rights Act (see page 182). However, despite the Civil Rights Act, little had changed in Selma, Alabama.

Key dates
Civil Rights Act: 1964
Selma to Montgomery march: 1965

(j) Selma (1965)

(i) The situation in Selma

Key question
Why was Selma so important?

About half of Selma's 29,000 population was black. Blacks had segregated schools, buses, churches, restaurants, playgrounds, public toilets and drinking fountains. They used a different library and swimming pool. They could only have certain jobs and houses. In white neighbourhoods the streets were paved. In black neighbourhoods there were dirt roads. The average white family income was four times that of black families. The local newspapers kept the black and white news separate. Despite an SNCC campaign, only 23 blacks were registered to vote. Lawsuits initiated by Robert Kennedy's Justice Department were still bogged down in the courts. The Civil Rights Act of 1964 had not brought any great improvements.

(ii) Why Selma?

King announced Selma 'has become a symbol of bitter-end resistance to the civil rights movement in the Deep South'. It promised exploitable divisions within the white community. Selma's Sheriff Jim Clark could be trusted to react as brutally as Bull Connor, which would result in national publicity and revitalise the SCLC and the whole civil rights movement. While some local black activists feared the SCLC would 'come into town and leave too soon' or ignore them, others said that as the SNCC had lost its dynamism there it was an ideal opportunity for the SCLC. Concentration on Selma was the most specific thing the SCLC had done for a year, a year in which King said he and the others had 'failed to assert the leadership the movement needed'.

(iii) Events at Selma

King led would-be voters to register at Selma County Court house, but despite a federal judge's ruling, there were no registrations. Several incidents made headlines. A trooper shot a black youth who was trying to shield his mother from a beating. Whites threw venomous snakes at blacks trying to register. Keen for the media to show brutality, King held back men who tried to stop Clark clubbing a black woman. King publicly admitted that he wanted to be arrested to publicise the fact that Selma blacks were not allowed to register to vote. His effective letter was published in the *New York Times*:

> This is Selma, Alabama. There are more Negroes in jail with me than there are on the voting rolls.

However, Selma had not proved as explosive as King had hoped. The SCLC and SNCC therefore organised a march from Selma to

Montgomery (Alabama's capital) to publicise the need for a Voting Rights Act. Eighty Alabama whites joined the march. State troopers attacked the marchers with clubs and used tear gas. 'Bloody Sunday' aroused national criticism of Selma's whites.

President Johnson asked King to call off the next march, but King felt that constituted a betrayal of his followers. Without informing the SNCC, King got the marchers to approach the state troopers then retreat. The SNCC felt betrayed and accused him of cowardice.

How many Southern whites helped blacks?
Bob Zellner, son of an Alabama Methodist minister, was one of the few Southern whites who had the courage and convictions to help blacks. Looking back on the segregated society of his youth, he recalled: 'It was just the way things were. You didn't think about it. Sometimes when you are inside the system, you can't see it very well.' At college, he became sympathetic to the civil rights movement. The Ku Klux Klan threatened him. He joined the SNCC and was jailed for working on voter registration in Mississippi. He joined a Mississippi march in protest against the murder of a black SNCC worker. He marched from Selma to Montgomery, despite death threats from his grandfather and uncle. As blacks grew more suspicious of white assistance, he was excluded from the SNCC. From 1967 he helped underpaid black and white workers.

Key date

Voting Rights Act finally ensured blacks could vote: August 1965

(iv) How significant was Selma?

The historian Stephen Oates described Selma as 'the movement's finest hour'. King thought the national criticism of 'Bloody Sunday' was 'a shining moment in the conscience of man'. There were sympathetic interracial marches in cities such as Chicago, Detroit, New York and Boston. Johnson and Congress probably would not have delivered the Voting Rights Act without Selma.

On the other hand, although the NAACP had been very supportive in the law courts, the SNCC was publicly critical of the SCLC: all the SCLC ever left behind was 'a string of embittered cities' such as St Augustine, which were worse off than when the SCLC had first got there; the SCLC just used people in those cities to make a point. Disgruntled St Augustine activists claimed King and the SCLC had 'screwed' them. One said, 'I don't want him back here now.' Selma's activists felt betrayed by the SCLC's withdrawal. The SCLC had raised a great deal of money because Selma was in the headlines, then the SCLC left and spent the money in the North (see page 141). The SNCC gleefully quoted an arrogant SCLC representative who said, 'They need us more than we need them. We can bring the press in with us and they can't.' The SNCC also accused the SCLC of 'leader worship' of King. Black divisions were worsening.

(k) Going West – Watts (1965)

In 1965, the nation's attention began to turn to the ghettos of the North, Midwest and West. On Friday 13 August 1965, riots erupted in Los Angeles' Watts ghetto.

Black mobs set fire to several blocks of stores. Local churchmen asked King for help. Despite his previously unsuccessful intervention in New York, King felt it was his duty. The scenes of devastation in Watts shocked him. Bayard Rustin, King's ex-Communist friend, recalled how King was:

> absolutely undone, and he looked at me and said, 'You know, Bayard, I worked to get these people the right to eat hamburgers, and now I've got to do something ... to help them get the money to buy it' ... I think it was the first time he really understood.

King told the press this had been 'a class revolt of underprivileged against privileged ... the main issue is economic'. Others were leading the leader towards a new philosophy. Previously King had thought of 'freedom' in the traditional American sense of the democratic right to vote. That right had been confirmed for blacks by the recent legislation but other grievances remained in the poverty-stricken ghettos. Now King began to define 'freedom' in terms of economic equality rather than political equality. He was turning to socialism, calling for 'a better distribution of the wealth' of the USA.

Key question
What was the impact of Watts upon Martin Luther King?

Key dates
Watts riots: 13 August 1965
Chicago campaign: January–August 1966

(l) Going North – Chicago (1966)

(i) Why Chicago?

After Southern blacks had sought and gained greater social and political equality, King turned North, where the problem was social and economic equality. King had hoped the struggle in the South would help Northern blacks. It had not. He had to do something to stop the increasing tendency toward violence and radicalism amongst blacks. King therefore sought a Northern ghetto upon which the SCLC could concentrate. Why did he choose Chicago?

Key question
What was the significance of Chicago?

- The SCLC said: 'if Northern problems can be solved there, they can be solved anywhere.' Chicago was America's second-largest city, with a three million population, 700,000 of whom were black and concentrated in the South Side and West Side ghettos. Chicago blacks suffered chronic employment, housing and education problems. Chicago's black schools were so overcrowded that students attended in half-day shifts.
- Other great Northern cities were effectively shut off to King. He was told to keep out of New York City by Adam Clayton Powell and out of Philadelphia by the local NAACP leader.
- Although Chicago activists warned SCLC not to just 'come in and take over', they did so relatively amicably.
- Chicago had a tradition of sporadic protest. Inspired by the Southern sit-ins, CORE was revitalised in 1960. In 1961, there were 'wade-ins' in protest against the customary segregation of South Side beach. In October 1963 over half of Chicago's half a

million black students boycotted their inferior, segregated schools for a day in protest, although no improvement had resulted.
- Chicago's influential religious community supported the civil rights movement.
- King hoped he could demonstrate his leadership skills for the first time in the North, which he thought suffered from 'bankruptcy of leadership'.
- Chicago's Mayor Daley relied heavily on black voters and was no racist. He had total political domination. If he could be won over, things could get done. Chicago could become an inspirational symbol.

However, throughout the winter of 1965–6, King and his lieutenant, Andrew Young, did not know what the SCLC could do in Chicago: 'we do not have a programme yet for the North'. Young talked vaguely of mobilising Chicago blacks, and 'pulling things together'. In late spring 1966, the SCLC finally concentrated upon discrimination in housing sales that stopped blacks moving out of the ghetto slums.

(ii) What happened in Chicago?

In January 1966 the SCLC rented a West Side ghetto apartment for King's use during the campaign. When the landlord found out who his new tenant was, an army of repair men moved in to make it habitable. Chicagoans joked that the easiest way for King to improve ghetto housing would be for him to move from building to building! King led reporters around rat-infested, unheated ghetto dwellings. King and his aides dramatically seized a Chicago slum building and, dressed in work clothes, began repairing it. King told the press that the SCLC had collected the tenants' rents to finance this. When he said that moral questions were more important than legal ones in this case, the press cried 'anarchy!'. The usual divisions between local Chicago activists and the SCLC members materialised and the lack of a clearly defined issue did not help. The July 1966 Chicago rally turnout was 30,000, disappointingly below the anticipated 100,000. The subsequent meeting between King and Daley was unproductive. King said Daley did too little, Daley said he did his best.

King's own family neared disintegration as they sampled Chicago ghetto life. There were neither pools nor parks in which his children could escape the suffocating heat of their small, airless flat. The surrounding streets were too crowded and dangerous to play in. King's children screamed and fought each other, as never before. With the temperature nearly 40°C, the police shut off a fire hydrant that black youths had been using to cool themselves. After some youths were arrested, angry blacks ran through the streets. King persuaded the police to release the youngsters. King encouraged ministers to join him in walking the ghetto streets to try to calm people. Black crowds derided and walked away from him, but he persuaded Mayor Daley to make fire hydrants and pools available. Daley implicated the SCLC in the riots, which had caused $2 million damage.

Chicago whites feared black neighbours would hit property values, increase crime, and threaten cultural homogeneity. So, when 500 black marchers defiantly and provocatively entered a white Chicago neighbourhood to publicise the fact that they could not as yet reside there, they were greeted with rocks, bottles, and cries of 'apes', 'cannibals', 'savages', and 'The only way to stop niggers is to exterminate them'. Several such incidents occurred. The police, shocked at being called 'nigger lovers' by fellow whites, did little to protect the blacks. When a rock hit King, it made the national press. The marches then became more peaceful: 800 policeman protected 700 marchers on one occasion. Many influential whites blamed King for the riots and invited him to leave. King himself blamed Daley. 'A non-violent movement cannot maintain its following unless it brings about change.' He warned that discriminatory house-selling practices would lead to 'Negro cities ringed with white suburbs', which was dangerous: hatred and fear developed when people were thus separated. The *Chicago Tribune* denounced King as a 'paid professional agitator' and asked how he could justify demonstrations that turned violent. He said demonstrations might stop greater violence and that the problem was not the marches but the conditions that caused people to march. He pointed out that:

> We don't have much money [or] education, and we don't have political power ... you are asking us to give up the one thing that we have when you say, 'Don't march' ... We're trying to keep the issue so alive that it will be acted on. Our marching feet have brought us a long way, and if we hadn't marched I don't think we'd be here today.

In autumn 1966 King left Chicago, leaving the SCLC's dynamic young Jesse Jackson in charge of 'Operation Breadbasket', which successfully used economic boycotts to help increase black employment.

(iii) Assessment of the SCLC in Chicago

In Chicago, King had tried to lead. Because of the threat of black marches into racist white areas, Daley agreed to promote integrated housing in Chicago, but the agreement was a mere 'paper victory' (*Chicago Daily News*). Most blacks remained stranded in the ghetto. Although the SCLC obtained a $4 million federal grant to improve Chicago housing and left behind a significant legacy of community action, local blacks felt SCLC had 'sold out' and lapsed into apathy. An SCLC staffer in Chicago said the voter registration drive there was 'a nightmare', 'largely because of division in the Negro leadership' and partly because Chicago blacks were uninterested. 'I have never seen such hopelessness.' 'A lot of people won't even talk to us.' Many disillusioned blacks turned to black power (see Chapter 7). Chicago's race relations had always been poor (see page 65). King could be considered to have worsened the situation. Black hopes were raised then dashed, and there was a white backlash. Whites increasingly thought of blacks as troublemakers on welfare.

The *New Republic* said, 'so far, King has been pretty much of a failure at organising'. One of King's closest admirers described the Chicago venture as a 'fiasco' and 'disaster'. Why had King and SCLC failed in Chicago?

- The SCLC had been inadequately briefed and ill-prepared – they even lacked warm clothing for the Chicago winter.
- The Meredith March (see next page) distracted the SCLC in mid-1966.
- SCLC could not effect a social and economic revolution in Chicago within months. Ella Baker had pointed out how SCLC's failure to develop grassroots participation often lead to disaster. King went into Chicago hoping to effect a miraculous transformation without educating and organising the local population for a long-term haul after he and the media had gone.
- Chicago's near million black population was too big to mobilise, unlike Selma's 15,000 blacks.
- Neither NAACP nor all the local black churches joined King's Chicago Freedom Movement. Radical Black Muslims (see page 152) were unhelpful, as were conservative blacks, who loathed SCLC's attempt to recruit and convert violent young gang members. Black Congressman William Dawson, who had represented Chicago since the Second World War, disliked mass action, which he thought caused trouble. Most slum land was owned by blacks, who resented King's criticism of slum landlords.
- The Chicago Movement never called in outside help, unlike Selma.
- Mayor Daley brilliantly out-witted the SCLC. Unlike Bull Connor's police, Daley's police protected the marchers. He stopped the marches by threatening fines (which the SCLC could not afford) rather than filling the jails. He did not want to alienate his white working class voters and his many black Chicago supporters did not want to offend him.
- The federal government had not helped the Chicago Freedom Movement, because Mayor Daley was a political ally of President Johnson.
- President Johnson had turned against King after King's criticism of the Vietnam War.
- The anti-Vietnam War movement was taking funds and energies from the civil rights movement.
- National press coverage of the Chicago Freedom Movement was limited. Black marchers attempting to register to vote in Selma gained national sympathy, black marchers going into white neighbourhoods did not. When CORE defied King and lead a march into the working class white suburb of Cicero, marchers clashed violently with hecklers. White Americans were tired of black protests that led to violence, tired of black ghetto riots (see page 159) and resistant to radical change that affected their property rights.
- Jesse Jackson thought Chicago was a success, because it had woken up Northern black America. However, awakening led to violence in the Northern ghettos. Coretta King considered

violence counter-productive: it 'unleashed' the 'vastly superior' white force that her husband had predicted.

(m) The Meredith March 1966

Key question
Why was the Meredith March so important?

(i) Why did the March take place?

Key date
Meredith March: June 1966

James Meredith was inadvertently responsible for the first major non-violent protest since Selma 15 months before. Famous as the University of Mississippi's first black student, Meredith planned a 220-mile walk from Memphis to Mississippi's capital Jackson, to encourage blacks to vote. He was shot on the second day of his walk and temporarily immobilised. Black organisations therefore declared that they would continue his walk. King came from Chicago and with 20 others began the walk. There were 400 marchers by the third day, including the new SNCC leader, Stokely Carmichael. Born in the West Indies, brought up in Harlem and educated at Howard, Carmichael was a founder member of the SNCC. Charismatic, handsome and a good organiser, he was involved in the SNCC's voter registration campaigns in Mississippi.

(ii) Divisions on the March

Black divisions damaged the March. The NAACP and the National Urban League wanted the March to focus national attention on the new civil rights bill, and withdrew when Carmichael criticised the bill. King welcomed white participants, the SNCC rejected them. The SNCC and CORE had become increasingly militant, following the lack of federal protection for their voter registration projects in the 'Mississippi Freedom Summer' of 1964. Carmichael was arrested. As white bystanders waved Confederate flags, shouted obscenities and threw things at the marchers, the SNCC people sang:

> Jingle bells, shotgun shells, Freedom all the way,
> Oh what fun it is to blast, A [white] trooper man away.

Upon release, Carmichael urged the burning of 'every courthouse in Mississippi' and demanded 'black power' (see Chapter 7). Crowds took up the chant. King and the SCLC tried to encourage chants of 'freedom now'. King disliked 'black power', because the words would alienate white sympathisers and encourage a white backlash. He had reluctantly agreed to the black paramilitary group 'Deacons for Defense' providing security. Tired of violence, King urged blacks to avoid violent retaliation against tear gas. He begged Johnson to send in federal troops but, as in Selma, Johnson refused.

Meanwhile Meredith felt excluded and began a march of his own. Some SCLC leaders joined him to disguise the split. The 15,000 main marchers ended at Jackson with rival chants of 'black power' and 'freedom now'.

(iii) Results and significance of the March

King despaired. 'I don't know what I'm going to do. The government has got to give me some victories if I'm going to keep people non-violent.' He felt he could no longer co-operate with the SNCC. 'Because Stokely Carmichael chose the march as an arena for a debate over black power,' King told the press, 'we did not get to emphasise the evils of Mississippi and the need for the 1966 Civil Rights Act.' He admitted that blacks were 'very, very close' to a public split. The NAACP no longer wanted to co-operate with the SCLC or the SNCC.

King had frequently been led by others, but had previously managed to put himself at the forefront of their movements. Now it seemed likely that leadership might pass into the hands of extremists such as Carmichael who rejected 'passive resistance'.

Key question
Did King achieve anything after 1966?

(n) 'Where do we go from here?'

After the Chicago and Meredith March debacles, King was depressed and unsure what to do next. He was marginalised by black extremists such as Carmichael, who called for black and white separation, and said blacks should use 'any means necessary' to obtain their rights. Black extremists, the white backlash and the distraction of white liberals by the Vietnam War resulted in the collapse of the civil rights coalition that had effected so much (see Chapters 7 and 8). In his 1967 book *Where Do We Go From Here?*, King highlighted the problem: giving blacks the vote had not cost money, but improving their economic situation would be expensive. No one wanted higher taxation. He urged demonstrations to seek **affirmative action**, on the grounds that 'a society that has done something against the Negro for hundreds of years must now do something special for him, in order to equip him to compete on a just and equal basis'.

Key term
Affirmative action
Also known as 'positive discrimination'; helping those who have had a disadvantageous start in life.

King urged blacks to broaden their movement and bring the Hispanic, Indian and white Appalachian poor into the war on poverty. He planned to bring all the poor together to camp out in Washington DC in a civil disobedience campaign. King had gone way beyond being a black civil rights leader, but had lost his old constituency, and failed to gain a new one. Adam Clayton Powell christened him 'Martin Loser King'. Even sympathisers expected his Poor People's Campaign to fail, to end in violence and an even greater white backlash. His final strategy (to represent a wider constituency) and his final tactics (yet another protest) were, in the climate of the time, unwise and unrealistic. Even friends and colleagues opposed his Poor People's Campaign. 'It's just isn't working. People aren't responding,' he admitted.

Key dates
Poor Peoples' Campaign: 1968
Death of Martin Luther King: 1968

Others, who recognised his publicity value, orchestrated King's last public appearances. In March 1968, King was asked to visit Memphis, Tennessee, to give support to black sanitation workers faced with discrimination from the city authorities. King joined a protest march, wherein a radical black power minority got violent and broke shop windows. King was exhausted, confused, frightened and in despair. 'Maybe we just have to admit that the day of violence is here, and maybe we have to just give up'. Within hours, King was dead.

Summary diagram: The leadership of the civil rights movement

Events	Involvement				
	King and SCLC	NAACP	CORE	SNCC	Grassroots
Montgomery Bus Boycott (1956)	✓✓	✓✓			✓✓
Sit-ins (1960)	✓		✓	✓✓	
Freedom Rides (1961)			✓✓	✓	
Albany (1961–2)	✓	✓		✓✓	✓✓
Brimingham (1963)	✓✓				✓
March on Washington (1963)	✓✓	✓	✓	✓	✓
Mississippi Freedom Summer (1964)				✓✓	✓✓
Selma (1965)	✓✓				
Meredith March (1966)	✓✓			✓✓	
Chicago (1966)	✓✓				✓
✓ minor or ✓✓ major					

4 | King and the Leadership of the Civil Rights Movement – Conclusions

(a) King's radicalism

Key question
Was King a political, social and economic revolutionary? Or an Uncle Tom?

Contemporaries who accused King of deferring to white authority figures were usually young 'black power' militants who rejected non-violence (see Chapter 7). He in turn criticised them. He told the *New York Times* 'black power' was dangerous, provocative and cost the civil rights movement support. King knew violence stood little chance against the military strength of the US government. King was moderate in comparison yet even he aroused hatred and a refusal to make concessions amongst many whites.

King was no Uncle Tom. He frequently criticised presidential policies. Some of his demonstrations were deliberately provocative. They invited white violence, making nonsense of his advocacy of non-violence. Within the Southern context, King was a political radical who sought the vote for the disfranchised and a social radical who sought racial equality. The Northern ghettos confirmed his economic radicalism: 'something is wrong with the economic system of our nation … with capitalism'. King's tactics could be considered revolutionary, particularly with his Poor People's Campaign. He envisaged representatives of all America's poor living in a temporary 'Resurrection City' in Washington, until Congress acted. King wanted to cause 'massive dislocation

… without destroying life or property'. Bringing Washington to a halt would be 'a kind of last, desperate demand for the nation to respond to non-violence'. By the winter of 1967–8 the Johnson administration considered King a revolutionary who advocated 'criminal [not civil] disobedience'. In 1995 King's family had a bitter argument with the federal National Park Service who played down the radicalism of King's later career in information they handed out at Atlanta's King National Historic site.

Key question
How much had King contributed to the progress toward equality, 1956–68?

(b) Achievements

Although much remained to be done, much had been achieved by 1968. The federal government had played an important role as had white extremists (President Kennedy joked that Bull Connor was a hero of the civil rights movement). Black activism had played a vital part in producing the legislation (see Chapter 8) by which Southern segregation had been shattered and a mass black electorate had gained a voice in the political process. American blacks had gained greater self-confidence. Black organisations such as the NAACP, CORE and the SNCC, churches, local community organisations, and thousands of unsung field workers all played an important part.

The extent of King's contribution has always been controversial: Ella Baker insisted, 'the movement made Martin rather than Martin making the movement'. Although we have seen that King was frequently led rather than leading, his actions and involvement always gained national attention and sometimes provided the vital impetus for some reform. His organisational skills were limited, but his ability to inspire was peerless. Although his tactics and strategy were sometimes unsuccessful (and unappealing), the problems blacks faced were long-standing and enormous. He was a relatively moderate leader who made a massive contribution to the black cause. In so doing, he inevitably roused white and black antagonism and extremism in a nation in which blacks had been too long oppressed.

The best way to judge his significance might be to look at what followed his death: the national direct action phase of the civil rights movement died with him. The Poor People's Campaign fizzled out under his successor Ralph Abernathy. Without King, the SCLC collapsed. However, it is not certain that the civil rights movement would have progressed any further had King lived. We have seen that King failed in Chicago. Other black activists were becoming more impatient and their frequent extremism was important in generating a white backlash.

Summary diagram: King and leadership of the civil rights movement – conclusions

Some things King did	Some reactions				
	Southern blacks	Ghetto blacks	White liberals	Federal government	Other whites
Talked about non-violent protest	✓	✗	✓	✓	✗
Provoked violence	–	–	–	✗	✗
Kept communicating with white authorities	✓	✗	✓	–	✗
Helped persuade federal government to pass civil rights legislation	✓	–	✓	–	✗
Moved toward Christian socialism	–	–	✗	✗	✗
Criticised Vietnam War	✗	✗	✓	✗	✗

Key: ✓ = positive; ✗ = negative; – = in-between.

5 | Key Debates

(a) Was there a 'New Negro' after 1956?

Martin Luther King claimed the Montgomery Bus Boycott signalled the emergence of 'the New Negro', but Roy Wilkins disagreed:

> The Negro of 1956 who stands on his own two feet is not a new Negro; he is the grandson or the great grandson of the men who hated slavery. By his own hands, through his own struggles, in his own organised groups – of churches, fraternal societies, the NAACP and others – he has fought his way to the place where he now stands.

Wilkins was jealous of King's increasing prominence, keen to emphasise NAACP's importance, and opposed to King's strategy of direct, non-violent action. Nevertheless there was much truth in his claim.

Historians argue over whether the civil rights movement of about 1956–68 constituted a great break with the past or represented continuity. Harvard Sitkoff (1997) and Glenn Eskew (1997) claimed that the mass direct action of the 1960s was definitely something new. However, local studies such as Adam Fairclough's on Louisiana (1995) Charles Payne's on Mississippi (1995) and Stephen Tuck's on Georgia (2001) all concluded that the 1960s owed everything to the activism of 'an earlier, socially invisible generation'.

(b) How important was King?

Historians differ in their assessment of King's importance in the civil rights movement. Professor Clayborne Carson contends that:

> If King had never lived, the black struggle would have followed a course of development similar to the one it did. The Montgomery

> Bus Boycott would have occurred, because King did not initiate it. Black students ... had sources of tactical and ideological inspiration besides King.

Professor Anthony Badger disagrees, believing that there was a 'revolution in Southern race relations' due to the civil rights movement, in which 'no person was more important' than King. Historians also disagree about the strengths and weaknesses of King as an organiser and visionary within the civil rights movement.

(c) Why was the civil rights movement a success?

Historians also disagree over the relative importance of factors contributing to the success of the civil rights movement in the 1960s. Mark Newman (2004) emphasises the needs to look at factors external to the black community: for example, NAACP litigated increasingly successfully, but that owed much to Franklin Roosevelt's liberal appointments to the Supreme Court.

While some historians argue that the federal government was crucial to activists and their success, others emphasise that the government simply responded to increased black voting power after the Great Migration and to world events and opinion. In the Cold War, the United States did not want to be seen to be racist and undemocratic. So, it could be argued that black activism needed particular, even unique, circumstances in which to flourish.

The importance of the church in the civil rights movement is also controversial. Aldon Morris (1984) stressed the role of the black churches, while Clayborne Carson (1981) pointed out that the church was frequently conservative and often held back activists.

(d) What were the major turning points?

Historians disagree as to the turning points in history of the civil rights movement. William Chafe (1980) described the Greensboro sit-ins as a great turning point. He saw the sit-ins as spontaneous, owing little to existing civil rights organisations, in contrast to Aldon Morris (1984) who links to them to a pre-existing network of churches, colleges and civil rights groups.

Similarly, Clayborne Carson rejected the terms civil rights movement, preferring 'black freedom movement' as a term that recognises the continuity and longevity of the black struggle for equality. Harvard Sitkoff (1993) dated the beginning of the civil rights movement to BROWN.

Those who pick out major events and/or individuals as 'starting' the civil rights movement subscribe to a 'top-down' view of the movement, in contrast to those who emphasise less well-known grassroots activism that had been in operation years before BROWN or Martin Luther King and that continued to operate in the years dominated by King. Steven Lawson (1991) brings those two schools of thought together, describing the civil rights movement as a mixture of local and national groups and events.

Since the rise of feminism or 'women's lib[eration]' in the 1970s, the role of women in the civil rights movement has been increasingly studied and emphasised, for example, Lynne Olsen (2001) wrote about the unsung heroines of the civil rights movement from 1830 to 1970.

Some key books in the debate

Anthony Badger and Brian Ward, eds, *The Making of Martin Luther King and the Civil Rights Movement* (New York, 1996).

Clayborne Carson, *In Struggle: SNCC and the Black Awakening of the 1960s* (Harvard, 1981).

William Chafe, *Civilities and Civil Rights: Greensboro, North Carolina, and the Black Struggle for Freedom* (Oxford, 1981).

Glenn Eskew, *But for Birmingham: The Local and National Movements in the Civil Rights Struggle* (North Carolina, 1997).

Adam Fairclough, *Race and Democracy: The Civil Rights Struggle in Louisiana, 1915–72* (Georgia, 1995).

Steven Lawson, *Freedom Then, Freedom Now: The Historiography of the Civil Rights Movement* (American Historical Review, 1991).

Aldon Morris, *The Origins of the Civil Rights Movement* (New York, 1984).

Mark Newman, *The Civil Rights Movement* (Edinburgh, 2004).

Lynne Olsen, *Freedom's Daughters: The Unsung Heroines of the Civil Rights Movement from 1830 to 1970* (New York, 2001).

Charles Payne, *I've Got the Light of Freedom: The Organising Tradition and the Mississippi Freedom Struggle* (California, 1995).

Harvard Sitkoff, *The Struggle for Black Equality* (New York, 1993).

Stephen Tuck, *Beyond Atlanta: The Struggle for Racial Equality in Georgia, 1940–1980* (Georgia, 2001).

Study Guide: AS Question

In the style of Edexcel

Describe the ways in which Martin Luther King contributed to the civil rights movement. (20 marks)

Exam tips

The cross-references are intended to take you straight to the material that will help you to answer the question.

When the question says 'describe', you are not expected to simply 'describe' all the things King did. As you only have 15–20 minutes in which to answer these 20-mark questions, you need to select three key areas of contribution, for example:

- King's inspirational contribution (for example, March on Washington speech – page 135)
- his organisational contribution (for example, Montgomery Improvement Association – page 106)
- his non-violence doctrine (for example, marching at Selma, which provoked white racist violence and elicited sympathy and action from the federal government – pages 138–9).

7 The 1960s – II: Black Power

POINTS TO CONSIDER
The period of the 'classic' civil rights movement in the South also saw the development of what became known as the black power movement in the 1960s. This chapter looks at:

- The Nation of Islam and Malcolm X
- The rise of black power in the 1960s
- black power and the Black Panthers
- The reasons why black power declined
- The achievements of the black power movement

Key dates

1930	Nation of Islam established
1959	Television documentary, *The Hate that Hate Produced*, made the Nation of Islam famous
1964–8	Annual riots in black ghettos
1964–5	Malcolm X left the Nation of Islam; killed by Nation of Islam gunmen
1966	CORE and SNCC advocated black power
	Black Panther Party established in Oakland
1968	Kerner report
1967–9	Black Panthers destroyed by police and FBI
1973	Demise of SNCC

1 | The Nation of Islam and Malcolm X

Key question
How and when did black radicalism develop?

The black power movement of the 1960s did not develop out of nothing. The black separatist tradition emerged in the nineteenth century, when some blacks advocated 'back to Africa'. Marcus Garvey's separatist **black nationalist** movement flourished briefly in the 1910s and 1920s (see pages 67–8). When Garvey's UNIA went into decline, the nationalist and separatist banner was taken up by the Black Muslim movement or Nation of Islam.

Key term
Black nationalist
Black nationalists want a separate black nation either within the USA or in Africa.

(a) Elijah Muhammad and the Nation of Islam

The Nation of Islam (NOI) (a name suggesting a nation within the US nation) was founded by Wallace Fard in Detroit in 1930. When Fard disappeared in 1934, leadership of the new religious group passed to Elijah Poole, who was born in Georgia in 1897. Under his adopted name of Elijah Muhammad, Poole led the Nation of Islam from 1934 until he died in 1975.

Key dates

Nation of Islam established: 1930

The Hate that Hate Produced on television: 1959

Although Elijah Muhammad said he was the prophet of Allah, the 'Messenger of Islam', his teachings frequently differed from those of orthodox Islam. He rejected ideas of spiritual life after death, and claimed that Allah originally created people black. Other races were created by an evil scientist, Yakub, whose last evil creation was the white race. Whites would rule the world for several thousand years, but then Allah would return and end their supremacy. 'We believed', said Malcolm X (see page 155) years later, 'in some of the most fantastic things that you could ever imagine'. The NOI aimed to provide blacks with an alternative to the white man's Christian religion, to persuade members to live a religious life, to increase black self-esteem, to keep blacks and whites separate and to encourage blacks to improve their economic situation.

From the 1930s to the 1950s, the NOI set up temples in northern black ghettos such as Detroit, New York and Chicago. In the 1950s, the NOI's most brilliant preacher, Malcolm X, attracted the attention and devotion of frustrated ghetto-dwellers with his rejection of integration and his bitter attacks on white America. However, the movement did not gain much publicity until a television documentary called *The Hate that Hate Produced* brought the NOI national prominence and white hostility. Addressing 10,000 people in Washington DC in 1959, Elijah Muhammad attacked the 'turn the other cheek' philosophy of Martin Luther King and Christianity, which perpetuated enslavement. He advocated separatism and armed self-defence against white aggression. The NOI's most famous recruit in the 1960s was the boxer, Muhammad Ali.

An illustration of racism in the West

One of Elijah Muhammad's many large and luxurious homes was in Phoenix, where the hot, dry climate helped his asthma. The situation of Phoenix's black population illustrates racism in the American West. In the early 1960s, there was still segregation, enforced by custom in theatres, restaurants and hotels, and by law in schools. Blacks constituted around five per cent of Phoenix's population, and they were concentrated in a neighbourhood characterised by unemployment, poor housing and poor schools.

(b) Achievements of the NOI

Key question

What were the achievements of the NOI?

(i) Negative

Some of the Nation's solutions to black problems (a return to Africa or a separate black state in the Deep South) were unrealistic. NOI teachings exacerbated divisions between blacks and whites and between blacks. While the NOI derided Martin Luther King as an Uncle Tom, a 'fool' who humiliatingly begged

Profile: Muhammad Ali (Cassius Clay) 1942–

1942 – Born in Louisville in the border state of Kentucky. His father was a sign painter, his mother a domestic servant

1960 – Almost did not go to the Rome Olympics because of his fear of flying, but won a gold medal for boxing. Claimed that when he returned from Rome, 'with my gold medal around my neck, I couldn't get a hamburger in my home town'

1964 – Became world heavyweight champion. Admitted membership of the NOI, called himself Muhammad Ali. This was interpreted, rightly, as a rejection of white America

1966 – Drafted, but refused to join the army to fight in Vietnam – 'No VC [Vietnamese Communist] ever called me nigger'. While Ali had some sympathy from fellow blacks ('Draft beer – not Ali' said some demonstrators' placards), white America turned against him and deprived him of his boxing titles and his right to earn a living in the ring. The NOI disowned him

1970 – Increased black political power and anti-Vietnam War sentiment in Atlanta, Georgia, enabled Ali to fight there

1971 – NAACP obtained Supreme Court ruling that said he was not a criminal for refusing to fight in Vietnam. NOI adopted him again!

1975 – Ali won back his world heavyweight title. Lost and regained it several times until his retirement in 1981

2001 – A popular film about his life starring Will Smith demonstrated his popularity amongst whites and blacks in America and the world

Ironically, for one who became an icon of black militancy, Ali never joined any civil rights protest marches. He said he did not want to face fire hoses and dogs. Ali was important in bringing US attention to the NOI and the new assertiveness and discontent of American blacks. In the 1960s, his unpopularity reflected white American discontent with the NOI, but his later, gentler version of Islam in the 1970s and his boxing come-backs generated great affection for him and also reflected white America's increased adulation of great black athletes.

for access to a white-dominated world and urged non-violence on his defenceless followers, King described the NOI as a 'hate group'.

The NOI's image suffered greatly in 1964 from the departure of Malcolm X and of two of Elijah Muhammad's sons, all of whom publicised the rampant materialism and hypocrisy among the movement's leadership and what one of the sons called the 'concocted religious teachings' of Elijah Muhammad.

The assassination of Malcolm X further decreased Elijah Muhammad's popularity amongst some blacks. One newspaper believed 'Black Nationalist Civil War Looms'. Many politically minded members left the NOI for the black power movement. However, the NOI soon began to expand again. Its relations with the black power movement (see page 158) were ambivalent. Both groups favoured separatism, cultural revival and self-help, but Elijah Muhammad's dismissive attitude towards non-Muslim African culture alienated some black power activists, especially when, in 1972, Elijah Muhammad said, 'I am already civilised and I am ready to civilise Africa'. Elijah Muhammad hated what he called 'jungle styles', such as Afro haircuts or colourful African-style garments. Nevertheless, most black power advocates revered Elijah Muhammad and the NOI as forerunners of the new black nationalism.

Malcolm X (right) meeting Martin Luther King in 1964.

(ii) Positive

In the ghettos, NOI membership was possibly as high as 100,000 in 1960, and possibly a quarter of a million by 1969. More conservative estimates say membership never reached more than 25,000. Commitment inevitably ranged from total to token. The NOI newspaper *Muhammad Speaks* had a weekly circulation of 600,000 by the mid-1970s. Blacks who were not members but sympathetic to the NOI bought the paper, finding comfort in its message of separatism and self-defence. The NOI attracted and inspired ghetto-dwellers because of its self-confidence and emphasis on racial pride and economic self-help. Elijah Muhammad and his son Wallace created many businesses, such as restaurants, bakeries and grocery stores. These symbolised black success and gave rare employment opportunities in the ghettos. The NOI expected converts to live a religious life, emphasising extramarital chastity and the rejection of alcohol, tobacco and flamboyant clothing.

When Elijah Muhammad died in 1975, his obituaries in the white press were surprisingly favourable. *Newsweek* described him as 'a kind of prophetic voice in the flowering of black identity and pride' while the *Washington Post* said he inculcated 'pride in thousands of black derelicts, bums, and drug addicts, turning outlaws into useful, productive men and women'. After Elijah Muhammad's death, the NOI split into two groups. One followed more orthodox Islamic teachings, led by Wallace Muhammad. The other retained Elijah Muhammad's teachings, led by Louis Farrakhan, who remains the leader of the NOI into the twenty-first century.

Key question
What were Malcolm X's aims, methods and achievements?

(c) The aims, methods and achievements of Malcolm X

(i) Aims and methods

Malcolm X aimed to improve the lives of black Americans. His main methods were to advertise (through sermons, speeches and writing) and encourage critical thinking on race problems, and, some would say, to encourage racial hatred and violence. Towards the end of his life, Malcolm claimed that he put forward the extremist position in order to make King's demands more acceptable to the white population. In Washington in 1964, Malcolm attended the debate on the civil rights bill, saying, 'I'm here to remind the white man of the alternative to Dr King'.

(ii) Achievements

Thurgood Marshall was particularly critical of the NOI ('run by a bunch of thugs') and of Malcolm ('What did he achieve?'). Black baseball player Jackie Robinson pointed out that while King and others put their lives on the line in places like Birmingham, Malcolm stayed in safer places such as Harlem. Many considered him to be irresponsible and negative. While he criticised civil rights activists such as Martin Luther King, he never established organisations as effective or long lasting as the NAACP or the SCLC. His suggestions that blacks were frequently left with no

Profile: Malcolm X 1925–65

1925 – Born Malcolm Little in Omaha, Nebraska. His father supported Marcus Garvey's separatism and nationalism. Some attributed Malcolm's father's death in 1931 to white supremacists. Malcolm's mother could not cope with Depression-era poverty and was committed to an insane asylum in 1939

1925 – Left school, full of resentment. Despite his intelligence, a teacher told him to forget his ambition to become lawyer – an '[un]realistic goal for a nigger'. Malcolm subsequently described his white foster parents as patronising

1941 – Moved to Boston's black ghetto. Took traditional black employment – shoeshine boy and railroad waiter, but switched to drug dealing, pimping and burgling

1946 – Sentenced to 10 years' imprisonment, where he joined the NOI, which taught him 'The white man is the devil' – 'a perfect echo' of his 'lifelong experience', he said

1952 – Released from prison. Adopted the name Malcolm X; the X replaced the African name that had been taken from his slave ancestors. Quickly rose within the NOI, recruiting thousands of new members in Detroit, Boston, Philadelphia and New York

1954 – Minister of Temple Number 7 in Harlem

1959 – After *The Hate That Hate Produced* (see page 152), attracted national and international attention. Famously said blacks should defend themselves 'by any means necessary'

1963 – Always critical of Martin Luther King's 'non-violence', christened the march on Washington the 'farce on Washington'

– Suspended by Elijah Muhammad for making unpopular remarks about the assassination of President Kennedy

1964 – Announced his split with the NOI, disappointed by Elijah Muhammad's romantic affairs and refusal to allow him to join those risking their lives in Birmingham in 1963. 'We spout our militant revolutionary rhetoric,' said Malcolm, but 'when our own brothers are … killed, we do nothing'

– On pilgrimage to Mecca, he established good relations with non-American Muslims of all colours. He rejected the racist theology of the NOI. Some historians consider Malcolm's development genuine, although it has been contended that his 'sudden realisation' of the 'true' Islam was a ploy to recreate his public image

– Established the Organisation of Afro-American Unity (OAAU), which aimed to unite all people of African descent and to promote political, social and economic independence for blacks. Like Martin Luther King, Malcolm moved towards socialism, propelled by economic inequality in the USA

1965 – Assassinated by NOI gunmen

Malcolm was important as the harbinger of black power of the 1960s and as a role model, inspiration and icon for discontented ghetto blacks. He also played a big part in the alienation of white America.

alternative other than violence seemed negative, irresponsible and unhelpful.

On the other hand, Malcolm rightly drew early attention to the dreadful conditions in America's ghettos, and he brought American blacks more closely in contact with oppressed black people throughout the world. He became a black icon and role model for black youth, particularly through his exploration of his feelings of rejection and his search for his identity in his 1965 *The Autobiography of Malcolm X*. 'Primarily,' said historian Claude Andrew Clegg, 'he made black nationalism in its various forms appealing to the angry generation of black youth who came of age just as American segregation and European colonial empires were collapsing'.

Perhaps most important of all, Malcolm inspired the new generation of black leaders such as the SNCC's Stokely Carmichael and CORE's Floyd McKissick and the black power movement in general. He was the first really prominent advocate of separatism and what subsequently became known as black power during the great civil rights era.

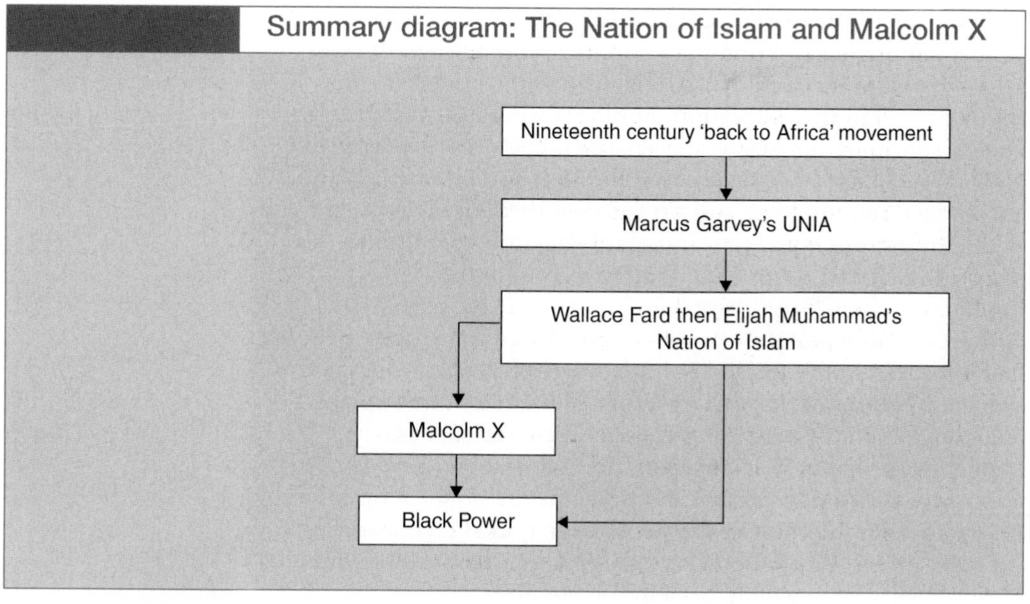

2 | The Rise of Black Power in the 1960s

Key question
Why did black power become a major force in the 1960s?

The origins of black power are controversial, but the influence of Malcolm X, ghetto problems, and the experiences of the SNCC and CORE (many of whose members were Northerners) in Mississippi (see page 136) were all contributory factors.

(a) The ghettos

Key dates
Ghetto riots: 1964–8
Kerner Report: 1968

(i) What was the problem in the ghettos?

Although the great civil rights movement of 1954–65 effected change in the South, it did nothing for the problems of the ghettos in the North, Midwest and West. As King saw in Chicago in 1966 (see page 141), ghetto life was soul destroying. Housing was poor, amenities were few. Those born in the ghetto found it hard to break out of the cycle of poverty. Only 32 per cent of ghetto pupils finished high school, compared to 56 per cent of white children. Ghetto schools did not provide a solid educational foundation for good jobs. Increased automation decreased the number of factory jobs for unskilled workers in the 1950s and 1960s, which led to a disproportionate amount of black unemployment. In the early 1960s, 46 per cent of unemployed Americans were black. Some ghettos, including Chicago's, had 50–70 per cent black youth unemployment.

From 1964 to 1968, America's ghettos erupted into violence each summer. The many city, state and federal government investigations into the violence helped explain the causes of the riots and the consequent rise of black radicalism. The most famous investigation was the National Advisory Commission on Civil Disorders (commonly known as the Kerner Commission) set up by President Johnson in July 1967. Like the other reports, the Kerner Report (published February 1968) emphasised the social and economic deprivation in the ghettos.

(ii) What solutions were suggested?

Leaders of the black community had long differed over how to improve ghetto life. The NAACP had worked through the law courts for integrated education, hoping it would provide better quality education for blacks and enable them to escape from the ghettos (see page 102). A. Philip Randolph and others encouraged unionisation and pressure on the federal government as the way toward equal pay and employment opportunities (see page 74). Martin Luther King had drawn attention to ghetto problems in the Chicago Freedom Movement (see page 141).

However, although the economic situation of some black people had improved in the first half of the twentieth century, the ghettos remained centres of poverty, unemployment, poor housing and schooling, and ever-increasing violence. The violence was frequently fuelled by black reaction to what were perceived as oppressive police policies and indifferent white political machines. Reports such as the Kerner Report recommended increased expenditure on the ghettos, but that seemed an impossible dream. Most whites were unwilling to help the ghettos.

(iii) Why were whites unwilling to help?

American Cold War anti-communism ensured that sympathy for the poor was often equated with sympathy for Communist doctrines of economic equality. Anyone who protested against ghetto poverty was likely to end up reviled and/or marginalised, as was Martin Luther King (see page 145).

Black children from a deprived background might hold back white children and damage their employment prospects. Black entry into a white neighbourhood would cause property prices to plummet. Thus white self-interest ensured poor prospects for better education and housing for ghetto blacks.

White voters did not want to pay extra taxes to end ghetto poverty, particularly after the Vietnam War led to tax rises. Neither the federal government nor state nor city authorities wanted to bear the expensive burden of improving the ghettos.

While whites increasingly perceived blacks as seeking 'handouts', blacks increasingly perceived whites as uninterested and unsympathetic. Not surprisingly then, the black power movement emerged out of the impoverished ghettos. By the late 1960s a new generation of black radicals was demanding improvements in the social and economic situation of America's black ghetto-dwellers.

Key dates

Massive tax rises due to Vietnam War: 1967

Ghetto riots: 1964–8

(iv) The ghetto riots

During the five so-called 'long hot summers' of 1964–8, US ghettos erupted. The first major race riot was in Watts (Los Angeles) in 1965. With 34 deaths, 1000 injuries, 3500 rioters and looters arrested, and over $40 million damage done to largely white-owned businesses, the Watts riots gained national attention. There were 238 other race riots in over 200 US cities from 1964 to 1968. Virtually every large US city outside the South had a race riot, for example, Newark, New Jersey (1967), and Detroit, Michigan (1967). Some had several, for example, Oakland, California (1965 and 1966), Cleveland, Ohio (1966 and 1968), and Chicago, Illinois (1966 and 1968). There was certainly a 'copycat' element. Sixteen cities experienced serious riots in 1964, and 64 in 1968. From 1964 to 1972, ghetto riots led to over 250 deaths (the fatalities mostly resulted from police shooting rioters), 10,000 serious injuries, 60,000 arrests, and a great deal of damage to ghetto businesses.

(b) Ghetto rejection of the civil rights organisations

The civil rights organisations tried to respond to ghetto frustration. Martin Luther King and the SCLC went to Chicago in 1966 and initiated the Poor People's Campaign from 1967. From 1964, CORE established 'Freedom Houses' in the ghettos to provide information and advice on education, employment, health and housing. Whitney Young's National Urban League (NUL) launched a programme to develop economic self-help strategies in the ghettos (1968). In 1971 President Richard Nixon's administration gave the NUL $28 million. However, none of this was enough. Many ghetto blacks felt that organisations such as the NAACP and the SCLC knew little about ghetto life and were of little help in improving matters. Many younger black activists criticised 'de great lawd' Martin Luther King. They rejected his emphasis upon the South, the 'white man's' Christian religion, and non-violence, none of which seemed to be contributing to progress in the ghettos. However, ghetto-dwellers recognised that civil rights activism had led to improvements, and were therefore inspired to be active themselves.

Ghetto blacks perceived the civil rights movement to be unhelpful and ineffective, so they looked to new leaders such as Malcolm X and Stokely Carmichael whose condoning of violence seemed a more appropriate response to white oppression than Martin Luther King's 'love thine enemy'.

(c) The radicalisation of the SNCC and CORE

Key question
How and why did SNCC and CORE change in the late 1960s?

By 1966, SNCC members were impatient with what they considered to be the slow progress of blacks toward equality. They were also disillusioned by the lack of federal protection in the Mississippi Freedom Summer (see page 136) and by the refusal of the Democratic Party to seat the MFDP delegates at Atlantic City (see page 183). They turned to a more militant leader: John Lewis was replaced by Stokely Carmichael. Similarly, when James Farmer resigned leadership of CORE in December 1965, the radical Floyd McKissick was elected in his place. The divisions between the increasingly radical SNCC and CORE and the SCLC and NAACP were publicly demonstrated in the Meredith 'March against Fear' in 1966 (see pages 144–5).

Key date
CORE and SNCC advocated black power: 1966

In July 1966, the annual CORE convention in Baltimore, Maryland, endorsed 'black power', and declared non-violence inappropriate if black people needed to defend themselves. The 1967 annual CORE convention excised the word 'multiracial' from CORE's constitution. By summer 1968, whites were excluded from CORE's membership. McKissick resigned in September 1968, and was replaced by a more militant figure. Similarly, in December 1966, the SNCC voted to expel whites. In *Black Power: The Politics of Liberation* (1967), Carmichael and Charles Hamilton urged American blacks to ally with other black victims of white colonialist oppression in developing countries. In May 1967, Carmichael was replaced by Henry 'Rap' Brown, who advocated armed self-defence. On 25 July 1967, Rap Brown addressed a black audience in Cambridge, Maryland. He urged them to take over white-owned stores in the ghettos, using violence if necessary. Soon afterwards, there was a race riot in Cambridge. At a rally in Oakland, California, in February 1968, the SNCC effectively emerged with the Black Panthers, the most radical of all black organisations.

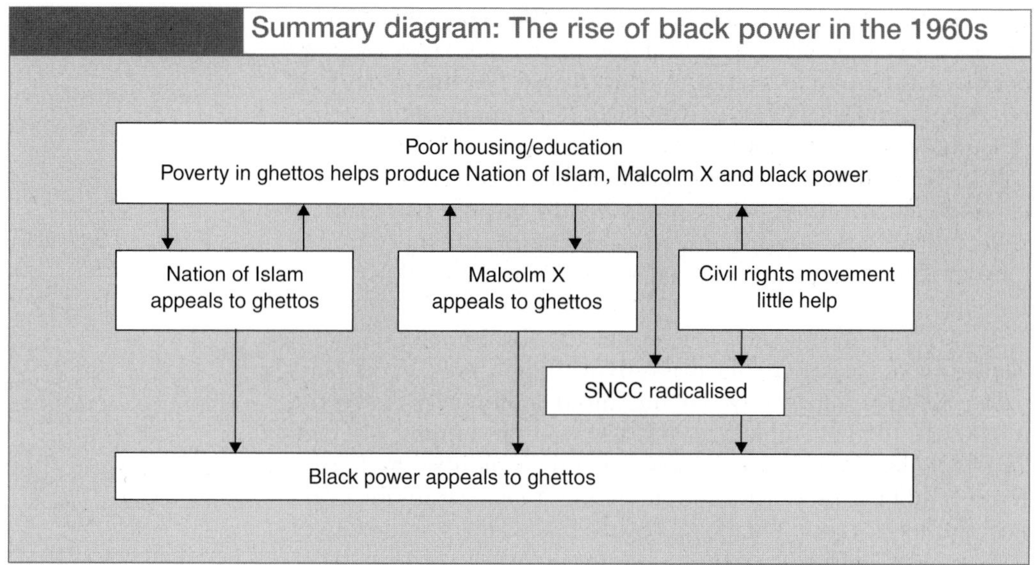

Key question
What was 'black power'?

Key term
Black power
A controversial term, with different meanings for different people, for example, black pride, black economic self-sufficiency, black violence, black separatism, black nationalism, black political power, black working class revolution, black domination.

3 | Black Power and the Black Panthers

(a) Black power

The term '**black power**' first came to prominence during the Meredith March (see pages 144–5), when the SNCC chairman, Stokely Carmichael, cried 'black power' in Greenwood, Mississippi. What did it mean? It meant different things to different people.

For some black people, black power meant black supremacy or revolution. In 1968, Elijah Muhammad said, 'Black power means the black people will rule the white people on earth as the white people have ruled the black people for the past six thousand years'. During 1968–9, black car workers at the Chrysler, Ford and General Motors plants in Detroit, Michigan, thought black power meant a black working class revolution. They united in a black power union, the League of Revolutionary Workers.

The older generation of civil rights leaders were hostile. Roy Wilkins of the NAACP felt black power supporters were racist and no better than Hitler or the Ku Klux Klan. Martin Luther King said, 'When you put *black* and *power* together, it sounds like you are trying to say black domination'. He called for 'striped power – black and white together'! King called black power 'a slogan without a programme'. When people persisted in using the phrase, King tried to give it more positive connotations:

> The Negro is in dire need of a sense of dignity and a sense of pride, and I think black power is an attempt to develop pride. And there is no doubt about the need for power – he can't get into the mainstream of society without it … black power means instilling within the Negro a sense of belonging and appreciation of heritage, a racial pride … We must never be ashamed of being black.

The SNCC's Floyd McKissick also attempted a positive definition: 'black power is not hatred'. It 'did not mean black supremacy, did not mean exclusion of whites from the Negro revolution, and did not mean advocacy of violence and riots', but 'political power, economic power, and a new self-image for Negroes'.

The *New York Times* probably got it right when it said, 'Nobody knows what the phrase "black power" really means'. Cleveland Sellers (SNCC) believed 'There was a deliberate attempt to make it [black power] ambiguous ... [so that] it meant everything to everybody'.

Black power meant economic power to some people. Conservative black Republican, Nathan Wright, proposed a black power capitalist movement. He organised conferences in Newark in 1967 and Philadelphia in 1968, and won the support of SCLC and NUL. In 1968, Republican presidential candidate Richard Nixon said black power meant, 'more black ownership, for from this can flow the rest – black pride, black jobs, black opportunity and yes, black power'.

Clearly black power was amorphous and ever-changing. One of the few areas of unanimity was the emphasis on black pride and black culture. In a highly popular book, which became an equally popular television series, black author Alex Haley went back to his African *Roots*. Blacks frequently adopted 'Afro' hairstyles and African garb. Black college students successfully agitated for the introduction of black studies programmes.

Huey Newton, founder of the Black Panthers in his San Francisco, California headquarters in 1967. Behind him is the iconic photo in which he advertised his African ancestry and weapons.

Key date

Black Panthers established in California: 1966

(b) The Black Panthers

(i) Establishment

In 1966 the SNCC had helped establish an all-black political party, the Lowndes County Freedom Organisation, in Alabama. That party's logo, the Black Panther, became more famous when used by the 'Black Panther Party for Self-defence', established in Oakland, California, in October 1966 by 24-year-old Huey Newton and 30-year-old Bobby Seale. Newton explained that he chose the Panther as a symbol because the panther 'never attacks. But if anyone attacks him or backs him into a corner the panther comes up to wipe the aggressor or that attacker out.' The Black Panthers adopted a predominantly black paramilitary uniform, with berets and leather jackets.

Key question

What were the aims and achievements of the Black Panthers?

(ii) Aims

Newton and Seale were greatly influenced by Malcolm X and by Communist revolutionaries such as Che Guevara and Mao Zedong. From 1969 to 1970, the Black Panthers aimed to become involved in the world-wide non-white working class struggle. They forged links with liberation movements in Africa, Asia and South America, and aligned themselves with other radical groups in the USA, especially the Mexican 'Brown Berets' and Puerto Rican and Chinese American radicals. The Black Panthers' manifesto was radical and nationalistic. Their demands/aims were very similar to those of Garvey and Elijah Muhammad and included:

- Payment of reparations [compensation] to black Americans by the federal government as compensation for slavery. (This demand is still being made by some black Americans.)
- Freedom for incarcerated blacks, who should be jailed only if tried by a black jury.
- Exemption of blacks from military service.
- A United Nations-supervised referendum of black Americans 'for the purpose of determining the will of black people as to their national destiny'.
- Less police brutality.
- Improvements in ghetto living conditions.

(iii) Achievements

Key term

Chapters
Branches of an organisation.

The Black Panthers never boasted more than 5000 members. Their 30 **chapters** were mostly in urban centres on the West coast, such as Oakland, and major Northern cities such as New York, Boston and Chicago. The Black Panthers won a great deal of respect in the ghettos, especially for their emphasis on self-help. The Black Panthers set up ghetto clinics to advise on health, welfare and legal rights. In 1970 the Southern California chapter of the Free Breakfast programme served up over 1700 meals weekly to the ghetto poor.

Citing the 2nd Amendment to the US constitution (which said citizens had the right to carry arms), armed Black Panthers followed police cars in the ghettos, in order to expose police brutality. This led to some violent shoot-outs. In May 1967 Black

Panthers surrounded and entered the California State Capital Building in Sacramento, accusing the legislature of considering repressive legislation. Some plotted to blow up major department stores in New York City, according to one FBI infiltrator.

(c) Black Panther leadership

The Black Panthers had a 'shadow government', including Newton as Minister of Defence, Seale as Central Committee Chairman, and Eldridge Cleaver as Minister of Information. After the Black Panthers allied with SNCC in February 1968, Stokely Carmichael became Prime Minister, James Forman of SNCC became Minister of Foreign Affairs, and Rap Brown was Minister of Justice, although the last three quickly resigned. In July 1969 the SNCC split from the Black Panthers because of personality clashes and ideological tension between the black radical leaders. SNCC advocated separatism and nationalism, while the Black Panthers advocated a multiracial working class struggle against oppression.

(d) The end of the Black Panthers

Key date

Black Panthers destroyed by white authorities: 1967–9

The Black Panthers routinely engaged in petty crime, sought confrontation with, and advocated the killing of, the police. Not surprisingly, the Black Panthers suffered from police attention, some would say persecution. Many Black Panthers had prison records from their pre-Panther days. Eldridge Cleaver, ranked 'No. 3' in the Black Panther hierarchy, had been released from prison in 1966, having served a sentence as a serial rapist. He justified his crimes as a righteous rebellion against 'white man's law', in the form of 'defiling his women'. The Black Panthers were targeted and destroyed by the police and FBI from 1967 to 1969. By 1970, most of the Black Panther leadership was killed, imprisoned, or in enforced exile like Eldridge Cleaver. A 1970 poll revealed 64 per cent of blacks took pride in the Black Panthers, although Newton's biographer Hugh Pearson claimed the Panthers were 'little more than a temporary media phenomenon'.

What happened to the Black Panther leadership?

- Huey Newton was shot in 1989 in an Oakland drug dispute.
- Eldridge Cleaver fled to Cuba and then Algiers. He returned to California, served as a Christian minister for prisoners, and was an unsuccessful Republican Senate candidate in 1986. He was recently charged with burglary.
- Angela Davis, imprisoned for radical activities but acquitted, is now a leading American academic, as is Kathleen Cleaver.
- Bobby Seale wrote two autobiographies and a best-selling cookbook, *Barbecu'n with Bobby*. After a spell as a stand-up comedian and a cameo appearance in the Malcolm X movie, he concentrated on his university lectureship.

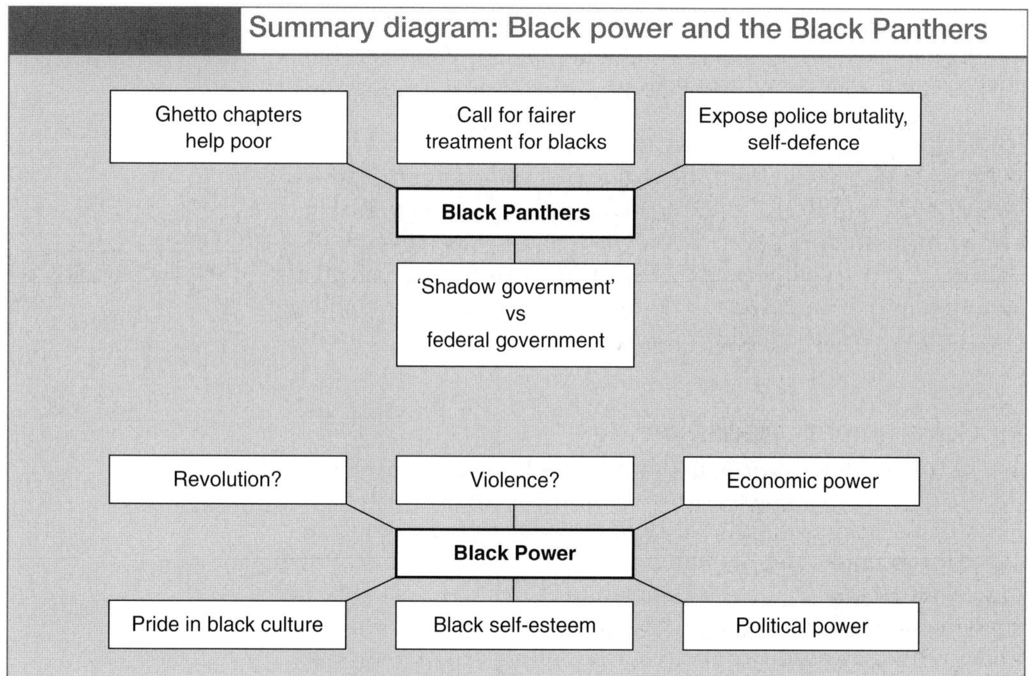

Key question
Why was black power unfashionable by the early 1970s?

4 | Why did Black Power Decline?

Black power 'peaked' in 1970, but this was followed by a swift decline. Why?

(a) Poor definition and organisation

The black power movement was always relatively ill-defined and consequently poorly organised. Initially, the lack of definition worked to the movement's advantage, ensuring a considerable amount of support. However, supporters had differing ideas as to what they meant by and wanted with black power. Therefore, as the years passed, the divisions became pronounced and open. For example, from 1967, SNCC was increasingly divided, with black separatists opposed to social revolutionaries who favoured multiracial co-operation in the struggle against poverty and inequality.

(b) Unrealistic aims

While black power was an attractive slogan to discontented blacks, the movement never really produced a persuasive and effective blueprint for change. The Black Panthers' talk of violence brought down the effective wrath of the federal government upon their heads. Similarly, Black Panther talk of socialism was ill suited to the USA with its capitalist culture. Talk of a separate black nation within the USA was equally unrealistic.

Key date
Rise of feminism: late 1960s

(c) Sexism

Feminism became very popular in the late 1960s, and appealed to many black women. Male black power advocates were often sexist.

When female supporters of black power found their black power activities limited because of their gender, they frequently concentrated upon feminism instead.

(d) Finance and the collapse of the SNCC and CORE

White liberals had financed the major civil rights organisations. When SNCC and CORE became more militant and expelled whites, their funding suffered. By 1970, SNCC was reduced to only three active chapters (New York City, Atlanta and Cincinnati) and no full-time employees. The New York City chapter could not even afford a telephone. In December 1973, the SNCC ceased to exist.

Key date
Demise of the SNCC: 1973

(e) Government opposition

The worst problem for the black power movement was probably the Nixon administration's sustained and effective pursuit of black power leaders. Even civil rights activists were targeted. In 1972, for example, the 'Wilmington Ten' (all civil rights activists) were arrested and charged with arson in North Carolina. The jury contained three known Ku Klux Klan members and the FBI bribed witnesses hostile to the ten, who were given extensive jail sentences.

Summary diagram: Why did black power decline?

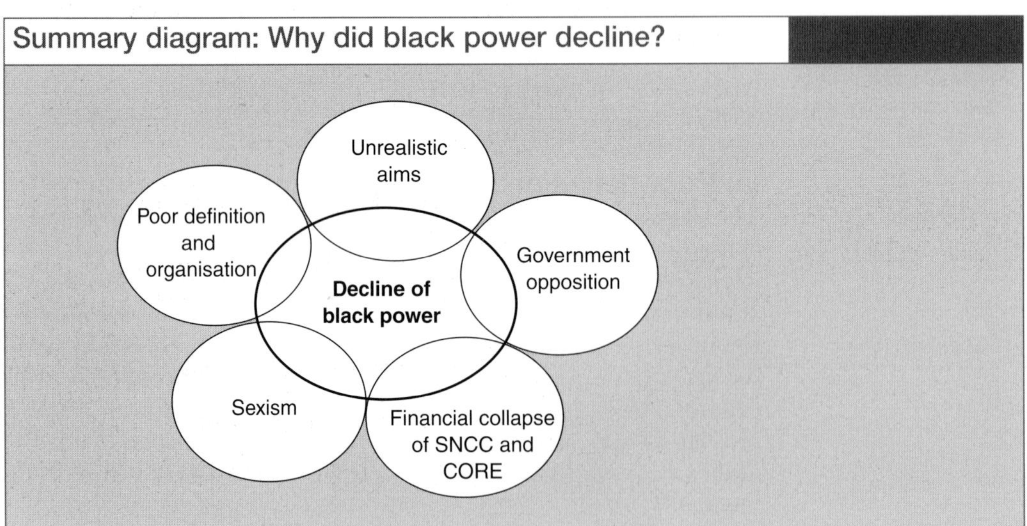

5 | What Had the Black Power Movement Achieved?

Key question
Was the black power movement a success or failure?

The achievements of the black power movement are as controversial as the movement itself.

(a) Positive achievements

- Talk of and/or participation in the black power movement raised the morale of many black Americans. Perhaps the main legacy with regard to black pride was the establishment of courses on black history and culture in American educational institutions.

- Groups such as the Black Panthers gave useful practical help to ghetto-dwellers.
- It could be said that black power activists, like civil rights activists, kept the ghetto problems on the political agenda.

(b) Negative achievements

- Black power contributed to the demise of what had been an effective civil rights movement. The older generation of civil rights leaders lost support and momentum. Their replacements failed to match their achievements. Under the leadership of its founder, James Farmer, CORE had played a vital role in non-violent protest such as sit-ins and freedom rides. Those protests contributed to desegregation in the South. After the radical Floyd McKissick replaced Farmer in 1965, CORE achieved little until, under McKissick's even more radical successor, it collapsed. The SNCC followed a similar line of development. (It could be argued that the civil rights movement would have lost momentum and effectiveness without the development and rivalry of black power. Once successes had been achieved in the South, the Northern ghetto problem proved insoluble.)
- Black power adherents failed to find an answer to the ghetto problem.
- Ghetto rioters and armed Black Panthers helped decrease the white sympathy that had been a key to progress for the non-violent civil rights activists.

Summary diagram: What had the black power movement achieved?

✓ Raised black morale
✓ Some practical help in ghettos
✓ Drew attention to ghetto problems

× Ghettos remained the same
× Alienated whites
× Damaged civil rights movement

6 | Key Debates

From the start of their enslavement in colonial America, some black Americans have sought self-determination and sovereignty, but this separatist and nationalist movement has not captured historians' interest and imagination in the manner of the civil rights movement.

Joseph Peniel (2001) tried to explain why scholars pay little attention to black power:

- American politics became increasingly conservative after the early 1970s.

- Scholars disliked the 'evil twin' that helped to wreck the civil rights movement.
- There is little archive material.
- Mainstream scholars do not take the topic seriously.

UNIA

Historians' interpretation of the success or failure of Marcus Garvey and UNIA (see page 67) depend on how the historian views black nationalism. Liberal, integrationist black historian John Hope Franklin (1988) acknowledged UNIA's mass appeal, but nevertheless declared it an unrealistic movement, doomed to fail. However, historians such as Theodore Vincent (1972), stressed UNIA's influence on the civil rights movement and black power.

Malcolm X

In a balanced biography of Elijah Muhammad, Claude Andrew Clegg (1997) recognised his positive and negative achievements and characteristics. Bruce Perry's (liberal) biography of Malcolm X, attributed Malcolm's struggles to an unhappy home life and psychological damage, whereas nationalist scholars see Malcolm within the long tradition of black nationalism within the USA. Historians' backgrounds similarly affect their interpretations of Malcolm's philosophical changes in his final year. The genuine nature and extent of his embrace of 'toleration' are much debated. One thing scholars agree on, is the great and lasting impact of Malcolm.

Black power

In 1979, feminist Michelle Wallace ignited debate by criticising the sexist black power leadership. The historian Gerald Horne (1997) criticised black power for promoting a black male macho culture that was anti-intellectual, anti-female, violent, and so militantly anti-white that it isolated blacks and made them even more vulnerable to repression and exploitation. Clayborne Carson claimed (1996) that while failing to give greater power to black people, black power militancy actually led to a decline in the ability of African Americans to affect the course of American politics. The black power movement promised more than the civil rights movement but delivered less. William Van Deburg (1992) said that black power's greatest contribution to the black community was intellectual and cultural, in university courses and in increased black self-esteem and identity.

Some key books in the debate

Clayborne Carson, 'Rethinking African-American political thought in the post-revolutionary era' in *The Making of Martin Luther King and the Civil Rights Movement*, eds Anthony Badger and Brian Ward (1996).

Claude Andrew Clegg, *An Original Man: The Life and Times of Elijah Muhammad* (New York, 1997).

John Hope Franklin and Alfred Moss, *From Slavery to Freedom: A History of Negro Americans* (New York, 1988).

Gerald Horne, *Fire This Time: The Watts Uprising and the 1960s* (New York, 1988).
Joseph Peniel, *Black Liberation Without Apology: Reconceptualising the Black Power Movement* (Black Scholar, 2001).
Bruce Perry, *Malcolm: The Life and Legacy of a Man who Changed Black America* (New York 1991).
William van Deburg, *New Day in Babylon: The Black Power Movement and American Culture, 1965–75* (Chicago, 1992).
Theodore Vincent, *Black Power and the Garvey Movement* (San Francisco, 1972).

Study Guide: AS Questions

In the style of Edexcel

1. In what ways did Martin Luther King and Malcolm X differ as black American leaders? (20 marks)
2. Why did more radical black movements emerge in the late 1960s? (40 marks)

Exam tips

The cross-references are intended to take you to some of the material that will help you to answer the questions.

1. Selection is a key skill when dealing with these shorter questions. Choose what you consider to be the three main differences – perhaps their different aims (integration versus separation) (pages 135, 155), methods (non-violence versus violence) (pages 123, 156) and achievements (King obtained vital white help, including legislation, while Malcolm terrified whites) (pages 135, 152).
2. This is a straightforward 'causes' question, for which you can get higher marks with a good range of reasons, some of which should be covered in depth. Take care when dealing with any question on the 1960s to check whether all aspects of the era need to be covered – in this case, you need to look at:
   - the ghetto problems (page 158)
   - the success of the civil rights movement in the South but its apparent failure with regard to the Northern ghettos (page 160)
   - the failures of the federal government with regard to the ghettos, which is covered in the next chapter (page 187).

   For higher marks you should look at the way the causes interrelate, for example, the Watts riots occurred within days of the passage of the Voting Rights Act – a clear indication of the relationship between the success of the civil rights movement in the South and the ghetto-dwellers' 'what about us?' feeling.

8 The 1960s – III: Kennedy, Johnson and the 'Black Problem'

POINTS TO CONSIDER

Many Americans idealise President Kennedy and demonise President Johnson, primarily because of Kennedy's untimely death and because of riots in the ghettos and anti-Vietnam War protests under Johnson. Some Kennedy supporters contend that while Kennedy 'really cared' about blacks, Johnson was only helpful for political advantage. This chapter looks at:

- How and why Presidents Kennedy and Johnson helped blacks
- Why they could/would not do more

It does this through the following sections:

- President Kennedy 1961–3
- Lyndon Johnson before the presidency
- President Johnson 1963–9

Key dates

1961	Kennedy became president Freedom Rides began
1962	James Meredith entered University of Mississippi
1963	Kennedy introduced civil rights bill Alabama began university integration Birmingham crisis March on Washington Johnson became president
1964	Civil Rights Act
1965	Education Acts Voting Rights Act
1965–72	Vietnam War
1966	Unsuccessful housing bill

Key question
What role did race play in the 1960 presidential election?

1 | President Kennedy (1961–3)

(a) Kennedy before the presidency

When Kennedy was 12 years old, his wealthy Boston Irish family moved to New York to escape snubbing by upper class Bostonians of Anglo-Saxon ancestry. The Kennedys' experience of discrimination did not make them embrace blacks as brothers. One friend 'never saw a Negro on level social terms with the Kennedys'. Future president John's brother Robert admitted that before 1961, 'I didn't lose much sleep about Negroes, I didn't think about them much, I didn't know about all the injustice.'

As a senator, John Kennedy considered it politically advantageous to oppose Eisenhower's civil rights bill. However, as civil rights became a more prominent national issue, Kennedy's interest increased proportionately. Although he employed a black secretary and two black attorneys as advisers, some blacks regarded him with suspicion and hostility.

In his 1960 presidential election campaign speeches, John Kennedy promised to help blacks if elected and said racism was immoral and damaged America's international image. Eisenhower believed that Kennedy's much-publicised sympathetic phone call to Coretta King, about her imprisoned husband, gained Kennedy black votes that helped him win the election. Historians disagree over whether the phone call was politically motivated or a gesture of spontaneous decency.

Key date
John Kennedy became president: January 1961

Key question
What was the racial situation at Kennedy's accession?

(b) The situation at Kennedy's accession (1961)

The new president inherited a nation with great inequalities. Most Southern blacks lacked the vote and suffered segregated housing, schools, transport and other public facilities. The great majority of Southern politicians were committed to the status quo. Some white racists used violence to prevent change. Other whites were disinclined to stop them. Southern blacks were politically, legally, economically and socially inferior. Northern blacks were in ghettos, where they had to attend inferior ghetto schools. Banks, realtors and property owners excluded them from better housing because property values plummeted when blacks moved into an area. Whites simply did not want to live alongside blacks. The 1960 Civil Rights Commission report adjudged 57 per cent of black housing substandard. Black life expectancy was seven years less than that for whites. The black infant mortality rate was twice that for whites.

(c) Why was Kennedy slow to help blacks?

There were several ways in which Kennedy could help blacks. He could try to get Congress to pass legislation, use his executive authority, and make symbolic appointments and gestures. However, despite his campaign assurances, he did not move quickly on civil rights legislation, for several reasons. He had no great popular mandate for action. His had been a narrow electoral victory. Opinion polls showed most US voters believed integration should evolve gradually, rather than be enforced by federal action. One poll showed civil rights at the bottom of the list of voter concerns. Civil rights legislation would be unpopular with most voters, and with Congress, which contained many influential Southern Democrats. Finally, Kennedy planned legislation for better health care and wages for the poor. If he pushed civil rights and alienated Southern congressmen, his whole legislative programme might suffer. If Kennedy failed to promote civil rights, black Americans would at least benefit from other legislation. Kennedy could also help in other ways.

(d) How Kennedy helped blacks

Key question
How did Kennedy help blacks?

(i) Appointments

Kennedy was shocked to learn how few blacks were employed in important positions by the federal government: of the FBI's 13,649 employees, only 48 (mostly chauffeurs) were black. Roy Wilkins noted that Kennedy put so much pressure on the civil service to employ blacks, 'that everyone was scrambling around trying to find themselves a Negro in order to keep the president off his neck'. No previous president made so many black appointments to the federal bureaucracy. Kennedy appointed 40 blacks to top posts, such as associate White House press secretary. He chose five black federal judges, including Thurgood Marshall. On the other hand, 20 per cent of his Deep South judicial appointments were segregationists, one of whom had referred to black litigants as 'niggers' and 'chimpanzees', and had unlawfully obstructed black voting registration drives in Mississippi. Why did Kennedy appoint segregationists? It was difficult to do otherwise down South. Kennedy had to balance morality and practicality. He had no desire to alienate Southern white voters.

(ii) Justice Department

The Justice Department had responsibility for civil rights. The president appointed his brother Robert as **Attorney General**. Believing that a legalistic approach would be the least emotive and most productive way forward, the Kennedy Justice Department brought 57 suits against illegal violations of black voting rights in the South, compared to six under Eisenhower. When Attorney General Kennedy threatened Louisiana officials with contempt of court sentences for denying funds to newly desegregated schools in New Orleans, it hastened desegregation in New Orleans, Atlanta and Memphis. On the other hand, the Kennedy Justice Department remained cautious. It backed down on voting rights in Mississippi when influential Democratic senators protested in 1963.

Key term
Attorney General Head of the Justice Department in the federal government.

(iii) Symbolic gestures

Symbolic gestures were the easiest and most politically painless way for President Kennedy to give the impression that he was committed to racial equality. He invited more blacks to the White House than any previous president. Although he rejected their requests for legislation, Wilkins said 'everyone went out of there absolutely charmed by the manner in which they had been turned down'. Kennedy ostentatiously resigned from an exclusive club that refused to admit blacks. The Washington Redskins was the last great football club to refuse to hire blacks. When Kennedy said the team could no longer use its federally supported stadium, the Redskins signed three black players.

(iv) Equal Employment Opportunity Commission

Blacks found the Kennedy administration disappointing on more substantial issues, such as equal opportunities in employment. Although Kennedy refused to endorse affirmative action, he used his executive powers to create the Equal Employment Opportunity Commission (EEOC). It aimed to ensure equal employment opportunities for federal employees and in companies that had contracts with the government. EEOC encouraged companies to hire more blacks. It had a few triumphs, for example, the integration and promotion of blacks at the Lockheed aircraft plant in Georgia. However, EEOC failed to bring about a great increase in black employment by federal agencies or companies doing business with the federal government. It exaggerated its successes, boasting a rise from one to two black employees as a 100 per cent increase in black employment! The Kennedys blamed EEOC chairman Vice-President Lyndon Johnson for the failures, but it was a difficult task. Employers frequently and rightly complained they were simply complying with demands from their workers for segregated facilities.

Key question
How and why did Kennedy react to the civil rights movement?

(e) Reacting to civil rights activists

President Kennedy had not planned extensive use of executive authority to help blacks. However, civil rights activists forced his hand, beginning with the Freedom Rides in 1961 (see pages 130–1).

Key date
Freedom Rides began: 1961

(i) The Freedom Rides (1961)

White racist responses to the Freedom Riders gained national attention, especially when a white mob poured and then lit kerosene on a black Freedom Rider in Montgomery. Kennedy was reluctant to intervene. He accused the Freedom Riders of lacking patriotism because they exposed US domestic problems during the Cold War. Attorney General Robert Kennedy wanted to protect the constitutional rights of the activists, but did not want to alienate Southern Democrats or the 63 per cent of Americans who, opinion polls indicated, opposed the Freedom Rides. When Robert Kennedy's federal marshals could not control a white mob bombing a meeting at Ralph Abernathy's church, Kennedy pressured Alabama's governor to call out the National Guard and state troopers.

The Freedom Riders' persistent pressure forced Robert Kennedy to get an Interstate Commerce Commission ruling supporting the Supreme Court rulings (1946, 1960) that terminals and interstate bus seating should be integrated. Although supposedly achieved by autumn 1961, historian

W.T.M. Riches records seeing *de facto* segregation in the Selma, Alabama, bus station as late as 1966. While black activists had to force the administration into action, it had done quite well.

(ii) Southern black voter registration (1961)

Later in 1961, SNCC worked on Southern black voter registration in Mississippi (see page 136). Robert Kennedy condemned white attacks on would-be voters, but said the national government could not interfere with local law enforcement unless there was a total breakdown of law and order:

> Mississippi is going to work itself out … Maybe it's going to take a decade and maybe a lot of people are going to be killed in the meantime … But in the long run I think it's for the health of the country and the stability of the system.

Key dates

SNCC began work in Mississippi: 1961

James Meredith entered University of Mississippi: 1962

Alabama began university integration: 1963

Why were the Kennedys so reluctant to interfere with Southern justice? The president felt the SNCC 'sons of bitches' were unnecessarily provocative: 'SNCC has got an investment in violence'. The Justice Department lacked sufficient staff, and the Kennedys feared using force against the South's white racists, most of whom voted Democrat. Kennedy inaction alienated blacks, and increased black militancy.

(iii) James Meredith and the University of Mississippi (1962)

Key question
To what extent did Kennedy help university integration?

Twenty-eight-year-old James Meredith, grandson of a slave and son of a sharecropper, had served in the US Air Force for a decade. He wanted a university education. His local black college had poorly qualified teachers so Meredith applied for the white University of Mississippi, which did not want him. When Meredith got legal aid from the NAACP and a Supreme Court decision in his favour, Robert Kennedy had to send 500 marshals to help him enrol. The ill-equipped marshals clashed with a racist mob. Two people were shot and one-third of the marshals were injured. President Kennedy sent the Mississippi National Guard and US Army regulars to the area. Meredith finally enrolled, inspiring other blacks to do likewise. Historians disagree over whether the administration handled the crisis well. They 'had been extremely lucky that none of the marshals had been killed, and that Meredith had not been lynched', according to historian Hugh Brogan.

(iv) University integration in Alabama, June 1963

Alabama was the last state to begin university integration. Kennedy sent in federal troops, marshals and the federalised Alabama National Guard. Governor George Wallace made a gesture of protest (proving his racist credentials to white voters), then gave in. To Martin Luther King's delight, President Kennedy publicly declared black inequality immoral, appealing to the Bible and the US Constitution. Kennedy asked how many whites would be content with the 'counsels of patience and delay' given to blacks.

As usual, Kennedy had been prodded into action. However, as so often, his administration contributed to a satisfactory solution.

Key dates
Birmingham crisis: 1963
March on Washington: 1963

(v) Birmingham (1963)

When Bull Connor turned his hoses on protesters in Birmingham (see page 133), President Kennedy said the television pictures sickened him and that he could 'well understand' black exasperation. Robert Kennedy sent in Justice Department representatives whom Andrew Young later acknowledged to have done a 'tremendous' job in bringing both sides together in preparation for changes to segregation. Birmingham's public facilities were soon desegregated and black employment prospects improved. The Kennedy administration had helped greatly, albeit reluctantly at first.

(vi) The March on Washington (1963)

In summer 1963 Kennedy opposed the proposed March on Washington. He considered it a rebuke for his slowness over civil rights. He feared it would antagonise Congress and jeopardise his civil rights bill. 'I don't want to give any of them a chance to say, "Yes, I'm for the bill, but I'm damned if I'll vote for it at the point of a gun"'. However, Kennedy eventually endorsed the March, and worked hard to make it interracial, peaceful and supportive of the bill. Critics consequently charged the administration with taking over the March. Malcolm X christened it 'The Farce on Washington'. Some historians claim Kennedy aides were ready to 'pull the plug' on the public address system if hostile words were spoken against the administration. That proved unnecessary. The March was a great success and facilitated the passage of the civil rights bill.

There is no doubt that black activism pushed Kennedy further and faster than he had intended. The civil rights movement was more important than the president was in initiating change.

Key question
How much legislative aid did Kennedy give blacks?

(f) Legislation

(i) Housing

Although Kennedy promised in his presidential election campaign that discrimination in housing could be ended at a 'stroke of the presidential pen', he did nothing. Disappointed blacks inundated the White House with pens to jog his memory, but Kennedy thought that if he pushed legislation on this issue, Congress would reject other important legislation. Also, with the congressional elections of 1962 looming, Northern Democratic Congressmen did not want their white voters upset by the thought of living next door to blacks. After those elections, Kennedy introduced a half-hearted measure that only applied to future federal housing. It was always difficult to obtain congressional co-operation: the 1962 administration literacy bill (enabling blacks with a sixth-grade education to vote) failed because of a Southern filibuster.

(ii) Civil rights bill

Kennedy introduced civil rights bill: 1963

Key date

Kennedy took a long time to ask Congress for a major civil rights law, maintaining that a Southern filibuster would surely overcome it. Kennedy finally proposed a civil rights bill, disappointed that businessmen and local authorities were slow to respond to his pleas to employ blacks and desegregate public facilities. Also, he was influenced by increasing Southern violence, particularly in Birmingham, and by criticism from civil rights activists. He was no doubt aware that black votes were useful, but there were probably elements of sympathy and idealism. He had suffered bigoted comments about his religion and ethnicity in the presidential election campaign. He was impressed by his friend J.K. Galbraith's 1958 book *The Affluent Society*, which drew attention to the great disparity in wealth and opportunity in the USA.

Kennedy knew it would be hard to get congressional co-operation. 'A good many programmes I care about may go down the drain as a result of this – we may all go down the drain'. So, his proposed bill of February 1963 was a moderate attempt to guarantee desegregation in public places, to help blacks to use their vote, and to help black workers.

The bill got stuck in Congress, partly because liberal 'sons of bitches' (Robert Kennedy) tried to push it too far for Republicans. It is difficult to decide whether the bill became an act in the next administration because of sadness over Kennedy's assassination, because of Kennedy's efforts with congressmen, or because of President Johnson (see page 182).

(g) President Kennedy and civil rights: conclusion

Key question
Had Kennedy helped civil rights?

Kennedy's record on civil rights was mixed. Kennedy made several gestures that publicised his commitment to racial equality at little or no cost, but combined appointments such as Thurgood Marshall with appointments of segregationist judges. Although his EEOC achieved little, its existence at least reminded employers of their obligations.

Black activists pushed the reluctant administration into unprecedented intervention in Southern states. Kennedy used federal force and injunctions to get interstate buses and terminals and universities desegregated (none of which directly affected the majority of Southerners). However, civil rights activists felt that Kennedy was a great disappointment. Sometimes, as with SNCC voter registration efforts, the administration remained steadfastly unhelpful.

Kennedy was slow in promoting change, because it was politically risky. A September 1963 poll showed 89 per cent of blacks approved of his presidency, but 70 per cent of Southern whites felt he was moving too quickly on integration. A total of 50 per cent of Americans agreed with that. Kennedy's approval rating in the South dropped from 60 per cent in March 1963, to 44 per cent in September 1963. He had probably gone as far as he could go. Southern whites were very resentful of Kennedy's changes. There was still much violence in the South, as in the church bombing that killed four children in Birmingham, Alabama (1963). A white backlash against the civil rights movement had begun in the North. In Congress, Southerners were increasingly uncooperative and the civil rights bill had stalled.

However, Kennedy had paved the way for the great 1964 Civil Rights Act and had morally committed the presidency to reform. This damaged his Democratic Party in the South, as he knew it would. It takes considerable courage for a politician to compromise his own party and his own presidential re-election prospects. Kennedy and his successor Johnson both risked this and could perhaps both be called genuine statesmen rather than mere politicians in their commitment to black equality.

Summary diagram: President Kennedy and civil rights

	◀ Unhelpful								Helpful ▶	
	1	2	3	4	5	6	7	8	9	10
Before president			✓							
1960 election						✓				
Speed of helping		✓								
Appointments						✓				
Justice Department					✓					
Symbolic gestures										✓
Freedom Rides					✓					
Voter registration	✓									
University integration						✓				
Birmingham					✓					
Legislation				✓						

Key question
Was Johnson an idealist or an unprincipled politician?

2 | Lyndon Johnson Before the Presidency

> I'll tell you what's at the bottom of it. If you can convince the lowest white man that he's better than the best colored man, he won't notice you picking his pocket. Hell, give him somebody to look down on, and he'll empty his pockets for you. (Lyndon Johnson)

(a) Johnson's early career

Some people believe that Johnson was nothing more than an unprincipled politician. However, he claimed to be an idealist who wanted to make the USA a better and fairer place for its inhabitants.

Key question
Did Johnson help blacks during the New Deal?

(b) Teacher and New Dealer

Johnson began helping minorities in 1928, teaching in a segregated school in what he described as 'one of the crummiest little towns in Texas'. Johnson recalled his 28 Mexican American pupils as 'mired in the slums', 'lashed by prejudice', 'buried half-alive in illiteracy'. He believed that education would be their escape route. He bribed, bullied, cajoled and encouraged his pupils. They adored him. What motivated Johnson? Idealism ran in his family. His father had stood up to the Klan in the Texas state legislature. Johnson was motivated by memories of his own childhood poverty and by his belief that giving help to minorities would bring spiritual and economic benefit to all Americans, particularly his beloved South. He was ambitious, but also caring and compassionate. 'I wanted power to give things to people … especially the poor and the blacks.'

During the Depression (see page 71) Johnson worked for a New Deal agency. Johnson said he would be 'run out of Texas' if he accepted Washington's order to have a black leader as a close adviser. He explained that 'long established' and 'deep rooted' racial customs 'cannot be upset overnight'. Johnson worked hard to alleviate black unemployment (nearly 50 per cent in 1932). Although he privately referred to blacks as 'niggers', he sometimes slept at black colleges to see how the New Deal was working, and blacks thought him unusually helpful. However, Johnson did little for Hispanics. There was no political pressure from Washington to help them (many Texas Mexicans were not US citizens). Also, Johnson believed that because their landlords helped them, Mexicans were better equipped to survive the Depression than blacks.

Key dates

Johnson working for New Deal Agency: 1930s

Johnson became a congressman: 1940s

(c) Congressman Johnson

Key question
Did Johnson help blacks in Congress?

Texas was 15 per cent black and 12 per cent Hispanic, so when Johnson became a congressman, he wanted their votes. He considered employing 'a talented and good-looking Mexican' or a Spanish American girl as a secretary to show his 'appreciation' of his Mexican supporters. In 1949, a segregated Texas cemetery would not bury a Mexican American war hero. Johnson arranged a burial in Arlington National Cemetery, thereby gaining front-page praise in the *New York Times*. Some white Texans interpreted that as a cynical publicity stunt, but any Texan who sought to represent that segregated state had to appear to be a segregationist. It took courage to make gestures such as this. On the other hand, it was an easy way to win minority votes, and it made a politician with national ambitions look free from **sectional** prejudices.

As black voters were relatively few, political expediency dictated that Johnson vote with his fellow Southern Democrats in Congress against civil rights measures that aimed to prevent lynching, eliminate poll taxes and deny federal funding to segregated schools. Johnson's opposition to Truman's civil rights programme (see page 94) disgusted Texas blacks. His explanations (or excuses) are valid (if not admirable) within the contemporary Southern political context. He said the bills would never have passed anyway. He recognised that he could only 'go so far in Texas'. He also trotted out the standard Southerner's excuse for refusal to help blacks. He said he was not against blacks but for **states' rights**. He thought civil rights legislation

Key terms

Sectional
Relating to a particular area of the United States, such as the South.

States' rights
Throughout US history, there has been constitutional conflict between upholders of the powers of the individual states as opposed to that of the federal government.

that tried 'to force people to do what they are not ready to do of their own free will and accord' would lead to a 'wave of riots' across the South. Finally, Johnson argued that civil rights legislation would not help blacks and Hispanics as much as better housing, schooling and healthcare.

Johnson worked quietly to get black farmers and black schoolchildren equal treatment in his congressional district. In 1938 he managed to get federal funding for housing in Austin, Texas, which benefited Mexicans, blacks, and white slum-dwellers. He appealed to white self-interest when he told the press the USA would not have to worry about the appeal of ideologies such as communism if it gave everyone good housing and a job.

The need to keep in with voters of all colours, coupled with his own ambition, idealism and racial ambivalence, made Johnson appear inconsistent on race relations. From the mid-1940s, Robert Parker worked for Johnson as a part-time servant at private dinner parties in Washington. Parker recalled it as a 'painful experience'. He feared:

> the pain and humiliation he could inflict at a moment's notice … In front of his guests Johnson would often 'nigger' at me. He especially liked to put on a show for [Mississippi] Senator Bilbo, who used to lecture: 'the only way to treat a nigger is to kick him' … I used to dread being around Johnson when Bilbo was present, because I knew it meant that Johnson would play racist. That was the LBJ I hated. Privately, he was a different man as long as I didn't do anything to make him angry. He'd call me 'boy' almost affectionately. Sometimes I felt that he was treating me almost as an equal … Although I never heard him speak publicly about black men without saying 'nigger', I never heard him say 'nigger woman'. In fact, he always used to call his black cook, Zephyr Wright, a college graduate who couldn't find any other work, 'Miss Wright' or 'sweetheart.'

Key question
Was Johnson really changing his mind on race?

Key date
Senator Johnson orchestrated passage of diluted civil rights bill: 1957

(d) Senator Johnson, BROWN and the Civil Rights Acts (1957 and 1960)

By the mid-1950s, Senator Johnson appeared to be changing his position on civil rights issues. He was one of the few Southern politicians who supported the Supreme Court's BROWN (see page 102) decision. However, Johnson remained careful to appease Southern racists. In 1956 he killed a civil rights bill in Congress, but changed his position in 1957. While assuring Texans there was 'no foundation' to rumours that he was promoting a civil rights bill and 'forced integration of the races', he orchestrated the passage of the 1957 Civil Rights Act. However, he diluted the parts most offensive to Southerners. He turned Eisenhower's bill into a voting rights law that was largely unenforceable, because of white domination of Southern juries. The part that allowed the federal government to promote integrated Southern schools was lost. Johnson was also very important in the passage of Eisenhower's second Civil Rights Act.

There were many reasons why Johnson changed his position on civil rights. He believed that the South had to accept desegregation in order to make economic advances: racial tensions made the South unattractive to investors. He felt a great debate about BROWN would only weaken the country. He said it was important to uphold the US Constitution and the place of the Supreme Court within it: 'However we may question the judgement,' it 'cannot be overruled now'. His presidential ambitions meant that he could not be seen to be too narrowly Southern, which helps explain why he was one of the three Southern senators who refused to sign the Southern Manifesto against BROWN (see page 102). He needed some dramatic legislative achievement if he was to become a serious presidential candidate – hence the civil rights legislation, which he hoped would show his talent for creating consensus. Northern black voters were beginning to switch to the Republicans, so the issue was increasingly important to Johnson and the Democrats.

Key date

Senator Johnson important in passage of Civil Rights Act: 1960

As always, Johnson's motivation was and is debatable. While one senator described his support of BROWN as 'one of the most courageous acts of political valour I have ever seen', Hubert Humphrey said Johnson used his stance on BROWN for political gain, hoping to win Northern black and white voters. Many of those close to Johnson said he had a genuine sympathy for greater racial equality, even though he talked in 'good ole boy' language to other Southerners. Furthermore, the time was ripe for change, following the Montgomery Bus Boycott and BROWN. If change was inevitable, it made sense to go along with it. As Johnson said:

> The Negro fought in the [Second World] war, and … he's not gonna keep taking the shit we're dishing out. We're in a race with time. If we don't act, we're gonna have blood in the streets.

(e) Vice-President Johnson (1961–3)

Key question
Did Vice-President Johnson help blacks?

Vice-President Johnson's greatest challenge was chairing Kennedy's Equal Employment Opportunity Commission (EEOC). Johnson did not want the job: he told Kennedy that EEOC lacked the necessary money and power. Kennedy insisted, so Johnson, as always, did his best. Johnson believed the USA was 'just throwing aside one of our greatest [economic] assets' by racism, which was 'un-American' and damaged the USA's reputation. CORE's James Farmer believed Johnson's motivation was genuine, not political. Farmer and Roy Wilkins both rated Vice-President Johnson higher than President Kennedy on civil rights issues. However, EEOC failed to win many plaudits. Johnson could not push contractors too far and too fast on equal employment, lest it damage him and the administration. Federal jobs held by blacks increased by 17 per cent in 1962 and 22 per cent in 1963 but black activists were still dissatisfied.

Summary diagram: Lyndon Johnson before the presidency

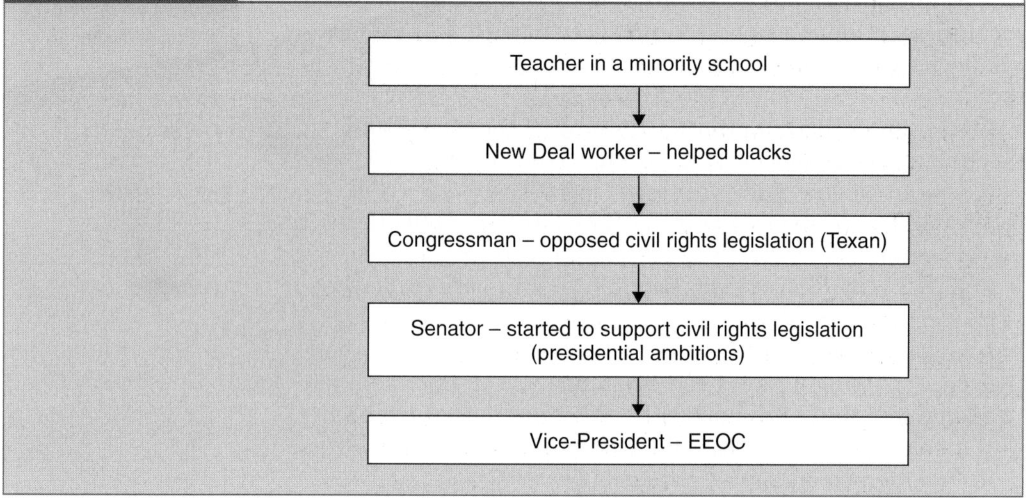

Teacher in a minority school
↓
New Deal worker – helped blacks
↓
Congressman – opposed civil rights legislation (Texan)
↓
Senator – started to support civil rights legislation (presidential ambitions)
↓
Vice-President – EEOC

Key question
How much did President Johnson help blacks?

Key date
Johnson became president: November 1963

Key term
Great Society
Johnson's plan to decrease poverty and inequality in the USA.

3 | President Johnson (1963–9)

(a) The 1964 Civil Rights Act

(i) Why Johnson supported the civil right bill

Lyndon Johnson became president after Kennedy's assassination. He announced his vision of a '**Great Society**' for the USA, with 'an end to poverty and racial injustice'. He was determined to get Kennedy's civil rights bill through. When a Southern senator told him the price would be the 1964 presidential election, Johnson said, 'I'll pay it gladly'. Johnson insisted that discrimination was morally wrong, and described how, when his black cook drove to Texas, she could not use the whites-only facilities in a gas station:

> When they had to go to the bathroom, they would ... pull off on a side road, and Zephyr Wright, the cook of the vice-president of the United States, would squat in the road to pee. That's wrong. And there ought to be something to change that.

He remained convinced that reform would help the economic, political and spiritual reintegration of the South within the nation. Also, as a non-elected president, he felt duty-bound to see the late president's bill through. His sense of obligation was increased by the tragic circumstances of Kennedy's death.

Johnson told Roy Wilkins he was 'free at last': freed from his Texas constituency and as president, he could now help blacks. Wilkins believed Johnson was 'absolutely sincere'. Andrew Young said while it was 'the way to really save the nation, he knew it was not politically expedient'. Although it ensured that Johnson got the black vote, he lost white racist votes.

(ii) How the bill was passed

Key question
How was the civil rights bill finally passed?

The civil rights bill faced considerable opposition in Congress, including the longest filibuster in Senate history. However, it finally became an act because:

- Black activists had drawn the attention of the nation and its legislators to injustices. 'The real hero of this struggle is the American Negro,' said Johnson.
- NAACP, trade unionists and the churches had lobbied Congress incessantly.
- Kennedy had won over the Republican **minority leader** before his death.
- Johnson thought the bill would have passed if Kennedy had lived, but it might have been emasculated like Eisenhower's bills. Now Johnson did not have to compromise the bill's contents. The nation was saddened by Kennedy's death. Passing his bill seemed an appropriate tribute.
- Important congressional leaders such as Hubert Humphrey worked hard on the bill.
- A Johnson aide gave the credit for the passage of the bill to Johnson himself. He devoted a staggering amount of his time, energy, and political capital to breaking the Senate filibuster and ensuring the passage of the act.
- Johnson made emotive appeals to national traditions and ideals and to Kennedy's memory.
- Johnson won over a few Southerners by appealing to their self-interest. He emphasised how the bill would help get blacks and Hispanics working:

> I'm gonna try to teach these nigras that don't know anything how to work for themselves instead of just breedin'; I'm gonna try to teach these Mexicans who can't talk English to learn it so they can work for themselves ... and get off of our taxpayer's back.

- The act had increasing national support: by January 1964, 68 per cent of Americans favoured the bill. After Birmingham, national religious organisations had increasingly supported the measure. Congress could not afford to ignore this marked swing in public opinion.

Key term
Minority leader
Leader of the party with fewer members in Congress.

(iii) The Significance of the Civil Rights Act

Key question
What was the significance of the Civil Rights Act?

Key date
Civil Rights Act: 1964

Johnson signed the civil rights bill in July 1964 before a national television audience. Historian Irving Bernstein described it as 'a rare and glittering moment in the history of American democracy'. The act gave the federal government the legal tools to end *de jure* segregation in the South. It prohibited discrimination in public places, furthered school desegregation and established an Equal Employment Commission.

However, the act did little to facilitate black voting, and little to improve race relations. There were signs of a Northern working class white backlash in the popularity of Alabama's racist Governor George Wallace in presidential primaries. Blacks felt

Profile: Fannie Lou Hamer 1917–77

1917	–	Born in Mississippi, the twentieth child of a sharecropping family
1923	–	Aged six, began working in the cotton fields
1929	–	End of her formal education
1961	–	Sterilised without her consent, a common practice to decrease the poor black population. (Hamer's only child haemorrhaged to death after giving birth, on a 100-mile journey to one of the few hospitals that would admit blacks)
1962	–	Attended SNCC meeting to urge blacks to register to vote and risked retribution by trying to register (Mississippi lynched more blacks than any other state: 539 between 1882 and 1968). Her attempt resulted in eviction from her sharecroppers' shack, jail, and a vicious beating from which her health never recovered
1962–5	–	Worked to persuade others to register, conducted citizenship classes, and took cases of election fraud and discrimination to court (HAMER v. CAMPBELL, 1965, and HAMER v. SUNFLOWER COUNTY, 1970)
1964	–	One of the MFDP delegates to the Democratic National Convention; in a dramatic televised speech, which infuriated President Johnson, she told the nation about poverty and the poor education and health care available in Mississippi
1965–77	–	Worked to make Mississippi blacks economically self-sufficient; ran frequently for political office, concentrating upon black rights, the exclusion of women from important positions in the Democratic Party, and the Vietnam War

Fannie Lou Hamer is important as an illustration of black social, economic and political problems in Mississippi and of the importance of grassroots activism in the civil rights era. MFDP helped to gain black equality within the Democratic Party.

the act had not gone far enough. Most still suffered from poverty and discrimination. The weeks following the passage of the act saw riots in the black ghettos of many East Coast cities. Furthermore, the predominantly black Mississippi Freedom Democratic Party (MFDP) demanded seats at the Democratic Party convention in Atlantic City, New Jersey, on the basis that they were more representative than the segregationists who represented Mississippi. Johnson was outraged. He knew 'we just delivered the South to the Republican Party for a long time to come'. He felt he had done a great deal and at great cost to help blacks and now black activists sought to repay him with demonstrations that would embarrass him and the party. Nevertheless, he pursued further legislation.

(b) Johnson's other legislation

Key question
How important and effective was the legislation initiated by Johnson?

(i) Education acts and medical help

Johnson hoped that his Elementary and Secondary Education Act (1965) would help children out of the ghettos. Poorer states like Mississippi benefited greatly from the federal funding. By the end of the 1960s, the percentage of blacks with a high school diploma increased from 40 to 60 per cent. However, a combination of reluctant local officials, and ghetto peer pressure and traditions, limited the act's effectiveness. His Higher Education Act (1965) was more successful. It gave significant aid to poor black colleges. The number of black college students quadrupled within a decade. Similarly, Johnson's introduction of health-care reform for the poor helped blacks: the black infant mortality rate halved within a decade.

Key dates
Johnson's Education Acts: 1965
Voting Rights Act: 1965
Social Security Act set up Medicare and Medicaid: 1965

(ii) The Voting Rights Act (1965)

Key question
What was the significance of the Voting Rights Act?

There were gaps in the 1964 Civil Rights Act that needed filling, but Johnson feared unco-operative Southerners in Congress. However, Selma and 'Bloody Sunday' (see page 139) forced Johnson to ask Congress for the voting rights bill.

Johnson's persuasive speech before Congress was one of his best:

> Rarely are we met with a challenge ... to the values and the purposes and the meaning of our beloved Nation. The issue of equal rights for American Negroes is such an issue ... The command of the Constitution is plain ...... It is wrong – deadly wrong – to deny any of your fellow Americans the right to vote in this country ... A century has passed, more than a hundred years, since the Negro was freed. And he is not fully free tonight ... A century has passed, more than a hundred years, since equality was promised. And yet the Negro is not equal ... The real hero of this struggle is the American Negro. His actions and protests, his courage to risk safety and even to risk his life, have awakened the conscience of this Nation ... He has called upon us to make good the promise of America. And who among us can say that we would have made the same progress were it not for his persistent bravery, and his faith in American democracy?

Martin Luther King said the speech brought tears to his eyes.

Johnson's Voting Rights Act disallowed literacy tests and 'constitutional interpretation tests' and established federal registrars. It had a dramatic effect on the South. By late 1966, only four of the old Confederate states had fewer than 50 per cent of their eligible blacks registered. By 1968, even Mississippi was up to 59 per cent. In 1980, the proportion of blacks registered to vote was only seven per cent less than the proportion of whites. Blacks elected to office in the South increased dramatically. Their numbers increased six-fold from

1965 to 1969, then doubled from 1969 to 1980. There was political gain for Johnson's Democratic Party: the enlarged black vote helped counter the loss of Southern white voters.

Key question
How did Johnson engineer a legislative revolution?

(iii) A legislative revolution

From 1964 to 1965, Johnson had engineered a legislative revolution. It was a 'unique set of circumstances', according to biographer Irving Bernstein:

- Due to his 24 years in Congress, for many of which he was Democratic Party leader, Johnson had unprecedented experience in getting legislation through Congress.
- He had an unusual two-thirds of Congress on his side (it is rare to have both a Democratic majority in Congress and a Democratic President).
- Congressmen knew their constituents were unusually receptive at this time to righting national wrongs, partly because they felt it would somehow atone for Kennedy's death.
- Most important of all, the president was exceptionally persuasive and determined, and had a lifelong commitment to helping the poor.

Key question
How did Johnson use executive authority to help blacks?

(c) Johnson and executive authority

Johnson, like Kennedy, used executive authority to help blacks.

(i) The manipulation of federal funding

In 1965–6 Johnson worked to help blacks through manipulation of federal funding, for example, offering federal subsidies to Southern districts that were cooperative on school desegregation. By September 1965 there was 88 per cent compliance down South. The numbers of black students attending desegregated schools tripled.

(ii) Black appointments

Johnson used black advisers, including future Congresswoman Barbara Jordan. A Supreme Court vacancy in 1967 gave Johnson the opportunity to make an appointment to help black morale. Every Supreme Court judge in 178 years of the nation's existence had been a white male. The President's wife, Lady Bird Johnson, suggested he should appoint the first woman, but he appointed the first black, 58-year-old Thurgood Marshall. Southern senators opposed the appointment, but on constitutional not racial grounds (they claimed Marshall was too liberal). Johnson got some hostile mail. 'You despicable bum. How do you have the guts to do it coming out of Texas?' asked one bigot who, like many other whites, felt Johnson had done more than enough for blacks.

(iii) The call for affirmative action

Johnson knew that the law alone could not ensure equality. As he told university students at Howard University, in 1965:

> You do not take a person who, for years, has been hobbled by chains and liberate him, bring him up to the starting line of a race

Profile: Thurgood Marshall 1908–93

1908 – Born in Baltimore, Maryland; father a railroad porter, mother a teacher, who worked for far less pay than white teachers. Marshall described Baltimore as segregated as any Southern city. Educated in an inferior segregated school

1920s – Organised a gang and got himself arrested for fighting a white man who called him 'nigger'; worked on Sundays for a bootlegger, making illegal booze

1930 – Graduated from Lincoln University, an old, all-male, all-black college in Pennsylvania. Wanted to study law but blacks could not attend the University of Maryland, so attended all-black Howard University. Inspired by Vice-Dean Charles Hamilton Houston (he could not be Dean: Howard depended upon federal funding and Congress insisted upon a white Dean)

1935 – Houston employed by the NAACP; hired Marshall as lawyer

1935–40 – Won great NAACP legal victories against segregated schools and lower pay for black teachers in Maryland and Virginia

1936 – Obtained entry for a black man to the University of Maryland Law School

1938 – Persuaded the Supreme Court to rule against states such as Missouri, which forced local black students to seek an out-of-state education if they wanted the same quality education as white Missourians (GAINES decision)

1946 – Narrowly escaped being lynched as he travelled around Southern courts

1950 – Argued successfully before Supreme Court in SWEATT v. PAINTER (see page 99)

1954 – Argued successfully before Supreme Court in BROWN (see page 102)

1958 – Argued successfully before Supreme Court in COOPER v. AARON (see page 113)

1962 – Kennedy appointed him judge in the US Court of Appeals in New York

1965 – Johnson appointed him US Solicitor-General

1967 – Johnson appointed him Supreme Court Justice, where he became the minority liberal voice in the increasingly right-wing court of the 1980s

Marshall's early life and career demonstrated that despite racial discrimination, some black men could get a good education and job. His court-room brilliance was crucial in dismantling segregation: Marshall contested 32 cases before the Supreme Court and won 29 of them. He helped and inspired fellow blacks for most of his life, although by the 1970s, black power critics attacked his promotion of integration, claiming that black-only schools had given teachers and pupils greater self-esteem and sense of community, and often greater opportunities.

> and then say, 'you are free to compete with all the others,' and still justly believe that you have been completely fair … This is the next and the more profound stage of the battle for civil rights.

Johnson said what was needed was positive discrimination to help blacks (this became known as 'affirmative action'). However, Johnson's plans to help blacks further were hit by the great white backlash after riots in Watts, Los Angeles in August 1965.

Key question
What stopped Johnson doing more?

(d) The factors that stopped Johnson doing more for blacks

Johnson had done more for blacks than any other president had, but after 1965 it became hard to do more, because of Congress, local officials, black violence and the cost of the Vietnam War.

Key dates

Ineffective act against discrimination in housing sales: 1968

Watts riots: 1965

(i) Congress

Congress was unhelpful. In 1966 Congress rejected an administration civil rights bill, one aim of which was to prohibit housing discrimination. Polls showed 70 per cent of white voters opposed large numbers of blacks living in their neighbourhood, especially after the Watts riots and Stokely Carmichael's call for 'black power' (see page 141). Johnson's proposed bill resulted in some of the worst hate mail of his presidency. When housing discrimination was finally prohibited in an act, the law proved difficult to enforce due to white resistance. Johnson found it hard to sustain national and congressional support for his war on poverty. He was angry with congressmen who jokingly called his rat extermination bill a 'civil rats bill' and suggested he send in a federal cat army. Johnson pointed out that slum children suffered terribly from rat bites.

(ii) Local officials

Johnson had to rely on local and state authorities, officials and employees to carry out his programmes. They were sometimes reluctant to co-operate, as in Chicago. The 1964 Civil Rights Act said federal funding should not be given to segregated schools, but Mayor Daley was a valuable political ally, so he got his funds and kept his segregated schools. This pattern was repeated in other Northern cities.

(iii) Ghetto riots, black power and the white backlash

From 1964 until 1968, successive summers saw rioting in America's black ghettos. These riots caused a white backlash. After the 1965 Watts riots (see page 140), the exasperated Los Angeles' police chief asked what else anyone could expect, 'when you keep telling [black] people they are unfairly treated and teach them disrespect for the law'. As television showed black youth shouting 'burn, burn, burn', whites feared black militants were driving the USA into race war. Throughout California, gun sales to suburban whites soared. Tired of being blamed for the black predicament, whites were turning against blacks and against Johnson's reform programme. Johnson could not believe what was happening in Watts: 'How is it possible, after all we've accomplished?' He was amazed and disappointed by what he later described as 'all that crazy rioting which almost ruined everything': could the rioters not see how their behaviour undermined his efforts to get public and congressional support for more legislation? How could they be so unappreciative of what he had done? Johnson secretly arranged that federal funds be poured into Watts but publicly he likened the black rioters to the Ku Klux Klan. He wanted to avoid accusations that his sympathetic policies encouraged rioters to demand more. Johnson told a colleague his fears:

> Negroes will end up pissing in the aisles of the Senate … [and] making fools of themselves the way … they had after the Civil War and during Reconstruction. Just as the government was moving to help them, the Negroes will once again take unwise actions out of frustration, impatience and anger.

Key dates

Ghetto riots:

Chicago, Atlanta, Philadelphia: 1966

Newark, Detroit: 1967

After the Watts riots, virtually every large US city outside the South had a race riot. Summer 1966 saw riots in 38 major cities, including Chicago, Atlanta and Philadelphia. In July 1967, amidst rumours of police brutality against a black taxi driver, Newark's black ghetto erupted. In six days of riots, 26 died, 1500 were injured, and much of the inner city was burned out. Then Detroit erupted. Forty died, 2000 were injured, 5000 were arrested, and 5000 were made homeless. The President had to send federal troops to settle Detroit. Inner-city riots became an annual summer event. An aide counted 225 'hostile outbursts' from 1964 too 1968, in which 191 were killed, 7942 wounded, and 49,607 arrested. There were several reasons for the ghetto riots.

The FBI blamed the misery of ghetto life, oppressive summer weather, and Communist agitation, while Johnson believed it was poverty and despair. Big city ghetto-residents could compare highly visible white affluence with their own situation. Whereas eight per cent of whites lived below the poverty line, 30 per cent of blacks did so; 18 per cent of whites lived in substandard housing, 50 per cent of non-whites did so. Between 1959 and 1965, the number of poor Americans decreased from 39 million to 33 million, but the percentage of poor blacks increased from 28 per cent to 31 per cent. Black unemployment (at seven per cent) was twice that of whites, but Johnson told journalists that the riots could not just have been about unemployment because there were training vacancies in most of the riot cities. In Detroit, 80 per cent of those arrested had well-paid jobs. He said it was more likely 'bad housing' and 'the hate and bitterness which has been developing over many years'.

Johnson's investigatory Kerner Commission blamed white racism above all. Blacks saw the police as 'the occupying army of white America, a hostile power'. The absence of black policemen fuelled ghetto tensions against white police 'outsiders'. A subsequent analysis of ghetto riots found 40 per cent involved alleged police abuse or discrimination. The *Boston Globe* described the 1967 Newark riots as 'a revolution of black Americans against white Americans, a violent petition for the redress of long-standing grievances'. It said Johnson's legislation had effected little fundamental improvement. Some suggest that false hopes raised by Johnson's extravagant Great Society rhetoric played a part in provoking the riots.

The assassination in 1968 of Martin Luther King by a white racist provoked major riots in 100 cities, with 46 dead, 3000 injured, 27,000 arrested. A total of 21,000 federal troops and 34,000 national guardsmen restored order following $45 million of damage to property.

The riots helped ensure that, after the 1965 Voting Rights Act, Johnson could do little more to help blacks. A 1965 poll showed 88 per cent of whites advocated black self-improvement, more education, and harder work, rather than government help. A 1966 poll showed 90 per cent opposed new civil rights legislation. In a 1967 poll, 52 per cent said Johnson was going 'too fast' on integration, and only 10 per cent said 'not fast enough'. Black militants also fuelled the white backlash. When the Black Panthers talked of carrying weapons for self-defence, they frightened and alienated whites.

Key date

Vietnam War: 1965–72

(iv) Vietnam War

The expense and distraction of the Vietnam War helps to explain why Johnson could not do as much as he wanted to alleviate the US's domestic problems. In 1965, the federal government deficit was $1.6 billion; by 1968 it was $25.3 billion.

(v) Rising taxes

Federal spending on the poor had increased by nearly 50 per cent and this helped make his programme increasingly unpopular among whites. In 1967, the Democratic governor of Missouri told Johnson that 'public disenchantment with the civil rights programmes' was one of the main reasons why he and the Democrats were so unpopular. White Americans were tired of paying out for America's oppressed minorities. The programmes were expensive and it appeared that political radicals were hijacking them.

(vi) Attempting the impossible

Johnson recognised that he could not work miracles. In June 1966 Johnson told a task force set up to report on black problems that:

> The dilemma that you deal with is too deeply rooted in pride and prejudice, too profound and too complex, and too critical to our future for any one man or any one administration to ever resolve.

He knew there was a limit to the amount of legislation that any administration could pass, particularly if most of the population were beginning to resist it. 'It's a little like whiskey,' said Johnson. 'It is good. But if you drink too much it comes up on you.' 'We have come too far too fast during your administration,' a leading Democrat told him.

Summary diagram: President Johnson

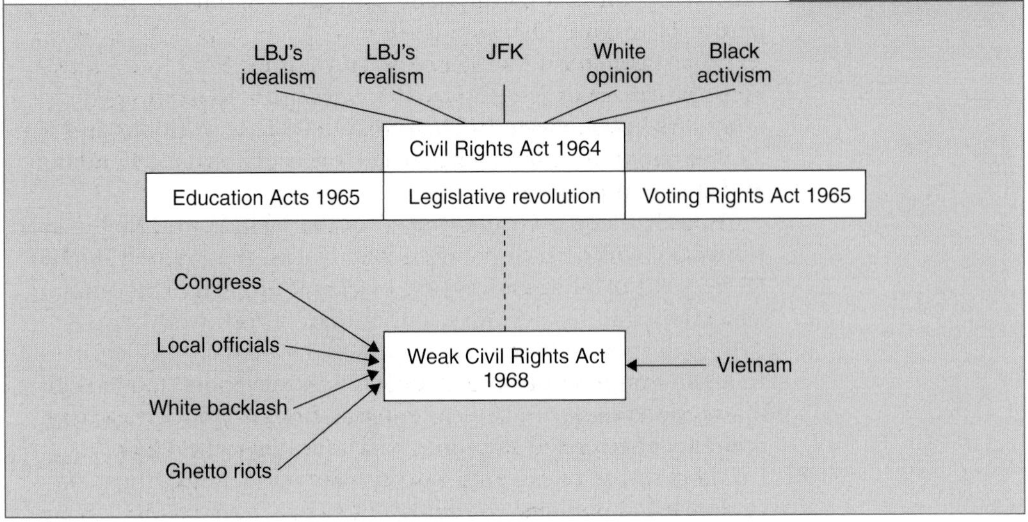

4 | Conclusions

Key question
What had Johnson achieved?

After Johnson died and his body lay in state in the Capitol Rotunda in Washington, around 60 per cent of those who filed past to pay their respects were blacks. One said, 'People don't know it, but he did more for us than anybody, any president, ever did.'

Johnson played an important role in ending *de jure* segregation in the South. Martin Luther King's old friend Bayard Rustin found the South transformed by 1980, 'from a reactionary bastion into a region moderate in racial outlook and more enlightened in social and economic policy'. Johnson's Voting Rights Act transformed Southern politics, by giving blacks the opportunity to vote without fear. In 1960 there had been no black officials in Mississippi; by 1980 there were over 300. His Education Acts speeded up school desegregation and helped black colleges. He had been instrumental in the passage of three Civil Rights Acts that gave blacks more political and economic opportunities. His civil rights legislation opened the way for a larger and richer black middle class. Black unemployment decreased by 34 per cent and the percentage of blacks living below the poverty line decreased by 25 per cent. Johnson's Great Society had contributed greatly to those statistics.

However, many blacks continued to suffer poor housing, poor schools, poor job opportunities and an inability to get out of the poverty trap.

Critics said the Great Society created a '**welfare dependency**' culture, and had caused federal expenditure to rocket.

Key term
Welfare dependency
Reliance upon federal aid.

Ironically, those like Johnson and King, who worked for equality believing it would lead to improved race relations, actually damaged them. While many blacks thought Johnson had done too little, many whites thought he had done too much. Johnson's Kerner Commission Report explained the 1967 ghetto riots as a result of white racism, and recommended greater federal expenditure, which was politically unrealistic. Back in Texas, Johnson had known there was only so much he could do. He overestimated what he could do as president, but his aims were surely admirable. Thurgood Marshall thought Johnson got it right: 'You didn't wait for the times. You made them'. Like Martin Luther King, Johnson probably did as much as was humanly possible in the circumstances.

As he left office, Johnson admitted, 'so little have I done. So much do I have yet to do.' The Kerner Report summed up the problem and demonstrated the limitations of what had been achieved:

> What white Americans have never fully understood – but what the Negro can never forget – is that white society is deeply implicated in the ghetto. White institutions created it, white institutions maintain it, and white society condones it … Our nation is moving toward two societies, one black, one white – separate and unequal.

5 | Key Debate

Although television documentaries usually credit Kennedy with greater concern for civil rights than Johnson, historians usually agree with Adam Fairclough's assessment (2001). Fairclough sees Kennedy as calculating in his approach to racial problems, only helping blacks when forced to do so. On the other hand, Johnson's biographers have often been very generous. 'This presidency made a difference,' insisted Vaughn Davis Bornet (1983). 'The nation was transformed in civil rights … education … [and] poverty'. Lyndon Johnson's reputation has been badly tarnished by 'his' Vietnam War. However, biographer Robert Dallek (1991–8) suggests: 'Johnson's role in reaching out to America's disadvantaged and combating racial segregation was perhaps his most important contribution to recent US history.'

Historians of civil rights perhaps inevitably give most of the credit elsewhere: 'African Americans were the principal architects of their own success', according to Robert Cook (1998).

Some key books in the debate

Vaughn Davis Bornet, *The Presidency of Lyndon B. Johnson* (Kansas, 1983).
Robert Cook, *Sweet Land of Liberty?* (Longman, 1998).
Robert Dallek, *Lyndon Johnson and his Times* (Oxford, 1991–8).
Adam Fairclough, *Better Day Coming: Blacks and Equality, 1890–2000* (Penguin, 2001).

Study Guide: AS Question

In the style of Edexcel

Why were the civil rights protests across the United States effective in the years 1954–64 and less effective thereafter? (40 marks)

Exam tips

The cross-references are intended to take you to some of the material that will help you to answer the question.

This question combines two traditional questions, the first being why the civil rights movement was effective up to 1964–5, the second being why it was less effective thereafter. This is another 'causes' question (see Chapter 5), so you should once more look at the links between the factors. The success of 1954–64 owed much to:

- inspirational black leaders (page 135)
- black grassroots support for protests and activism (page 183)
- considerable Northern white support for change (page 185)
- black and media exposure of Southern racism (page 134)
- the Cold War propaganda war (page 118)
- the sympathy of the federal government and of President Johnson in particular (page 185).

The failure of the civil rights movement after 1965 owed much to:

- increasingly radical black leadership (page 167)
- black divisions (page 145)
- decreased white support, as the focus shifted from the South and legal/social inequality to the Northern economic inequality (page 145)
- black rioting (page 188)
- decreased federal government support due to all the above and the cost of the Vietnam War (page 189).

Take care to interlink the factors, for example, the changed black leadership no longer communicated with nor had the sympathy of the federal government.

9 US Race Relations 1968–80

POINTS TO CONSIDER

After the death of Martin Luther King, the civil rights movement lost the sense of being a national movement. Organised direct action ended. Although Jim Crow had been destroyed, the problems of inner-city deprivation, drug abuse, rural poverty, job discrimination, unstable families and segregated schools remained. Blacks, Hispanics and Native Americans constituted a virtual under-class. This chapter looks at how Americans tried to solve these problems. It looks at:

- Federal intervention to help minorities
- Black involvement in politics
- Conclusions about black progress
- Native Americans and the black civil rights movement
- The impact of the civil rights movement on Hispanic Americans and Asian Americans

Key dates

1969	Native Americans occupied Alcatraz
1971	SWANN v. CHARLOTTE-MECKLENBURG and GRIGG v. DUKE POWER COMPANY – Supreme Court said school desegregation should be fully implemented and supported affirmative action
1972	Equal Employment Opportunity Act
1974	Supreme Court overturned a Detroit busing plan (MILLIKEN v. BRADLEY)
1975	Indian Self-determination and Education Act
1978	BAKKE v. REGENTS OF THE UNIVERSITY OF CALIFORNIA – Supreme Court upheld the University's affirmative action

Key questions
How much did the federal government help blacks 1968–80?

How much did President Nixon help blacks?

1 | Federal Intervention

(a) President Nixon (1969–74)

Nixon's record on civil rights was a strange mixture.

(i) Nixon's negative side

Compared to his contemporaries, Nixon had been exceptionally liberal on civil rights issues during the 1950s. However, he had a dim view of blacks, privately adjudging that 'there has never in history been an adequate black nation, and they are the only race of which this is true'. As president, Nixon:

- Did not want to meet black leaders and opposed the proposal that Martin Luther King's birthday should be a national holiday.
- Crushed black radicals like the Black Panthers
- Attempted a revision of the Voting Rights Act in order win the white Southern vote.
- Nominated an unimpressive Southern racist to the Supreme Court (a Nixon supporter contended that as many Americans were mediocre, they should have a representative on the court).
- Refused to back the Supreme Court when it said it was time for school desegregation to be fully implemented (SWANN v. CHARLOTTE-MECKLENBURG, 1971). This necessitated **busing** children considerable distances in order to ensure racially mixed schools, which Nixon considered bad for the child and the local community.

Key dates

SWANN v. CHARLOTTE-MECKLENBURG: 1971

MILLIKEN v. BRADLEY: 1974

Equal Employment Opportunity Act: 1972

GRIGG v. DUKE POWER COMPANY: 1971

Key term

Busing
Transporting white or black children to schools in an area other than that in which they live, to ensure integrated schools in that area.

However, the courts continued to endorse busing. So, whereas 68 per cent of Southern black children attended segregated schools in the first year of Nixon's presidency, it was only eight per cent by the time he left the White House. Busing made Southern schools amongst the US's best integrated by 1972, despite Nixon's funding of white segregationist private schools. On the other hand, thanks to Nixon's four conservative appointments to the Supreme Court, that body ruled (MILLIKEN v. BRADLEY, 1974) that white children could not be bused into inner cities, which facilitated the *de facto* re-segregation of schools.

(ii) Nixon's positive achievements

Nixon set up the Office of Minority Business Enterprise to encourage black capitalism, and embraced 'affirmative action' (or 'reverse discrimination' as its critics described it). Why?

He believed jobs were the way out of the ghetto. The NAACP had flooded the OEEC with protests over employment discrimination, so Nixon's 1972 Equal Employment Opportunity Act gave OEEC greater powers of enforcement through the courts. Nixon fought off congressional and trade union opposition to help ensure that over 300,000 companies with federal contracts employed a number of blacks proportionate to the size of the population. The Supreme Court supported affirmative action (GRIGG v. DUKE POWER COMPANY, 1971).

Thus the civil rights movement retained sufficient support in the courts, the federal bureaucracy, Congress and even a reluctant Nixon White House to facilitate progress in school desegregation, employment discrimination and voting rights. Although Nixon sometimes tried totally to turn back the tide, it sometimes proved too strong. His administration tried to undermine the Great Society agencies but nevertheless dramatically increased federal expenditure on poverty programmes. Although Nixon said he hated having to pretend any sympathy for 'all that welfare crap', social security and welfare payments doubled during his presidency. Statistics suggest federal anti-poverty efforts helped raise black living standards. A total of 87 per cent of blacks were below the poverty line in 1940, 50 per cent in 1960, down to 30 per cent in 1974. The civil rights movement had aimed to effect greater federal intervention on behalf of blacks. They had succeeded.

Key question
Was President Carter helpful to blacks?

(b) President Carter (1977–81)

The first Southern president since Woodrow Wilson, Jimmy Carter, grew up in segregated Georgia. He did not challenge segregation in his younger days. He claimed subsequently that he had been naively unaware. When campaigning to be governor of Georgia he opposed busing but, as governor, declared segregation was over and employed many blacks. While campaigning for the presidency, he declared he had 'nothing against' a community 'trying to maintain the ethnic purity of their neighbourhoods', which prompted Jesse Jackson (see page 197) to call him a Hitlerian throwback.

As president, Carter appointed more blacks and Hispanics to the federal judiciary than any previous president. The percentage of black federal judges rose from four per cent in 1977 to nine per cent in 1981. Carter made significant minority appointments. He appointed black women to his cabinet and made Andrew Young US ambassador to the United Nations. He renewed the Voting Rights Acts, ensured minority-owned companies had their fair share of government contracts, and deposited federal funds in minority-owned banks. He increased Justice Department power over voting rights, strengthened the OEEC, and supported the Supreme Court when it upheld affirmative action (BAKKE v. REGENTS OF THE UNIVERSITY OF CALIFORNIA).

After Richard Nixon had encouraged affirmative action, universities often gave priority to minority applicants. Marine veteran Allan Bakke challenged the University of California at Davis for rejecting his application to medical school, while minority candidates with lower scores gained places. The Californian Supreme Court ruled in his favour, but the Supreme Court (BAKKE v. REGENTS OF THE UNIVERSITY OF CALIFORNIA, 1978) upheld the University's affirmative action. Despite that setback, however, the white backlash against affirmative action continued and gained strength. In 1980, the Supreme Court weakened the Voting Rights Act in CITY OF MOBILE v. BOLDON, which made it harder to challenge discriminatory voting laws.

Key dates

BAKKE v. REGENTS OF THE UNIVERSITY OF CALIFORNIA: 1978

CITY OF MOBILE v. BOLDON: 1980

Summary diagram: Federal intervention

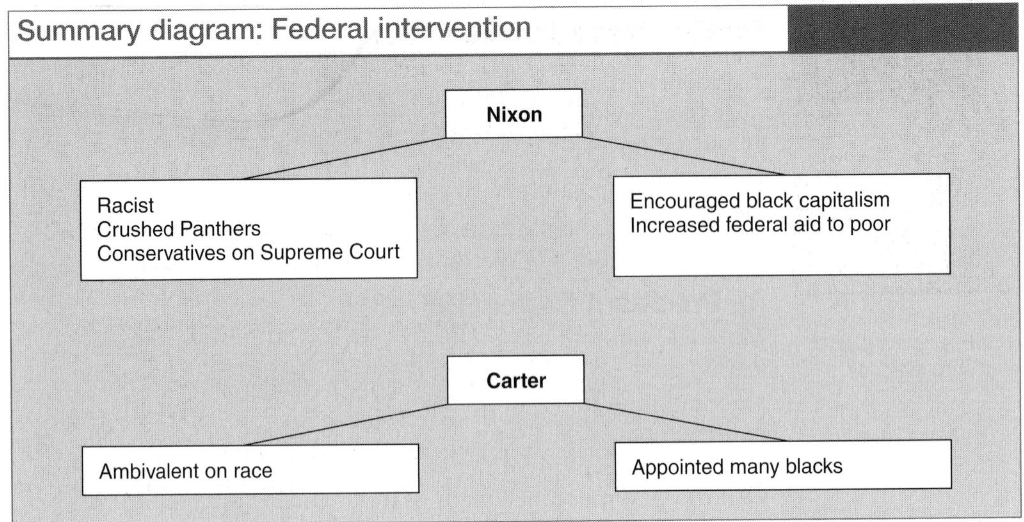

2 | Black Involvement in Politics

Key question
What effect had the civil rights movement had upon black involvement in politics?

(a) Black organisations

Blacks continued to try to influence the political process through organisations such as the NAACP, which continued lobbying and litigation. The NAACP launched school desegregation suits and backed integration orders. However, some blacks, worried about the loss of black cultural cohesion, criticised busing. They suggested that more resources for black schools was preferable to complex busing and less likely to cause a white backlash. The most ferocious backlash came from Irish Americans in Boston, who in 1974 set up alternative schools, and used protest marches and sit-ins! Across the USA there was a growth in private education and a white exodus from the cities to the suburbs. In 1974 the Supreme Court overturned a Detroit busing plan by five to four (MILLIKEN v. BRADLEY). Four out of the five judges were Nixon appointees.

Key dates
Boston Irish protests against busing: 1974
MILLIKEN v. BRADLEY: 1974

Other NAACP activities were less controversial and more clearly successful. NAACP was the most important black organisation in the Leadership Conference on Civil Rights, which represented blacks, Hispanics, women, the disabled and the elderly, and lobbied powerfully in Washington.

(b) Black politicians

Now securely within the Democratic Party, blacks used the vote to gain political power. In 1972 Andrew Young was elected to Congress. Birmingham had its first black mayor in 1979, Chicago in 1983. A total of 80 per cent of Chicago's poorest blacks turned out to vote, suggesting that civil rights activists had ended their apathy (see page 142) after all. Although black advancement should not be exaggerated (in 1980 only one per cent of the US's elected officials were black) the magnitude of black political progress is well illustrated by the career of Jesse Jackson.

Profile: Jesse Jackson 1941–

1941	–	Born to an illiterate South Carolina sharecropper
1961–4	–	Attended North Carolina Agricultural and Technical State University at Greensboro; leader of campus chapter of CORE, participated in Greensboro sit-ins
1965	–	Attended Chicago Theological Seminary; headed SCLC's successful Operation Breadbasket in Chicago
1968	–	Hoped to be Martin Luther King's successor. On the day after King's assassination, Jackson infuriated SCLC by appearing on television claiming to have King's blood on his shirt and to have been the last to speak to him
1971	–	SCLC leader, Ralph Abernathy, disciplined Jackson for financial impropriety in helping black businessmen. Jackson left SCLC and set up his own organisation, 'People United to Save Humanity' (PUSH). The 'save' was quickly and modestly changed to 'serve'! PUSH used black buying power to gain black employment
1984	–	Campaigned for the Democratic presidential nomination. His appeal owed much to fears of and antagonism toward Republican President Reagan's cutbacks in welfare spending and the Reagan Justice Department's opposition to affirmative action. Jackson was the third most popular Democratic candidate. He won 20 per cent of his support from whites
1988	–	Campaigned for the Democratic nomination again; increased appeal to white liberals; doubled his vote; 40 per cent of his supporters were white. His 'rainbow [all colours] coalition' appeal won him 60 per cent of New York's Hispanic vote. He came a close second to the eventual Democratic candidate
2001	–	His sexual indiscretions were publicised, forcing him into temporary retreat from the limelight

Jesse Jackson was universally recognised as the most influential African American of the 1970s, 1980s and 1990s. Although never of the same calibre as King, he helped keep civil rights on the political agenda after the death of King. His career illustrates both the changing black emphasis from protest to political participation and increased black political power.

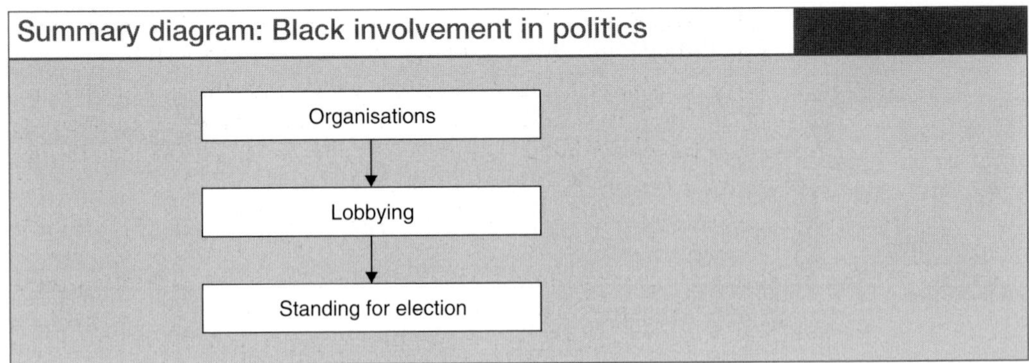

3 | Conclusions About Black Progress

Key question
How far had blacks progressed between 1863 and 1980?

(a) Political progress

In 1863 there were no elected black officials. In 1980, blacks were mayors of major cities, and controlled parts of the Deep South. However, during the 1970s, Klan membership tripled and violence increased. The United States Commission on Civil Rights reported 'white resistance and hostility by some state and local officials to increased minority participation in virtually every aspect of the electoral system'. Furthermore, political involvement alone did not solve all black problems. In 1980, blacks politically dominated Lowndes County, Alabama, but it remained the fifth poorest US county.

(b) Economic progress and social problems

In 1863 most blacks were enslaved, lacking mastery of their own economic destiny. Although by 1980 improved educational opportunities and affirmative action had helped make one-third of blacks middle class, black poverty had increased again during the 1970s because of US economic problems and increasing numbers of one-parent black families. The black infant mortality rate of 19 per cent was higher than that in some developing world countries. One-third of blacks and half of all black children lived below the poverty line. Another one-third had low status, low-skilled jobs in low-wage occupations. Average black earnings were half that of whites. Integrated schools caused 'white flight' to the suburbs and increased numbers of white private schools. Seventy per cent of blacks had concluded that, if equally funded, black schools were better. Blacks constituted around 12 per cent of the US population, but furnished 43 per cent of arrested rapists, 55 per cent of those accused of murder, and 69 per cent of those arraigned for robbery. Whites perceived blacks as responsible for the majority of crimes.

(c) The ghetto problem

After the Civil War, freed blacks gravitated to the cities. By the 1900s they congregated together in ghettos, which became increasingly unpleasant places in which to live. By 1980 it was clear that even black mayors such as Carl Stokes of Cleveland,

Ohio, could not solve the problem of ghetto crime, poverty and unemployment. They could not alienate white liberals by favouring blacks. They had to co-operate with the whites who dominated the local economy. Furthermore, some blacks, such as Supreme Court judge Clarence Thomas, became critical of liberal policies and 'welfare dependency'.

Black progress was thus limited by black divisions, the white backlash, and the financial and social problems associated with getting blacks out of the ghetto poverty trap. The lack of progress owed much to racial tensions, and contributed to more tension. The 1968 Kerner Report had warned that Americans were 'moving towards two societies, one black, one white – separate and unequal' – that remained true in 1980.

(d) Was the USA still a segregated society in 1980?

While whites were reconciled to equal black legal and political rights, and appreciative of black cultural and sporting contributions to US life, widespread racism and class prejudice remained. If the solution to black poverty was higher taxation, whites did not want to know. Housing remained effectively segregated, while, after the integration high-point of the late 1960s and early 1970s, schooling was becoming increasingly segregated once more. Although Southern blacks were integrated into the political process, there was a tendency for the Democrats to be the party of Southern blacks, and Republicans of Southern whites.

Summary diagram: Conclusions about black progress

	1863		1980
POLITICAL	No elected black officials	→	Number of elected black officials not too far off proportionate to black population
ECONOMIC AND SOCIAL	Most blacks were slaves	→	One-third of blacks were middle class, but the rest were poor *De facto* segregation for poor

Key question
What was the situation of Native Americans in the civil rights era?

4 | Native Americans and the Black Civil Rights Movement

(a) Continued Native American problems

While Indian reservation 'termination' (see page 117) had few defenders by 1960, the poverty, unemployment, poor housing and education on the remaining reservations was an embarrassment to the world's richest nation. Native Americans had worse housing, education and economic problems than blacks. Half of the 700,000 Native American population lived short, hard lives on the reservations, wherein employment ranged from 20 to 80 per cent, and where, in the 1970s, life expectancy was 44 years compared to the national average of 64 years. Tuberculosis continued to kill thousands. Unlike African Americans, Native Americans had an exceptionally high suicide rate. One of the main reasons for this was that Native Americans felt their unique culture as well as their ethnicity was despised by whites.

(b) The impact of increased black consciousness

Key question
What was the impact of the civil rights movement on Native Americans?

Native Americans were inspired by the African American campaign for equality and racial unity. The National Congress of American Indians (NCAI) was established in 1944. It was the first pan-Indian movement. In 1958 NCAI helped to stop the Eisenhower administration terminating reservation rights. It won Kennedy's promise of more jobs on reservations. NCAI copied NAACP's litigation strategy, suing state and federal governments over discrimination in employment and schooling, and also for breaking treaties. In PASSAMAQUODDY v. MORTON (1972), a tribe in Maine gained massive compensation from the federal government for breaking a 1790 treaty. Unlike NAACP, NCAI did not seek integration into US society. It worked for the survival of the separate Native American cultural identity.

Key dates
National Congress of American Indians established: 1944
PASSAMAQUODDY v. MORTON: 1972
Native Americans occupied Alcatraz: 1969

(c) Increased Native American militancy

Like African Americans, Native Americans became increasingly militant in the 1960s and 1970s. Their main target was the white-dominated Bureau of Indian Affairs (BIA), which had dictatorial powers over the reservations. NCAI leaders who co-operated with the BIA were despised as 'Apples' (red on the outside but white on the inside) or 'Uncle Tomahawks' (a variant on the African American 'Uncle Tom'). In 1969, 14 Native Americans occupied Alcatraz Island, the former federal prison in San Francisco Bay. They wanted to make it a Native American Museum. Over 10,000 Native Americans visited Alcatraz during the occupation.

Inspired by the black example, a Red Power movement developed. Some tribes occupied federal land. The Passamaquoddy collected tolls on a busy highway that crossed their land. Most militant of all was the American Indian Movement (AIM). AIM developed in one of the few Native American big city ghettos, in Minneapolis–St Paul. When young AIM members monitored police racism, the Native American population in the local jails dropped by 60 per cent. AIM worked to improve ghetto housing, education and employment, then gained members from the reservations. In their first national convention AIM stressed positive imagery, and attacked white Americans' use of names such as 'Washington Redskins' (football team) and 'Atlanta Braves' (baseball team): 'Even the name Indian is not ours. It was given to us by some dumb honky [white] who got lost and thought he'd landed in India'. Indians increasingly preferred the name 'Native American'. AIM participated in a Native American March on Washington. AIM activists occupied

BIA offices in 1972. The violence and destructiveness in AIM's 1972 occupation of BIA offices upset many other Native Americans, and alienated many whites.

Key question
How did whites react to increase Native American militancy?

(d) The white reaction to Native American militancy

White reactions to Native Americans and African Americans were frequently similar. When AIM occupied reservations, the Nixon administration used the same laws against them as were used against the Black Panthers. Although polls demonstrated white American sympathy for the Native Americans (whom they considered to be far less threatening than African Americans), most Americans were tired of demonstrations, and the Native Americans got little more than the sympathy. To a certain extent, like blacks, Native Americans were victims of the white backlash. However, as with African American activism (and perhaps partly because of African American activism), increased Native American assertiveness helped change the government's attitude. That changed attitude was the major reason for the improvement of the Indians' situation by 1980.

(e) Federal aid

Between 1946 and 1978, the Indian Claims Commission, created by Congress, gave $800 million to Indians to compensate for previous unjust land loss. That money contributed to tribal economic development. Like blacks, Indians were amongst the greatest beneficiaries of Johnson's War on Poverty. However, as with blacks, there were Indians who disliked the resulting 'welfare dependency' culture. Indians had to rely heavily upon federal job creation schemes on the reservations. Private industry found reservations unattractive with their limited pool of skilled workers, poor communications, and distance from markets.

(f) Self-determination

By 1980, Indians were near-dominant in the Bureau of Indian Affairs (BIA) and became as effective (proportionately) as blacks in lobbying Congress. However, tribal sovereignty for America's two million Indians was a contentious issue. Tribes saw self-government as essential to the improvement of the situation. Tribes took over several functions of the federal government. They rejected state police jurisdiction on tribal land, refused to collect state taxes, and issued car licence plates. Tribal sovereignty was assisted by the Indian Self-determination and Education Act (1975). The act encouraged tribes to manage their own affairs while retaining their special wardship status with the federal government.

Key dates
Indian Self-determination and Education Act helped increase Native American self-government: 1975
OLIPHANT decision: 1978

The rulings of Supreme Court Justice Marshall (1831–2) proved important precedents for Native American claims to tribal sovereignty. Marshall had described them as 'domestic, dependent nations'. He said states had no right to infringe upon tribal territory or authority. However, in the OLIPHANT decision (1978) the Supreme Court limited tribal authority over non-Indians and Indians of other tribes on the reservations. Whereas the Supreme Court declared 'the power to tax is an essential attribute of Indian sovereignty' (MERRION, 1982), states such as Oklahoma resented the loss of tax revenues occasioned by around 300 Indian 'smoke shops' wherein the state tax on cigarettes was not levied. White/red clashes over water and fishing rights demonstrated that while the Native American situation had greatly improved during the twentieth century, racial tensions remained, and, as so often in the past, land ownership was a root cause.

Key date
MERRION decision: 1982

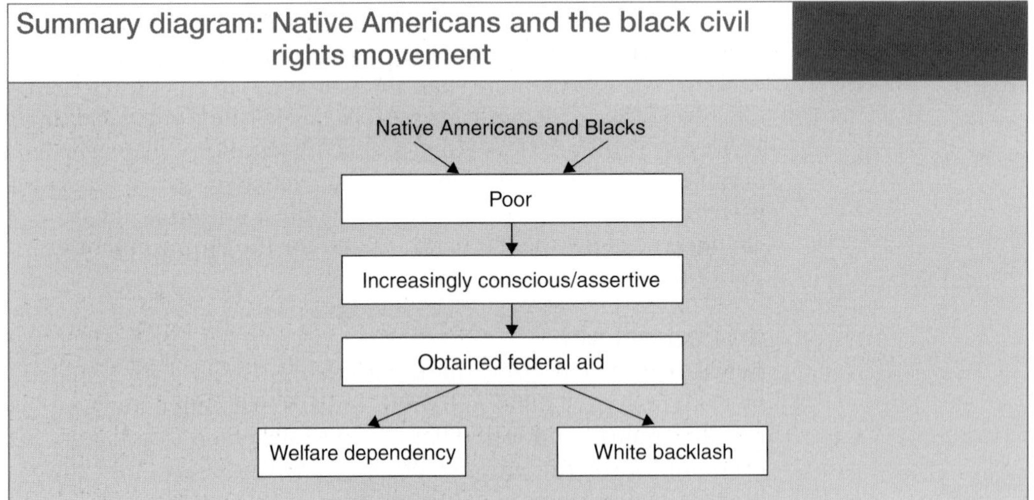

5 | The Impact of the Civil Rights Movement on Hispanic Americans and Asian Americans

Key question
How did the civil rights movement affect Hispanic Americans and Asian Americans?

For many years, Mexican Americans worked and lived in isolated rural communities or in their urban ghettos. As in Mexico itself, Mexican Americans wanted little to do with the federal government. However, when in the 1960s Americans became more aware of the rights and problems of minorities, Mexican Americans began to follow the black example. Cesar Chavez's agricultural workers' labour union mirrored A. Philip Randolph's encouragement of black political awareness through union organisation. The Brown Berets modelled themselves on the Black Panthers, but compared to blacks, Mexican Americans as a whole were less interested in and knowledgeable about such political movements and politics as a whole. They despised the 'Anglo' government that had taken the Far West from Mexico, and had discriminated against them. Interestingly, the ethnic groups that made the fastest and most remarkable economic advances in the face of racial prejudice and legal discrimination were those who deliberately avoided political involvement – the Japanese Americans and Chinese Americans.

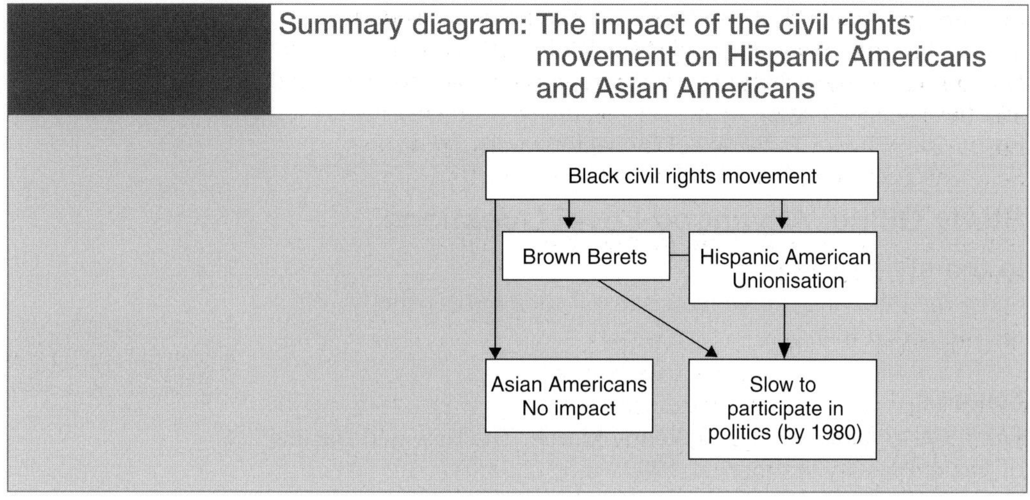

6 | Key Debates

Historians have disagreed far more over President Nixon's record than over President Carter's. While historians such as William Chafe (2003) condemn Nixon's civil rights record, others such as Joan Hoff (1994) emphasise his positive achievements. Hugh Davis Graham (1990) preferred to credit the judiciary and the Democratic Congress with helping to force Nixon to be more positive over civil rights, but Graham gives Nixon some credit.

Some historians claim that the civil rights movement in the South disintegrated soon after Selma. Adam Fairclough held that view in 1987, but by 1995 his study of Louisiana, confirmed by Stephen Tuck's of Georgia (2001), suggests that there was 'continuity of protest' at the local level, for example, in challenging electoral abuses. NAACP membership and activism grew again, while Tuck recorded SCLC as very active in early 1970s Georgia.

Perhaps the greatest debate on this period, because it is so relevant to the present, is the debate over the impact of BROWN. In 1984, Raymond Wolters studied the impact of BROWN and concluded that it had not helped to improve the academic performance of black schoolchildren and had led to new routes (such as white flight and private schools) to segregation. Wolters claimed that integration had lowered standards because of the presence of poorly-prepared and poorly behaved lower class black children. David Garrow (1985) accused Wolters of political bias. Such debates remind us that racial tensions remain in America and amongst those who write its history.

Some key books in the debate

William Chafe, *The Unfinished Journey: America Since World War II* (New York, 2003).

Adam Fairclough, *Race and Democracy: The Civil Rights Struggle in Louisiana* (Georgia, 1995).

David Garrow, *Segregation's Legacy,* Reviews in America History (1985).

Hugh Davis Graham, *The Civil Rights Era* (New York, 1990).
Joan Hoff, *Nixon Reconsidered* (New York, 1994).
Stephen Tuck, *Beyond Atlanta: The Struggle for Racial Equality in Georgia* (Georgia, 2001).
Raymond Wolters, *The Burden of Brown* (Knoxville, 1984).

Study Guide: Advanced Level Questions

In the style of AQA

Study the following source material and then answer the questions that follow.

Source A

From: Philip Klinkner, The Unsteady March: The Rise and Decline of Racial Equality in America, *1999.*

The fear of slave revolts and of racial mixing led whites to enact harsh and punitive slave codes to ensure the stability of the slave system and to maintain the supremacy of whites over blacks. African American slaves did not possess basic rights of life, liberty, or property to any meaningful extent.

Source B

From: Alan Farmer, Reconstruction and the Results of the American Civil War 1865–77, *1997.*

Black Southerners certainly wielded some political power. Having been given the vote, most blacks were determined to use it. The result was that in the two decades after 1867, Southern blacks were elected to national, state and local office. Two black Senators and 15 black Representatives were elected to Congress before 1877. Many blacks were elected to state legislatures and for a time blacks actually controlled the lower house of South Carolina's legislature. But while this was a revolutionary break with the past, black power and political influence never reflected black numbers. Very few of the top positions in state governments went to blacks. In five Southern states no black held a major office during Reconstruction. The majority of black office holders were local officials. But even at this level blacks did not hold a proportionate share of offices.

Source C

Adapted from: Stephen Tuck, Beyond Atlanta: The Struggle For Racial Equality in Georgia, 1940–80, *2001. Tuck is describing the 1946 election for state governor in Georgia.*

In the 1946 Georgia gubernatorial election, Eugene Talmadge made the repeal of black enfranchisement the essential issue of the campaign. Talmadge's victory was entirely dependent on a co-ordinated purge of black voters and fraudulent poll counts. FBI reports later revealed a sophisticated campaign through which Talmadge supporters across the state took advantage of a largely unknown constitutional provision allowing any citizen to challenge the right of another to vote. Some [white] challengers simply asserted that they did not think 'any nigger was qualified to vote'. In Savannah, political boss Johnny Bouhan brought voting to a standstill by minimising the number of polling booths. Consequently, thousands of black Savannahians were unable to vote, even though they had stood in line at the polls since dawn. None of the still-qualified hundred black voters in Schley County actually voted because the local state representative [stood] outside the polling booth with a shotgun, exclaiming that 'if a nigger votes in this election, he'll be a dead nigger'.

Source D

From: Steven Lawson, Civil Rights Crossroads, *2003.*

When Johnson entered the White House in 1963, approximately one-quarter of adult blacks were on the voter rolls in the South; by the time he left office, the proportion was approaching two-thirds. In some counties where no blacks had cast a ballot since the turn-of-the-century, thousands of Negroes were participating in the electoral process by 1969, and some were even winning office. Before his death, Johnson would see two Southern blacks take seats in the House of Representatives, and in the fall of 1973 a Negro was elected mayor of Atlanta.

1. **Use Sources B and C and your own knowledge.**
   How fully do Sources B and C explain why the number of elected black officials did not proportionately represent the number of blacks in the United States between 1877 and 1946?
2. **Use Sources A, B, C and D and your own knowledge.**
   How successful was the federal government in ensuring that African Americans were allowed to vote between 1877 and 1989?

Exam tips

1. 'How fully' is examiner-speak for 'Write about the way in which the sources (i) *do* explain, (ii) have not fully explained, or (iii) have not mentioned. A source 'omits' something *either* because the writer has prejudices that you ought to be able to detect *or* because the writer (or the person who selected the extract) has missed other points *or* because the writer does not think the other points are as important as the points he is making. Remember, all your references to omissions needs to be explained: why is that particular piece of omitted information needed? Remember, when discussing the contents of two sources, it is far better to deal with them simultaneously rather than doing one first, then the other.

2. When asked to use a source and your own knowledge, you should try to formulate an essay plan and then use the sources as evidence to support it. Try to inter-weave your own knowledge and the sources throughout your answer.
   Remember, 'How successful' is examiner-speak for 'Give me some indication of success, but also some indication of failure'.
   Finally, when asked to cover a period of around 100 years in your answer, ensure that you mention all periods – there are quite distinct phases in the period 1870 to 1946:
   - Reconstruction
   - the increasing number of Jim Crow laws
   - the rise and increase (and increasing effectiveness) of black activism
   - the post-1965 Voting Rights Act period.

In the style of Edexcel

1. How far do the actions of federal and state governments demonstrate continuity rather than change in dealing with the 'black problem' between 1865 and 1969?
2. How far do you agree with the view that the key factor in bringing about change in the status of black people in USA was the role of the federal government over the period 1865–1969?

Exam tips

The cross-references are intended to take you to some of the material that will help you to answer the questions.

1. When asked about change over a period of time, clarify the situation at the beginning and the end of the period. Contrasting situations between two given dates makes a good introduction to an essay. These two questions will have considerable overlap in factual content, but the style of your approach will be different. In question 1, basic factual content will be what the federal and state governments did (or did not do) over these years. You will need examples of laws, court rulings and executive actions from the Reconstruction period (pages 22–30), the 'decades of disappointment' (pages 46–59), the New Deal era (pages 71–3), and then the period of the civil rights movement (Chapter 8). You can try to 'measure' change by the amount of government activity and by its practical impact on blacks. Take care to give both continuity and change relatively equal coverage.

2. Question 2 is a 'causes' question. 'How far' is an invitation for you to look at other 'key factors' such as the impact of events (e.g. the Second World War, pages 80–4) on attitudes and opportunities, the role of black leaders and organisations (e.g. Ida B. Wells, NAACP, pages 40–6) and changes in the American economy (e.g. the mechanisation of Southern agriculture, the decreased demand for unskilled manual labour in the North. You could organise this essay in two ways. A paragraph on each factor, looking at its impact on the political/social/economic/legal status of blacks is the easier way. It is harder but more productive to look at the changing political status of blacks throughout the period in one paragraph. That paragraph would contain discussion of the role of each of your suggested key factors in bringing about the changes. You would then do similarly organised paragraphs on the social, economic and legal status of blacks.

In the style of OCR

1. To what extent were the activities of anti-civil rights groups the most important reason for the continued discrimination against African Americans from 1865 to 1980?

Source: OCR, January 2005

2. How far was Martin Luther King the most important African American leader in the development of civil rights from 1865 to 1980?

Source: OCR, June 2004

Exam tips

The cross-references are intended to take you to some of the material that will help you to answer the questions.

1. When studying any question, it is helpful to 'break it down' before you start. Here you are asked 'to what extent', a phrase that tells you that even if you agree with the 'most important' cause in the question, you need to put in other causes too. In your essay plan, you could devote one paragraph to each other 'cause'. You might decide to have a paragraph on:
   - white economic jealousies and fears (pages 61, 64–5, 70, 80, 145–6, 189, 195)
   - white racism (pages 27–9, 52, 61, 70, 74, 91, 95–6, 102–3, 111)
   - frequent lack of federal government support for blacks (pages 29–30, 50–1, 99–100, 113–4, 116, 136, 144, 159, 175, 187)

- frequent lack of state government and local support for blacks (pages 27–30, 43, 62, 99, 143, 159, 187)
- black disunity (page 34–5, 45, 49, 52–3, 66–7, 78, 125) and
- white fear of blacks due to black power, riots, crime, etc. (pages 40, 139–44, Chapter 7, 187–9).

The next step is to define 'anti-civil rights groups', which include the Ku Klux Klan and White Citizens' Councils (see pages 28, 54, 64, 102, 106–7, 134). You can then do a series of paragraphs on numbers on the points above, within each of which you weigh up the importance of the anti-civil rights groups compared to the other cause. In some paragraphs the groups are probably not as important as your other cause. However, in other paragraphs it can be seen that the connection between the groups and the other cause are very important. Having weighed up the relative importance of your six factors alongside the specified cause, it is probably best if you have led in this direction throughout the essay, to say which is the most important cause in your conclusion. If desperate, you could try leaving that to the conclusion, although that is a far less effective technique. Within each of your six paragraphs, you need to have examples to illustrate your generalisation from several periods across the 1865–1980 timespan, because the black situation changed over time. For example, within one paragraph, you might want an example from the Reconstruction period, another from the 'decades of disappointment', a third from the early part of the twentieth century, a fourth from the 'classic' period of the civil rights movement, and finally, one from the period following the 1964 and 1965 acts.

2. 'How far' is a phrase similar to 'to what extent'. Here, you need to look at the other important leaders, such as Booker T. Washington (page 47), W.E.B. Du Bois (page 55), A. Philip Randolph (page 76), Marcus Garvey (page 68) and Malcolm X (page 156). If you are looking at your leaders chronologically, explain what the situation was for blacks at the beginning and at the end of each leader's career. The best way to answer would be to make the assessment thematic, considering the significance of each leader in such areas as voting rights, equality before the law, employment rights, free access to education, etc. That way the relative importance of the individuals can be acknowledged. This will make it easier for you to judge who contributed most. As the greatest civil rights advances are generally considered to have taken place in the 1960s, you might well conclude that Martin Luther King was the most important leader.

Glossary

Abolitionists Those who wanted to end slavery.

Accommodationists Those who favoured initial black concentration upon economic improvement rather than upon social, political and legal equality.

Acculturation Making Indians live like whites.

Administration When Americans talk of 'the Truman administration' they mean the government as led by that particular president.

Affirmative action Also known as 'positive discrimination'; helping those who have had a disadvantageous start in life.

Amendment Under the Constitution, Congress could add 'Amendments' (changes or new points) to the Constitution. Amendments needed ratification (approval) by 75 per cent of states.

Attorney General Head of the Justice Department in the federal government.

Bills, Acts and **Vetos** If a member of Congress or the President wanted a law to be made, he introduced a bill into Congress. If the bill was passed by Congress and accepted by the President, the bill became an Act or law. Under the Constitution, the President had the power to veto (reject) a bill, although if Congress persevered, it could override that veto.

Biracial Black and white together.

Black nationalist Black nationalists want a separate black nation either within the USA or in Africa.

Black power A controversial term, with different meanings for different people, for example, black pride, black economic self-sufficiency, black violence, black separatism, black nationalism, black political power, black working class revolution, black domination.

Black Reconstruction The phrase was coined by the early twentieth-century white historian Dunning, who sympathised with Southern whites' 'suffering' when blacks gained political power during Reconstruction.

Black separatists Blacks who desired to live apart/away from whites.

Busing Transporting white or black children to schools in an area other than that in which they live, to ensure integrated schools in that area.

Chapters Branches of an organisation.

Citizenship Indians were recognised as legally equal to white Americans with all the same rights, for example, voting.

Civil rights Having the vote in free elections. Equal treatment under the law. Equal opportunities, e.g. in education and work. Freedom of speech, religion and movement.

Civil rights movement Aimed at legal, social, political and economic equality for blacks. Black and white activists campaigned, particularly in the 1960s, with some success. Historians disagree over the exact dates of the movement.

Cold War From about 1946 to 1989, hostility between the USA and the USSR was known as the Cold War.

Communism The ideology of the USSR and its allied states. Emphasised economic equality and state control of the economy. As the Communist Party was supposed to be the party of the people, Communist states were usually one-party states on the grounds that no other party was needed.

The Confederacy When the Southern states left the Union, they became the Confederate States of America, known as the Confederacy for short. Supporters of the Confederacy were called Confederates.

Congress The American equivalent to Britain's parliament, consisting of the Senate and the House of Representatives. Voters in each American state elect two senators to sit in the Senate and several congressmen (the number depends on the size of the state's population) to sit in the House of Representatives.

Constitution The rules and system by which a country's government works. The USA has a written constitution.

Daughters of the American Revolution A prestigious middle class society whose members could claim US ancestry back to the revolutionary war era, distinguishing them from newer immigrants.

Decolonisation After the Second World War, countries such as Britain allowed their colonies to become independent.

De facto In fact if not in law.

De jure Legal, in law.

Democratic Convention Democrats and Republicans each have a national convention in a presidential election year, to choose/confirm their presidential candidate.

Democratic Party Dominated American politics in the first half of the nineteenth century. It was pro-slavery and against a powerful central/federal government.

Depression When a country's economy is nearly ruined. Prices and wages fall, and many people are unemployed, as in the USA after 1929.

Disfranchise Deprive someone of their vote.

Dixiecrat A racist political party established in 1948.

Economic boycotts The use of black purchasing power to gain concessions, for example, not shopping at a store that refused to employ blacks.

Emancipation In this context, freedom from slavery.

Executive Orders The constitution reserved certain powers to the executive (the president). For example, the president could issue executive orders regarding the armed forces in his constitutional capacity as commander-in-chief.

Federal government The USA, as a federation of many separate states (such as South Carolina and New York), has a federal government. The federal government consists of the President, Congress and the Supreme Court.

Filibuster Prolonging congressional debates to stop bills being voted upon.

First-come, first-served Southern buses were divided into black and white sections. Sometimes blacks would be standing while the white section was empty. Blacks therefore wanted seating on a first-come, first-served basis.

Free blacks In the North in particular, many blacks had been freed from slavery by their owners.

Freedom Rides When integrated groups of civil rights activists rode on interstate buses to defy segregation and monitor whether Supreme Court rulings against segregation were being ignored.

Genocide The murder of an entire race.

Ghettos Areas inhabited mostly or solely by (usually poor) members of a particular ethnicity or nationality.

Graduate schools Universities.

Great Migration The Northward movement of Southern blacks during the twentieth century.

Great Society Johnson's plan to decrease poverty and inequality in the USA.

Hispanic Relating to Spain, for example, having Spanish ancestry and/or speaking Spanish.

Indian Bureau The federal agency with special responsibility for Indians.

Integration The social mixing of people of different colours and cultures.

Interstate Between states, for example, between Alabama and Georgia.

Jim Crow An early 1830s' comic, black-faced, minstrel character developed by a white performing artist that proved to be very popular with white audiences. When, after Reconstruction, the Southern states introduced laws that legalised segregation, these were known as 'Jim Crow laws'.

Justice Department Branch of the federal government in Washington DC with special responsibility for justice.

Korean War From 1950 to 1953, the USA, South Korea and the United Nations fought against Communist North Korea and China in Korea.

Left-wing Those whose political beliefs included greater economic equality, for example, Communists and socialists.

Liberals Generally more sympathetic than most to racial/social/economic equality.

Lynching Unlawful killing (usually by hanging) of blacks.

Marxist historian Believes that history has been deeply shaped by economic circumstances. Influenced by the ideology of philosopher Karl Marx.

Minority leader Leader of the party with fewer members in Congress.

Miscegenation Sexual relationships between blacks and whites.

National Guard and reserves Each state has its own 'army', ready to deal with state problems, but also available to be federalised if the federal government needed extra manpower. The reserves are federally controlled, trained and ready to supplement the regular armed forces in an emergency.

New Deal President Roosevelt's programme to bring the US out of economic depression.

Passive resistance Gandhi's sit-down protests against British imperialism in India were called 'passive resistance'. King felt 'passive' sounded negative.

Poll tax A tax levied on would-be voters, which made it harder for blacks (who were usually poorer) to vote.

Primaries When presidential candidates for a particular political party vie to be chosen as that party's candidate.

Progressive A historian who is an advocate of political policies that bring about rapid progress or social reform.

Public schools Schools financed and run by the government (called state schools in Britain).

Racial Pertaining to a group of people connected by common descent from distinct ethnic stock.

Radical Republicans Members of the Republican Party who were most enthusiastic about ending slavery.

Reconstruction The process of rebuilding and reforming the 11 ex-Confederate states and restoring them to the Union.

Renaissance A revival or exceptionally productive period for culture.

Repatriation In the context of American race relations this meant people of African descent (black Americans) being returned to Africa.

Representative Member of the House of Representatives, the lower chamber in Congress.

Republican Party Emerged in the 1850s. It was against slavery.

Revisionist A historian who changes a well-established interpretation.

Sectional Relating to a particular area of the United States, such as the South.

Segregation The separation of people because of race (for example, separate housing, schools and transport).

Self-help Booker T. Washington and Marcus Garvey emphasised black-owned businesses as typical of the self-help needed for black progress.

Sharecropper A white landowner provided the land, seed, tools and orders, while a black worker (the sharecropper) provided the labour. The crop produced was usually divided between the two men.

Sit-ins An example of economic pressure; black protesters would sit at segregated restaurants until they were served. If they were not served, they would be taking up seats, so white paying customers could not find places. The idea was to force the restaurant to desegregate.

State of the Union Address Annual presidential speech that sums up the situation in the USA and/or advertises the president's achievements.

States' rights Throughout US history, there has been constitutional conflict between upholders of the powers of the individual states as opposed to that of the federal government.

Tennessee Valley Authority A New Deal programme to bring prosperity to rural Tennessee.

Trade union A group of workers united to bargain for better working conditions and pay.

Uncle Tom The Northern abolitionist Harriet Beecher Stowe wrote the book *Uncle Tom's Cabin* in 1852. Her character was a slave who deferred to whites. Twentieth-century blacks called other blacks 'Uncle Tom' if they seemed too deferential to whites.

Welfare dependency Reliance upon federal aid.

Index